SMALL COMPUTERS

SMALL COMPUTERS

SMALL COMPUTERS

SMALL COMPUTERS

SMALL COMPUTERS

SMALL COMPUTERS

SMALL COMPUTERS
FOR THE
SMALL BUSINESSMAN

Nicholas Rosa & Sharon Rosa

DO NOT REMOVE
CARDS FROM POCKET

SMALL COMPUTERS FOR THE SMALL BUSINESSMAN

SMALL COMPUTERS FOR THE SMALL BUSINESSMAN

Nicholas Rosa and Sharon Rosa

dilithium Press
Portland, Oregon

FRANCESCA,

DEBORAH,

and MICHAEL

ISBN: 0-918398-31-2

Library of Congress catalog card number: 80-68531

Printed in the United States of America.

dilithium Press
30 N.W. 23rd Place
Portland, Oregon 97210

PREFACE

The computers described in this book are not the formidable roomfuls of machinery that most people think of when they hear the word "computer."

This book is about small computers that anyone can use — electronic servants, not masters, of human beings in business.

The new small computers — microcomputers — can be afforded by any business, however small, that needs one.

Computers are not yet appliances. Acquiring the right computer system for your business requires a little savvy. But there is nothing mysterious or even "technical" about it. This book is intended to help you develop that savvy.

The pronoun "we" that frequently appears in this book is not any kind of regal "we" or even an editorial "we." It is simply the first-person plural pronoun. The book has two authors, and we address you, the reader, directly. In so doing we perhaps violate some sacred canons of "literature," but we have no wish to be literary. We wish to be informal, clear, and useful to you. Our aim is to provide you with a friendly teacher, who happens to be a pair of friendly teachers, at your elbow.

We hope you will find this book completely nontechnical. We have written the book for business people, not for computer people. More and more these days, the computers themselves are being produced for business people, rather than for computer people. The trend could go a good deal farther than it has, but at least it is there. It can and will go as far as the business **community demands.**

We have written this book for *small business* people. And thus it is mostly about small computers, specifically microcomputers. The advent of the microcomputer has triggered a Small Computer Revolution, whose full flowering will change all our lives in countless ways, as the Big Computer Revolution did. Only, this time, the revolutionary computers will be in the hands of everyone. That is going to make quite a difference.

Campbell, California
February 1980

CONTENTS

Chapter One

THE SMALL COMPUTER REVOLUTION

Today the small business can own a complete computer system for less money than it takes to buy computing services or rent computer time. A computer can be yours for "about the price of a new car." This is the legacy of the Small Computer Revolution. The revolution resulted from the advent of a radically new device, the **microcomputer.** (We shall define that term later.) A small in-house computer can save your small business money, enhance your operational efficiency, save time, and thus make money, indirectly. The small computer can even increase revenue.

If a computer can save money for your business right now, you are losing money by not having one. That may seem obvious. But consider this: if you delay acquiring a computer, you will never gain back the money you are losing. That idea may seem rash or extreme. But it can be supported. We shall come back to it, with support.

Never think of a computer as a glorified calculator. A **data processor** is what a computer really is, and should properly be called. Yes, it can do your arithmetic. But it can do so much more. A computer can sort, list, compare, file, retrieve, summarize, report on, any items of business information you have. Much of what your staff does every day consists of these operations—over and over. A computer streamlines these operations, makes them faster, surer, and less expensive.

Any business is encumbered by innumerable files, including those drifting outside the filing cabinets, like today's invoices. You need to keep those files up to date—and for some things, up to the moment. Changing anything in one file necessitates updating other files. This applies even to that small sale just rung up on the cash register. The faster and more accurately you can keep those files updated and related, the better off you are. The faster you can retrieve crucial information, the handsomer your balance sheet.

You are constantly making decisions. Effective decisions depend on fresh and *relevant* information, concisely presented. How well is a particular item selling? by month over the past three or six months? this week? today? How smoothly is inventory keeping up with sales? How well do sales balance with inventory? That's the kind of information your own small computer can gin up for you on demand.

Think of all the money floating out there that morally and legally belongs to you—receivables that you haven't gotten around to billing yet, maybe even haven't invoiced yet (even though the shipments went out!). You have some billed accounts that are more than 90 days behind. Your bookkeeper is struggling to sort those out and tack on the service charges. Hey! A shipment just went out to Micawber & Co. even though they've been deadbeating on you for six months. Business is so good you're losing money. At today's interest rates, money you haven't got in the bank is really costing you. Could a small computer help you with this? It certainly could.

BUT WE'RE NOT TRYING TO SELL YOU

We don't have to. You must be thinking of "computerizing" or you would not have picked up this book. You already suspect that a computer might bring the solution to some problem that is driving you bonkers. Somewhere you have some chaos, some situation in which information comes too thick and fast, goes astray, gets lost, delayed, scrambled. Somewhere the number of similar repetitive clerical tasks is getting beyond everyone's stamina and attention span. You are beset with petty details. You are kept from repeating the feats that have made you a successful businessman. Or would have, if you were not up to your, um, ah, bellybutton in alligators. You are already wondering: could a computer eat up the alligators, or at least drain the swamp?

Yes. It could.

"THE PRICE OF A NEW CAR"

The saying in the microcomputer industry is that you can have an effective small-business computer system "for less than the price of a new car." That turns out to be a big four-door sedan, when all's said and done, not a dinky Honda. It's still reasonable. It is even possible to start out with the computer version of the Honda, and learn the ins and outs of using the computer as a business tool on it. Then you can upgrade.

Now we have to shift metaphors. The new metaphor is stereo components. You know how you can start with just a stereo receiver (tuner and amplifier combined) and speakers, then add turntable, tape deck, and so on *ad lib*. In other words you can start with a minimum system and add to it, or upgrade it piece by piece. The same goes for small computers.

A complete small business computer system, based on a Cromemco System Three microcomputer. The computer is in the desk pedestal at right, along with disk drives (external magnetic data files). The printer at left produces typewriter-quality printout. The terminal box has a full electric-typewriter keyboard, numeric key pad, and various computer function keys.

Courtesy of Cromemco

Ultimately the main cost of your computer system may not be the hardware—the intriguing black boxes you see through the computer-store windows. Your main upgrading and adding on will be the **software**—the programs that go into your computer, and tell it how to process your data. You may start with a minimum set of packaged programs to simplify routine items like general ledger and accounts receivable, but you will keep seeking programs that do your thing your way, and that do more and more for you, using the same hardware.

Software costs money: it is a product of professional human labor; it is inherently more expensive than the hardware. However, more and more good software is becoming available and its price is coming down, if you buy the right systems. This is partly because the better hardware vendors are subsidizing small-business software development, and amortizing its cost through the sale of more hardware. All this is a complex subject, covered in detail in Chapters 2, 3, and 8.

Any small computer system that calls itself a microcomputer will, in 1980 prices, cost you between $4000 and about $16,000, as an acquisition price. The higher prices include software. Beyond $16,000, you are into the realm of the **minicomputer,** and these run up to $30,000 and more. The minicomputers are the direct offspring of the giant main frame computers that everybody thinks of when the word "computer" is mentioned. You know: IBM and all that: a large, air-conditioned room full of big black cabinets. But we are talking about computers that occupy a desk top. Minicomputers and micros now look alike, are in the same physical size ranges, and—in regard to the better microcomputer systems—perform about the same.

When you buy a small "computer" you will actually buy a system consisting of a "computer proper" plus a number of accessories or peripherals (Chapter 2). The simplest system you might buy will have a keyboard and either a TV-like display screen or a simple printer, to enable you to make use of the computer electronics. Actually, the simplest practical system should have some external magnetic storage or "memory," whether tape or disk.

Now, the **central processing unit (CPU),** the computer proper, doesn't cost much: a few hundred to a thousand dollars or so. It usually comes in a cabinet the size of a stereo receiver. You could even buy a "complete" microcomputer, naked, on a single printed circuit board (PC board). We would not recom-

A bare-bones system for light business uses, by Radio Shack.
Courtesy of Radio Shack, a Division of Tandy Corp.

mend buying anything that simple for business purposes, even
though you might spot one advertised for as little as $50.00 But
the more elaborate "stereo-sized box" is still only a few hundred

The computer proper fits into a box about the size of a stereo amplifier or receiver. The Vector MZ shown here has built-in diskette drives
for external magnetic data storage (distinct from the computer's internal memory). The MSI 6800 computer works with external disk
drives. Both these computers are operated by means of separate
keyboard terminals and can be used with many kinds of peripheral
devices.
Courtesy of Vector Graphic, Inc.

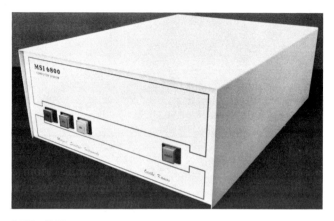

The MSI 6800 computer.
Courtesy of Midwest Scientific Instruments

dollars, up to $1000-$2000, depending on how elaborate the circuitry is inside the box.

Why the $4000 minimum then? First, the cost of **peripheral devices**—that TV-like cathode-ray tube (CRT) display, a good keyboard, a decent small printer for paper printouts, some magnetic storage, then some minimal software (programs and their documentation). As the price goes up, the peripherals and the software should get better. For example, the higher price covers a heavy-duty "fancy" printer, giving you type quality like that of the best electric typewriters. It covers more and better software, including some "hard-wired" into the circuitry. And it includes a bigger memory capacity. Memory is important, as later chapters will explain. (That $50 computer-on-a-card has the memory of an electronic rabbit. You want something more like the memory of a small elephant.)

For microcomputer circuitry, prices have about halved roughly every two years through the 1970s. During the same period, the performance of the basic circuitry doubled in quality every year or two. Less money buys you more computer. There have been three or four generations of microcomputers—based on the same families of microprocessor **chips,** to be explained later—since the first true microcomputer appeared in 1971. In 1979, three of the leading microprocessor chip manufacturers brought out new chips that promised about a tenfold increase in performance. For new equipment using these chips, prices may not rise unduly but performance will improve, some time soon.

THEN SHOULDN'T YOU WAIT?

This, of course, prompts an intelligent question from you: *Shouldn't I wait?* **No.** *But you're saying that performance will be even better soon, at comparable or lower prices, if the falling-price trend continues.* Yes, that's what we're saying; **BUT:** please consider the following:

1. If a computer will save or make money for you now, you are losing money by not having one, and you will never gain back the money lost during the time of delay before you acquire one.
2. The CPU or "computer proper," the electronics, costs a small fraction of your total system cost; you can upgrade the CPU in a few years, and the new electronics will run your old peripherals.
3. Therefore, it doesn't pay to wait until electronic prices come down further, or performance goes up; at this stage, you may not even be ready for the better performance. In practice today, most "minimum" systems are under-utilized!
4. "Computerizing" your business will involve a learning process for you and your staff, and some false starts and mishaps. Use today's computer to learn from, and gain from; switch to an "advanced" system if your circumstances really call for it, when both you and the advanced computer are ready. Then you'll be able to make the most of it. (Perhaps some day you will need a Learjet, but you will learn to fly in something like a Cessna 150.)

NOW, ABOUT THAT RASH IDEA...

We have mentioned more than once that if a computer can save or make money for you now, you are losing money by not having it. Furthermore, you will never gain back the money you will have lost by delaying acquisition.

We owe that idea to an analyst named Roger Williams, who developed it in four articles in *Interface Age,* a leading magazine devoted to applications of microcomputers, in mid-1978. (See Roger Williams, "Consideration for Computer Implementation in a Small Business," May through August, 1978 issues of *Interface Age.)* We can only hope to summarize Williams' exquisite reasoning. It would be worth your while to get hold of back issues and read the entire series. (These and other worthwhile business articles are published in their entirety in the BEST OF INTERFACE AGE: Volume 3: General Business. This book is available from dilithium Press.)

Williams makes a differential cash-flow analysis—continuously comparing what cash flow is like with a computer and without it. He uses three simple conceptual tools: differential revenue, differential cash flow, and differential expenditure. Differential revenue consists of the increase in revenue plus decrease in expenditure due to implementation of a computer. Differential expenditure is the decrease in revenue and increase in expenditure due to your having acquired a computer. The difference between the differential revenue and the differential expenditure is the differential cash flow.

What matters ultimately is differential accumulated cash, "the cash accumulated over a specific time interval as a result of the accumulated cash flow." In this case, the term means the cash you accumulate as a direct result of having the computer, as compared with the cash you could accumulate anyway without it.

A chart, like a picture, can be worth a thousand words. Figure 1-1 is adapted from Williams' own first graphs. The zero line represents cash flow as is, and as will be without the computer. Differential revenue begins to increase almost immediately as the computer begins simplifying some tasks and saving time. But differential *expenditure* is heavy at first—you have bought the computer outright, or have made a down payment and have a payment schedule, or you have a lease-purchase deal.

The stippled area above the zero line represents the differential accumulated cash. The little stippled area at the left, below the zero line, represents *negative* differential accumulated cash. This is during the time when you can feel the computer costing you. But the negative period does not last long: it is always being countered by the increase in differential revenue. Notice, too, that the differential expenditure bottoms out. There will come a time well before the amortization point where everything gets easier.

As Figure 1-1 points out, differential cash flow must go positive eventually because the computer will be amortized and

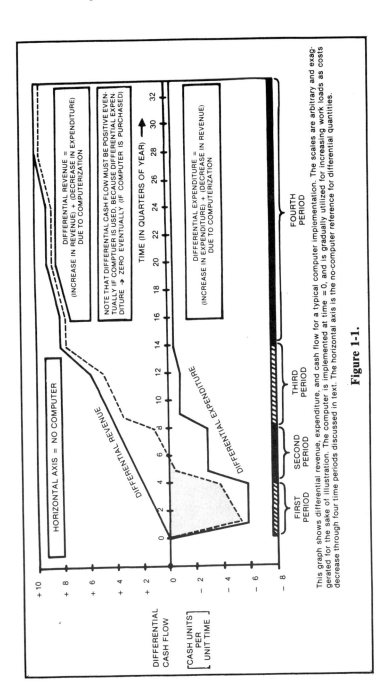

Figure 1-1.

This graph shows differential revenue, expenditure, and cash flow for a typical computer implementation. The scales are arbitrary and exaggerated for the sake of illustration. The computer is implemented at time = 0, and is gradually utilized for increasing work loads as costs decrease through four time periods discussed in text. The horizontal axis is the no-computer reference for differential quantities.

HORIZONTAL AXIS = NO COMPUTER

DIFFERENTIAL REVENUE =
(INCREASE IN REVENUE) + (DECREASE IN EXPENDITURE)
DUE TO COMPUTERIZATION

NOTE THAT DIFFERENTIAL CASH FLOW MUST BE POSITIVE EVENTUALLY IF COMPUTER IS USED, BECAUSE DIFFERENTIAL EXPENDITURE → ZERO EVENTUALLY (IF COMPUTER IS PURCHASED)

DIFFERENTIAL EXPENDITURE =
(INCREASE IN EXPENDITURE) + (DECREASE IN REVENUE)
DUE TO COMPUTERIZATION

DIFFERENTIAL REVENUE

DIFFERENTIAL EXPENDITURE

TIME (IN QUARTERS OF YEAR)

FIRST PERIOD   SECOND PERIOD   THIRD PERIOD   FOURTH PERIOD

DIFFERENTIAL CASH FLOW

[CASH UNITS PER UNIT TIME]

expenses attributable only to it will drop virtually to zero. This means that the computer purchase is *long-term viable*.

Another way of looking at this is through Figure 1-2. This shows differential accumulated cash for the same situation as in Figure 1-1. It is nearly self-expanatory. The horizontal line again represents cash flow without the computer. A point comes when the differential cash flow exceeds the non-computer cash flow and *continuously* increases thereafter. Of greater interest here is the brief swoop of the curve below the zero line. It bottoms out where differential expenditure equals differential revenue. There, differential cash flow is zero, and this is Williams' "extremum deficit." After that, the only way is up. If that area of the graph can be survived, the computer is *short-term viable*. That is, it is affordable.

What about never gaining back the money lost by delaying implementation of a computer? Try Figure 1-3. This repeats the curve of Figure 1-2, three times: for immediate implementation, for a delay of two quarters, and for a delay of eight quarters. the distance between repetitions of the curve show the permanent "cost," or *loss,* occasioned by the delays in implementation. The losses are not only permanent, they actually grow over time, just as differential accumulated cash grows over time. Every quarter, those curves grow farther apart.

The argument is clinched with Figure 1-4. This chart has an important difference: the horizontal line represents the cash flow *with* the computer in place. The plunging line represents the differential accumulated cash situation with the computer never implemented—"infinite delay." You can make profits without a computer, but every quarter, every year, the amount of *extra* profit you might have gained (but never will) gets bigger. And this is a total and real loss. The import of the other two graph lines is obvious.

As Williams points out, "this is real cash, not just paper! It is with this perspective in mind that a decision *not* to implement a computer *immediately* must be considered most carefully as a high risk option containing a high probability of irreversible and ever-increasing differential losses."

AFFORDING IT

Of course, the question is there as to whether you can afford
it. Your business may be undercapitalized for the $4,000-

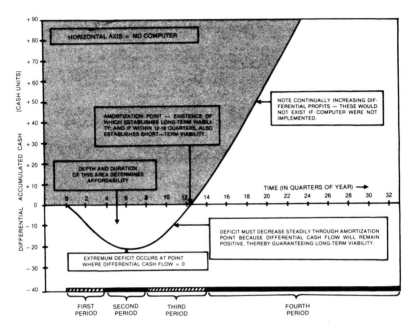

Figure 1-2. Differential accumulated cash for the typical computer
installation of Figure 1. The calculation for this graph is
known technically as a time integral of the differential
cash flow. Scales are arbitrary.

$10,000 typical cost of a microcomputer installation. To quote
Williams again, "...the rational decision to implement a computer is already clear merely by establishing affordability, and
nothing else. The question is not whether to implement a computer (the answer is already 'yes'), but when — the answer being
'as soon as the computer is affordable!'"

In his thinking, which is conservative, Williams estimates that
the small computer will save the labor of one-half to five
employees, or labor costs of $300 to $3,000 monthly. At today's

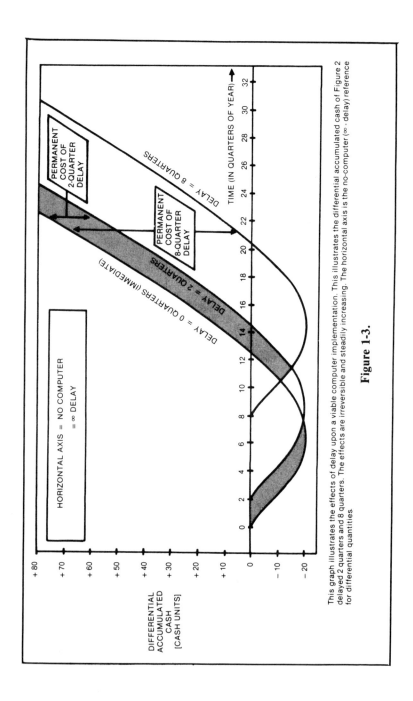

Figure 1-3.

This graph illustrates the effects of delay upon a viable computer implementation. This illustrates the differential accumulated cash of Figure 2 delayed 2 quarters and 8 quarters. The effects are irreversible and steadily increasing. The horizontal axis is the no-computer (∞ - delay) reference for differential quantities.

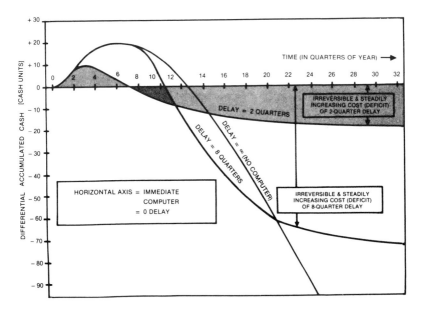

Figure 1-4. Actually Figure 3 repeated, but with "zero delay" (horizontal axis) as the reference. The no-computer or "infinite delay" graph shows increasing amount of cash that could have been earned but was not; this is real, not "theoretical," cash.

actual labor costs in many parts of the country, we think the savings could be greater. Williams puts the cost of acquiring the computer as between $7,000 and $10,000—his minimum is greater than ours ($4,000), but it includes more. His upper figure includes six months of half-time custom programming. You may want that for turning specific alligators into affectionate lap dogs. Farther along in his four-part series, Williams applies his differential cash flow analysis to a hypothetical business using real figures—an annual gross of so much, so many employees, and so on. We have only summarized his case; he establishes it powerfully.

So, if you can afford a computer, get one. But *caveat emptor.* You could buy the wrong horse for the wrong cart. And as in any other line, you could get stung. We do not recommend a two-quarter delay or even a one-quarter delay, but we want to

introduce you to some of the ropes before you encounter your
first computer dealer.

TURNKEY IN THE STORE

It is unlikely that you will be able to run out and buy a computer system that is just right for you right off the shelf. You,
your competitors, and your business neighbors will all purchase
about the same kind of hardware, but it's the software that does
specific things for each of you. That will be the trickiest part of
your computer-shopping. Nevertheless, you should expect some
high degree of **turnkey** capability in the system you buy. That is,
you should be able to have the computer doing something for
you almost as soon as you have it out of the crate. Your system
should have a number of applications programs delivered with
it, that can start handling a few items such as payroll, general
ledger, mailing list, accounts receiveable, and so on, in some
way that is satisfactory to you.

You certainly do not want to buy an all-hardware system and
then start casting about for programs to run on it. Your computer isn't going to do a damn' thing for you without a specific
program for each job. Not only that, the computer system needs
some programs just to run itself. If yours has the kind of external memory (actually, filing system) known as **floppy disk,** or
any kind of disk, it is going to need a **DOS,** or *disk-operating
system.* That "system" is a program in the machine.

The only way to find out specifically which available applications programs are best for you is to have them demonstrated.
You may go to the vendor, or the vendor may bring the whole
kit and kaboodle to you. Either way, *you* must try the programs
on your own data. Use obsolete data if you want to, but make it
real. You want lots of typical-case data, to see if the results
come out in a form satisfactory to you (and to a satisfactory
depth of detail). You also want to try your *worst-case* or *worst-
problem* data on the demonstration system. Have a game of
Stump the Computer, or rather, Stump the Program. The programs won't come through with flying colors on your worst-
problem stuff, because they were not specifically written for

your problems. But you will be able to see whether, and to what extent, you may need custom programming.

You will learn a lot during demonstrations—and you should have more than one system, from more than one vendor, demonstrated to you. Even so, you will learn still more after

Your employee who runs the computer need not be a computer expert, and no employee need be a computer specialist. The microcomputer is simply a business machine, like this Intellec MDS System from Intel Corp.

Photo courtesy of Intel Corp.

buying and installing the computer. The *best* implementation of your computer system will come after you and your staff have had day-to-day experience with it.

GRAPHICS

Some microcomputer systems offer graphics capability. We need not dwell on the value of this capability in the business environment (or in the engineering-company environment). A little more will be said about this in Chapter 4. If you need graphics capability, bring to demonstrations some not-too-hairy examples of the kind of comparison data you would like to see in graph form (curves or bar graphs), or bring some enginering drawing that will challenge the capabilities of the system. Graphics capabilities vary in quality; don't be discouraged if the first one demonstrated to you is a dud for your purposes. Some of them are extremely good; a few produce hard-copy graphics on a "printer" (a computer-run X-Y plotter) as well as displaying them on a screen.

Some microcomputer systems offer graphics capability. This Tektronix 4027 Color Graphics Terminal provides graphics in color.
Courtesy of Tektronix, Inc.

This book has an entire chapter on software — on programs and their documentation (Chapter 4). That chapter will try hard to fill you in on the software picture, but the nitty-gritty part of the learning curve will be mastered through your own experience. There is also a chapter on hardware (coming next). And a chapter on *analyzing your business* to determine your specific needs (Chapter 5). And other chapters to fill you in on what it's all about, plus an appendix that covers, *lightly,* the technicalities of how it all works.

HOW "BIG" A SYSTEM

You will hear and read plenty of advice about buying as big and "capable" a system as you can. We, the authors, belong to the opposing, or "start-small-and-learn" school. Even the conservative Williams has you starting with a rather complete, high-grade system at the $10,000 to $13,000 level. That, we think, might be proper for the larger small businesses that gross $250,000 to $5,000,000 a year. If you are struggling along at sixty to seventy thousand a year or less, but need a computer, a smaller system is probably closer to your needs (and to your affordability!).

This is all highly debatable and loudly debated, and we cannot prove a thing here. But we think it will stand up in court that you should never be put off by a $10,000 or $16,000 price tag and decide that a computer system is not for you. With shrewd shopping, you can break in at $4,000 to $7,000, learn, and enlarge the system later—especially once it is indeed making money for you. Don't let the "ideal" be the enemy of the workable.

A low-cost business computer system, the Commodore CBM series. The computer is in the same cabinet as its keyboard-and-screen terminal, and is here flanked by a dual disk drive and an advanced printer. The "32K" refers to the size of this CBM model's internal memory.

Courtesy of Commodore Business Machines, Inc.

Remember, most small computer systems are underutilized anyway. There are a number of reasons for this. For some time it was due to an unavailability of software to make the small computer do more. But in very large part it is because most small computer users simply do not know—have not learned—

how to make the most of the systems they have. The "minimum" amount of hardware varies rather little. If you are very small, you will still buy a "minimum" resembling your larger associates' "minimum." If you buy only $7,000 worth of computer, you are better off than buying $10,000-$16,000 worth that you underutilize. Your neighbor who buys the bigger system will probably underutilize his.

MAKING MONEY DIRECTLY

Since small computers tend to be underutilized, you can earn money directly by using your computer more fully. You can offer computer services at reasonable cost to business neighbors and associates. Once you have your own payroll, accounts receivable, and so on, under control, you can just use your same software for services you sell. What about that big gas station and garage down on the corner? The owner has perhaps a dozen employees, some part-time, but quite a bit of paperwork. He's a master mechanic and would as soon be relieved of that. But he probably doesn't want to get involved with a computer, even a small one. And he has accounts payable and an inventory — of gasoline, tires, and auto parts. His work you would keep filed on a separate disk or disks. But disks are relatively cheap, and you will already have the expensive disk drive, which you will be using part of the time (underutilized!).

Use your businessman's ingenuity. You will think of far more outlets for your computer services than we can. You have lunch, play golf, go to Lions or Kiwanis or Rotary meetings with other businessmen in other lines of work. You know quite a bit about their operations and about what kinds of problems they have. (And you can read our chapters on different lines of business, too.) Your opportunities are built-in, waiting.

Need we say it ? Every minute of computer time that you can sell helps pay the machine off faster. It gets you up over that "zero line" sooner, into gravy country — pure positive differential cash flow, pure positive differential cash accumulation. But you have already thought of this.

If your computer has **word-processor** software, you can do even more with it, and offer enhanced services to other small businesses. A computer readily processes verbal "data" as well as numerical data; anything you give it is going to be translated into binary code anyway and the computer doesn't care. A word processor can keep lists, write bills and checks, "personalize" form-letter mailings (each letter separately "typed" on the printer), and "individualize" boiler-plate items like contracts. It can edit text, do all kinds of things (see Chapter 4).

In fact, acquiring a word processor computer is a way to start small, even in the $4,000 range. Then you can add software to make the same computer a data-processing (or "number-crunching") computer. You may be a lawyer, or you may be a secretarial service, or something else that needs words processed. But you can offer *that* service, along with the data-processing facilities you later acquire, to others.

The natural cliche to use here is that "entire books could be written about this alone." Books have been written about this alone. Try *From the Counter to the Bottom Line,* by Carl Warren and Merl Miller, from this same press, dilithium, and *How to Make Money with Your Microcomputer,* by Carl Townsend and Merl Miller, from Robotics Press. There is also *How to Profit from Your Personal Computer,* by T. G. Lewis, from Hayden Books. We are personally acquainted with these authors; they are top men in the microcomputer applications field, and they write with clarity and verve. You can further benefit from frequent articles on this topic in magazines like *Interface Age, Small Business Computers,* and others.

"BUT I'M NOT A COMPUTER FREAK..."

That's right. If you were otherwise, we might have no book to write. Some businessmen *are* computer "freaks," or at least are deeply and fruitfully involved with computers. A plumbing contractor friend of ours got hooked—to his own surprise and ultimate delight. And profit. People like him don't need a book like this.

You don't have to become a computer freak, but you do need to make the effort to understand this *new* small business tool, and find out how to make the most of it.

Our plumber friend, by the way, had bought an expensive minicomputer. But he found no software that could handle the esoteric mysteries of plumbing contracting. Grumbling, he studied a computer language and set out to write his own software, on the computer itself. That took up all his nights and weekends for months. This was hard on his family—Daddy had "married" the computer, which took up big chunks of his business time, too. But the breakthrough came. He produced the software. And he copyrighted it. And he packaged it – and he sells it to other plumbing contractors, and at a good price!

He writes articles for the plumbing trade magazines on computerizing. He gets paid for those, too. He isn't at all literary (a plumber?) so he dragooned his wife and college-age daughter – an English Lit major – into "cleaning up" his writing. The daughter complained, but she complied. And when she finished college, she immediately got a high-paying job as a technical writer for a big-computer manufacturer. So there.

THAT MINI- AND MICRO- DISTINCTION

The famed minicomputers share some of the microcomputers' attractive traits – even though they were meant to be scaled-down versions of the forbidding main-frame or "maxi" computers. The major mini makers – IBM, DEC, Hewlett-Packard, and so on – have worked hard to simplify the operation of minicomputers so that they can compete functionally with microcomputers. So that Maisie from Bookkeeping can fearlessly operate them, the way she can a micro. Today's minis even use **microprocessor** chip circuitry, like the micros. There is no sharp dividing line. As a rule of thumb, the mini will come from some venerable giant whose name is a household word, or even a computer-industry symbol, like IBM. Another rule of thumb, the microcomputer is produced by some smaller, rather new company that you probably never heard of, like Cromemco or Northstar or Vector Graphic or Apple or Basic/Four. Or from a formerly "non-computer" firm like Commodore Business Machines, Radio Shack, or Heath. A final rule of thumb: *lower* mini prices are in the range of *upper* micro prices. Exceptions to any of these rules will stand out like sore thumbs and merely prove the rules.

We are apostles of the microcomputer, but the minis have some advantages if you can affort them. One is software compatibility – many tried-and-true programs developed (at great expense) for the maxis will work on them. They can use venerable, highly evolved programming languages like COBOL and FORTRAN. Since IBM and other giants have years ago said, "Okay, we'll publish our codes, and independent programmers may program for our equipment," you are assured that there are programmers all over who know how to custom-program for the minis. Another is the existence of reasonably far-flung service networks. If something goes wrong, you have a giant company's guarantee that a technician with a tool box will show up in a reasonable time. And he should be a highly qualified technician who knows your minicomputer from its table legs up. Also, any established mini has a whole catalog's worth of available peripherals. But see Chapter 6.

WHAT ABOUT JUST RENTING SERVICES?

First off, it now costs more to rent outside computer services (or to buy timesharing, discussed below) than it is to own your own microcomputer system. Of course you can't amortize or depreciate anything you merely rent—especially a service. And you acquire no assets.

Remember the Greek tale about Procrustes? He was the demigod who hung around by the side of the road. He had a bed with him. He enticed or forced travelers to lie down on this bed, which was a measuring instrument. Anyone who was too short was stretched to fit the bed. If anyone was too tall, Procrustes trimmed him or her at the ends. There was no getting by without lying down on the Bed of Procrustes.

Computer services are Procrustean. You do things *their* way. You accomodate your business methods to *them*. You submit data in periodic batches and you get back results in periodic batches—voluminous printouts. The results may be rather stale, not nourishing to the fast metabolism of your small business. You have no control over "computer error." If you need special programming, you pay for it, but you rent it—you never get to own it.

WHAT ABOUT TIMESHARING?

With timesharing, you get faster response. You have a device called a **terminal** in your office. This lets you feed data into the big remote computer and get results right back. Timesharing gives you the illusion of having the entire giant computer at your sole command. Except when you are bumped for mysterious priority traffic, or when the computer "crashes" or "goes down."

But timesharing, too, is expensive. You pay a monthly rental on the terminal. You may as well be making payments on your own computer. And timesharing is Procrustean. The timesharing outfit's big, vanilla-flavored all-user programs aren't just right for you. So you pay for custom software, but you rent it instead of owning it. Your connection with the computer is by telephone line; you pay, say, a dollar an hour to rent that line plus several dollars more for "connect" time. All this comes to much more than the cost of owning your own computer.

If you put the money into your own, you *can* amortize, you *can* depreciate, you do acquire an asset: a useful machine that is a thing of beauty and ultimately a joy.

We discuss services and timesharing more thoroughly in Chapter 6. *However, if you skimmed or skipped the foregoing it was because you have tried one or both of them, and it didn't work out for you.* Yes, you learned that your business could benefit from computerizing, but Procrustes had you limping and scalped. So here you are, considering buying your own.

NOW WHADDAYA MEAN, "REVOLUTION?"

We speak of a Small Computer Revolution because you can have the computing power of a multimillion-dollar main frame computer for a few thousand dollars. This is a rather sudden development. It was not the result of some gentle, predictable evolution. The microcomputer is not the offspring of the big granddaddy computers. It sprang into being on its own, independently of them. It is of practical importance to you to have some notion of *how come*. It will give you a perspective that will meaningfully affect your purchasing strategy.

The microcomputer is the outgrowth of developments in the **semiconductor** industry, not the computer industry. Transistors are examples of semiconductor industry products.

The first true, full-fledged, fully programmable digital computer, ENIAC, was completed in 1946. Its circuits employed 18,500 vacuum tubes. These were used for lightning-fast, automatic switching. You may have heard that digital computing is a matter of juggling combinations of ones and zeroes—that all numbers (and all other data, including words) are translated into **binary numbers** that can only have 1 and 0 as digits. (Why digital computers are built this way is a matter for the Appendix). The "1" and "0" can be represented by whether a switch is closed ("turned on") or opened ("turned off"). Obviously, a computer needs a lot of switches, and they ought to be fast. Vacuum tubes could operate as the fastest switches in existence in 1946.

In 1952, the first transistors became commercially available. The pea-sized early transistors were a tiny fraction of the size of a tube. They needed no heated filament. They ran at a few percent of the typical operating voltage of a tube. They operated at low current. This meant they could perform "tube" functions while using much less power than a tube.

The transistor hardly affected the computer industry at first. Not many computers were being built in the 1950s anyway. But a trend towards miniaturization in electronics, begun during the Second World War, took a big leap. Some devices got small quickly, such as hearing aids and portable radios. The transistors themselves became cheap. Ultimately, "transistor arts" were applied to computers. It became easier to make, sell, power, and maintain a computer. This set off the Big Computer Revolution. That revolution was barely up to speed when the Small Computer Revolution dry-gulched it.

THE INTEGRATED CIRCUIT

About 1960, somebody found a way to make two or more separate transistors on the same tiny chip of semiconductor metal. These could be combined, on the chip itself, with microminiaturized circuit elements to make a practical device. Thus was born the **integrated circuit,** or **IC.** The IC is now the dominant circuit module in practically all electronics.

Integrated circuits rapidly got "larger," that is, more complex, on the same-sized little chips. It became possible to have extremely sophisticated switching circuits on a tiny IC chip. And these were what computer engineers call **logic circuits.**

A semiconductor chip of typical size. Today, whether a chip holds one transistor or 100,000 of them, the size is about the same.
Courtesy of Intel Corp.

Their most common use was in industrial controls. A semiconductor chip could replace a small cabinet full of relays and motor-driven stepping switches. By the late 1960s, IC chips were appearing in clothes dryers and dishwashers, and even in toys. They were simpler, more reliable, and *cheaper* than the mechanical control devices they replaced.

BUT WHAT'S A SEMICONDUCTOR?

We just used that term "semiconductor" again and it is time to explain it. Familiar metals such as copper, aluminum, iron, and even silver and gold are *conductors.* Electricity flows through them readily. An electric current can flow every which way in a conductor. There is no preferred direction of flow. If you pass an electric current through a copper penny, it will flow as well from tails to heads as from heads to tails—and you can tap the current off the edges if you want to.

A few metals behave peculiarly as conductors. In their pure crystalline forms they have a preferred direction of current flow. While current moves readily in one direction, it flows weakly (hardly at all) in the opposite direction. These metals are *semiconductors.* A semiconductor device is a one-way-flow device, *and so was the vacuum tube.* (Now you have it in a nutshell why the transistor could come along and duplicate the functions of the tube.)

Silicon—one of the two most common metals in the Earth's crust—is usualy the semiconductor of choice. Ordinary quartz sand is silicon dioxide, SiO_2, and sand is the raw material for semiconductor silicon. This is one reason why semiconductor devices can be cheap.

And so you hear about "Silicon Alley" and "Silicon Valley" (or "Silicon Gulch"). The U.S. semiconductor industry has two centers. Silicon Alley is along Route 128, around metropolitan Boston. Silicon Valley (or Gulch) is at the northern end of the Santa Clara Valley, in California, along the south shore of San Francisco Bay. That's where most of the microcomputer action is.

LARGE SCALE INTEGRATION (LSI)

Through the 1960's, fabrication techniques kept improving. More and more transistors could be accomodated—not crowded! — within the area of a tiny silicon chip. Circuits could get more and more complex, and could do more.

These circuits were performing logic and "decision" functions, just like similar circuits in computers. For control applications, input on-off switching data was *processed* to provide patterns of output on-off switching. So the little chip circuits were called **microprocessors.** The microprocessor, with upwards of 100 transistors on a single chip, was an example of **large scale integration,** or **LSI.** (Other kinds of LSI circuits exist.)

One thing the microprocessor made possible was the pocket calculator. These have certainly proliferated. And they come down rapidly in price so that even schoolchildren can afford them. The chips became cheaper once they were mass-produced and their development costs were amortized.

AND SUDDENLY —

One day, *circa* 1970, somebody came up with a microprocessor chip with transistors arranged in a tictactoe matrix 100 on a side. Multiply 100 by 100 and you get 10,000 transistors on one chip. This is *something approaching the 18,500 vacuum tubes in ENIAC,* or the thousands of transistors in a 1970-model big computer. The 10,000-transistor chip could be designed with any kind of "computer-style" logic circuits the design engineer wished. One or two of these could run a complete computer...

The chip is delicate and needs protection — and connection points. This is an 8085 chip, successor to the famous 8080 of the first true microcomputer. A 1924 $20 gold piece, smaller than a dime, gives scale. The protective-connective device is called a dual in-line package, or DIP. The DIP's cover has been left off in this photo.
Courtesy of Intel Corp.

VOILA!

And so it came to pass. In 1975, the MITS Corporation brought out the first *microcomputer,* which it marketed as the *Altair.* A few miles down the road in Silicon Gulch, engineers at the IMSAI Corporation had had the same idea. When the *Altair* came out, the IMSAI gang did not despair. They responded with a stroke of genius. They finished their computer using the *Altair* "wiring harness," or **bus.** This gave both companies a "second source" for anything they marketed to go with their computers. It also encouraged outside designers of computer peripherals and auxiliary circuits, and outside software writers. Anything *anybody* marketed for either computer could be used with the other. (Had there been two completely different designs, nobody may have wanted to make anything for them.) And so, immediately, the microcomputer industry was on its feet. Tiny, yes; shaky, yes; but on its feet.

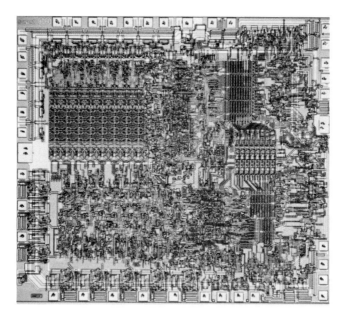

An Intel 8080A microprocessor chip, greatly magnified. Its complexity would be best conveyed in a wall-sized magnification. Metals are removed from and added to the pure silicon substrate in as many as 16 photo-etching and deposition steps. The photographic process involves reduction, the opposite of enlargement, from large templates.
Courtesy of Intel Corp.

Please notice that the microcomputer was not developed by
the computer industry. IBM, DEC, and the others were not in
the picture at all. The microcomputer did *not* evolve by some
process of scaling down a Goliath computer to make something
the small businessman could afford. The microcomputer was
not developed for business applications. It was believed hobby-
and-home, or "personal," applications made the most likely
market. It was believed that microcomputer sales could benefit
from the public enthusiasm for "computer games" and other
microprocessor-based toys. This belief was an error that the
microcomputer industry perceived after a couple of years, and
since 1978 the main emphasis has shifted to business.

The home-and-hobby market for microcomputers is healthy, but all
major manufacturers are now concentrating on the small business
market, which should grow indefinitely. Home and hobby markets
will experience peaks in the next few years and descend to lower
plateaus than the business market.
Courtesy of Radio Shack, a Division of Tandy Corp.

THE SIGNIFICANCE

The infant microcomputer industry is a branch or scion of the semiconductor industry. While the big computer firms are getting into microcomputers (most of today's minicomputers are microcomputers at heart, quite literally) it remains a separate computer field. You will look to it, and through it to the semiconductor industry, for major developments.

What kinds of developments? In pricing and performance. As has been said and written elsewhere, "progress in the microcomputer field keeps getting ahead of everyone's expectations." Performance rises and prices diminish faster than anyone dares predict. Prices for total systems at least hold their own against inflation.

A new microprocessor chip in its sealed DIP, the Intel 8086. This chip was introduced as this book was being written; it will be used in a new generation of microcomuters having faster operation and greater memory capacity. It is "hardware-compatible" but not always "software-compatible" with "classic" microcomputer designs.

Courtesy of Intel Corp.

But stop and consider. What "steadily" goes down in price is the semiconductor electronics at the heart of the microcomputer. Yes, as the industry tools up for *real* mass production, prices should diminish further. But as we—and Roger Williams and many other observers—have pointed out, the electronics represents only a small fraction of the cost of the total system. If chip prices are cut to one-half or even one-quarter of what they are now, it won't make much difference. As for upward leaps in performance, today's microcomputers have all the performance most small businesses can use. Once more, if you want for prices to come down still further, you lose money while you wait, and you will lose much more money than you will have "saved" by waiting. If you can use a computer now and can afford it now, get it now.

Chapter Two

THE SMALL BUSINESS COMPUTER

This chapter offers a completely nontechnical overview of the physical structure of a small computer system. It is intended only to familiarize you with the hardward and acquaint you with the major concepts. It will introduce some of the technical jargon you will inevitably encounter. For a more detailed explanation of how it all works, see Appendix A.

All computers, of any size and computing power, consist of three basic units: an **input device,** an **output device,** and a **central processing unit,** or **CPU.** The input device is used, of course, to feed the data and instructions to the CPU. The output device displays, records, or prints results. The CPU is the heart of the computer — or rather, the brain. In truth, the CPU *is* the computer, the part that does the real work.

Figure 2-1 shows three boxes, with arrows to indicate the information flow. The input and output devices are unspecified; they can each be of several kinds. You may just, for now, regard the three diagram boxes as three physical "black boxes" that in some "mysterious" way get a job done for you.

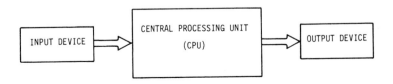

Figure 2-1. "The computer."

Most books use a similar diagram with four, five, or more boxes. One box may be labeled "storage" or sometimes, "memory." Another box may be labeled "clock" or "timer" or something that translates to one of those. However, every CPU has some inherent information-storage capability, or "memory," and every CPU relies on the clock as part of its auxiliary circuitry. The CPU itself maybe broken down into a "control unit" and an "arithmetic logic unit (ALU)." In our next diagram, Figure 2-2, this next level of detail is shown. Behold a whole bunch of boxes, with appropriate connecting arrows. It is really a matter of nit-picking as to whether the clock or storage or whatever is, or is not, to be considered an integral part of the CPU. What do you care? You probably don't. When you have come to care, see Appendix A. Meanwhile, for your present purposes, *a computer system consists of an input device, an output device, and a CPU.* (Don't worry if some manufacturer refers to his CPU as "the processor" or "the microprocessor.")

The input and output devices, however, are always distinct from the CPU. This will be true even if you buy a computer system that has everything in one cabinet. Input and output devices can be changed. You can literally just unplug one and plug in another. In practice, you leave them all plugged in and switch from one to another. Indeed, the computer will do this for you. You will probably come to own several of each.

Input and output devices are also known as **peripheral devices** because they are peripheral to the computer itself, the CPU. The computer neither knows nor cares what kind of device it is working with. It will still do its job, in the same way. But the peripherals are inert until the computer tells one of them to do something.

There are a number of possible and actual CPU structures or designs, but the CPU in your small business computer will be a **microprocessor chip**, also frequently nicknamed a "microprocessor." The advent of the microprocessor, which does the same job as the old giant "main frame" CPU's, was outlined in Chapter One. Most of today's "serious" small computer systems use additional microprocessor chips for auxiliary purposes, so it can become awkward to speak of "the" microprocessor. The term "CPU" is completely unambiguous and denotes a *function.* That's all you care about.

Fairly ample notes on input and output (and combined input-

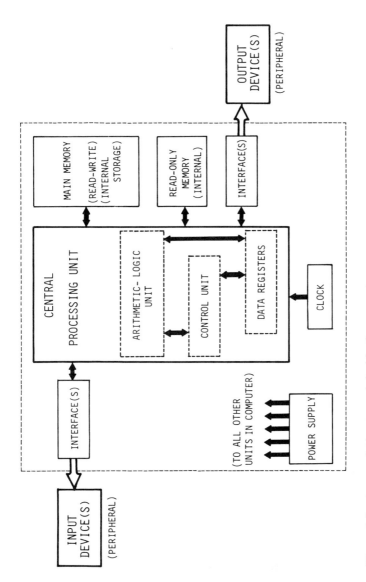

Figure 2-2. A more intimate peek inside the computer.

output) devices will be offered near the end of this chapter and also in Chapter 8. They are categorized in the microcomputer industry as **I/O devices**, and I/O, like CPU, is part of the jargon you are going to pick up. For the moment, it is enough to say that among the I/O devices (peripherals!) available for your microcomputer are *Teletype*™ machines and their relatives; electric *typewriters* with electronics added to afford an *interface* with your CPU; separate *keyboards* without a typing or printing mechanism, for entering data or instructions only; *CRT display units,* which resemble television screens; *cassette drives* using standard audio cassettes for entering or recording informaton; *floppy disk* and *diskette* drives which, like cassette or other tape, are magnetic read-in, read-out devices; a variety of *printers* having a variety of speeds (up to 300 characters a second, or perhaps higher: progress is rapid); and *modems*, which are devices that permit using a telephone line to communicate with another computer.

Rest assured that there are quite a few peripherals that offer convenient ways of getting information into and out of the magic box that is your microcomputer. There are even industrial control devices, though they are beyond the scope of this book.

Some small computer units now on the market have the CPU circuitry and one, two, or more I/O devices all in one cabinet. There are pros and cons to this approach that will be taken up later in this chapter.

It is now time to look at various aspects of your computer and its peripherals, in order to develop a clear understanding of what it is you will be investing in. We shall avoid technical jargon except where you would probably agree that it would be useful. You will also find its use inevitable in such places. This chapter will avoid depths of technical detail. (But do try Appendix A later; it is to your advantage to deepen your understanding of the computer as a tool.) Suppose we start with *interfacing.*

INTERFACING

An **interface** is some electronic circuitry that makes a particular I/O device compatible with your CPU. Usually, an interface fits on a single printed-circuit (PC) board that plugs in somewhere, either inside the CPU's cabinet (which some microcomputer manufacturers call the "main frame," although it's no bigger than a breadbox) or inside the peripheral's.

This is a printer interface circuit on its printed-circuit board or "card," known as a PCB. The various dual-in-line packages, or DIPs, on this board contain circuits that marry the computer to the printer. The printed circuit "wiring" can plainly be seen — even the back-of-board signal lines can be discerned. Connectors for flat ribbon cables are at the top of the board. Gold-plated "teeth" at the bottom edge plug into a connector on the motherboard or "bus."

Courtesy of Cromemco

All your input-output devices have to be compatible with your patricular CPU and its **bus**. This leads us immediately to an apparent digression but please bear with it: everything here is really on the same track. A "bus" is a sort of wiring harness. It is a set of signal lines, built to a protocol, that will carry data bits (and electric power, for operating) to and from the CPU. The bus affords the actual wiring into which the I/O devices and other accessories can be connected.

The necessity for the bus becomes clear when you consider that a microprocessor chip may have 40 or more pin connections on it. Of course each pin represents something definite inside the microprocessor circuit. Each pin has to connect to some sort of pin jack that is in turn connected to some conductor ("wire") that can be connected to something else. (True wires are not used. The circuitry employs **printed circuit board** or **PCB** technology, in which the "wires" are lines of conductive material literally printed onto an insulating plastic card.) A standard bus offers a standard, predictable way to connect devices to a CPU — and even to assemble the total CPU circuit, since the microprocessor chip and its auxiliary circuits can all plug into the bus.

Some manufacturers prefer to call their bus a "motherboard." There are some semantic niceties about this that we won't go into. You haven't got time. In a small computer, a **motherboard** is a bus. We have spoken.

If a particular peripheral is designed for connection to a certain bus type, the jargon saying is that the device "supports" that bus. Thus you read or hear that this CRT display or that floppy disk drive "supports the S-100 bus." The S-100 is the bus design that was used in the earliest true, flexible microcomputer, the Altair. The S-100 bus quickly became so common in microcomputer designs it can be regarded as a sort of standard. Myriad other computers, including all that use the famous 8080 chip and its descendants, use or "support" the S-100 bus.

Remember that word "support." *In this context* it means "is compatible with" or "is designed to be used with." The implication is that a device that "supports" the XYZ bus or the HAL *2001* CPU or whatever *does not* "support" some competing bus or chip or CPU. (There are other meanings of *support* in the computer lexicon that will become apparent later.)

Now, the key to interfacing: there is nothing about any keyboard, disk drive, CRT display, printer, or other I/O device that *inherently* causes it to support a given bus or CPU type.

Interface Circuits

What counts is that electronic circuitry, the interface, that meaningfully connects the particular device to the bus and CPU. This is much more than a matter of selecting the right pin connections. (In fact, several different peripherals may use the same pin connections on the CPU chip, through the bus "wires.") The interface makes sure that the electrical output of the I/O device is in the proper form for the computer — and that the device can respond to signals from the computer. Output and input, each way, must consist of electric pulses of a specified length, of a specified voltage, and in the proper coding. The device and the CPU must constantly exchange **handshaking** signals by means of which they stay coordinated. The interface extends the device's hand to the CPU.

A note on buses. The S-100 bus has been controversial. It has had its critics. Furthermore, not all manufacturers who use the S-100 bus use it in the same way. This makes hairy problems for programmers and may cause some inconvenience for periph-

This interface board enables a microcomputer to drive a cathode-ray tube or CRT display, to show up to 24 lines of 80 characters each. The integrated circuits on this board "remember" how to form 256 different characters on the display screen, including letters, numbers, and even graphics characters preprogrammed by the user. This is called a video interface.

Courtesy of Vector Graphic Inc.

eral-interface designers. For the past few years, a standards committee of the Computers Group of the Institute of Electrical and Electronics Engineers (IEEE) has been working up a set of standards for use of the S-100 bus. The new standards are expected to be ready soon. The matter will be discussed further in the Appendix. You may find yourself "involved" because you may be offered equipment that uses another bus (or "motherboard") design. Not long ago we might have said, "Stick with S-100 — it's not a perfect standard but it's the only standard we've got." However, the trend today is for manufacturers to offer systems — not just a "computer" (CPU) for which you are expected to find peripherals. If a system is complete — keyboard, CRT, disk drives, printers, whatever — and *proven*, but "has its own" bus, a non-S-100 bus, it's okay. It has an "internal" standard. At least it has internal consistency. And interfacing has been taken care of.

Caveat

Many models of various peripherals incorporate interfacing circuitry for a given bus or CPU, but beware. The peripheral manufacturer may assume that you can provide your own interfaces. Or, the interface cards may cost extra, whether supplied

H89 P.C. Board

The Heath Company (Heathkit) microcomputers have their own bus design or motherboard. This is acceptable because Heath computer systems have their own line of compatible peripherals available.

Courtesy of Heath Company

by the peripheral manufacturer or the computer manufacturer. However, the leading brands of small business computers do incorporate interfacing for certain peripherals, and nowadays at least a few basic peripherals are offered as part of this computer package.

MEMORIES ARE MADE OF THIS...

The data storage capability of your microcomputer is one of the marvels of electronic miniaturization. The main "memory" consists of semiconductor chips that each hold thousands of electrical on-off switches. The "on" position in any switch can represent a 1 and the off position a 0. Either a *one* or *zero* can represent a **bit** of information. ("Bit" is a condensation of "*bi*nary digi*t*.") Each of the switches, then, can "remember" either a 1 or a 0 depending on how it is thrown. Thus each switch can store *either* of two possible bits. When a switch that is "on" is turned "off," it then stores a zero instead of a one.

Storing information as either a 1 or a 0 is called **binary coding** (explained in Appendix A). We may safely ignore the details of binary coding for the moment.

Arbitrarily, computer designers call a set of eight bits a **byte.** In most microcomputers a single byte is also a **word** in the memory. Most larger computers use at least a two-byte "word," and so do a few microcomputers. For present purposes, the number of bytes in a word is unimportant. You only need to understand what bits, bytes, and those figurative "words" are.

Now, the bits in a byte may take any combination of ones and zeroes—there are 2^8 or 256 possible combinations. Thus a one-byte word can have 256 possible meanings. A two-byte word as 2^{16}, or 65,536, possible meanings.

A typical minimum microcomputer memory will hold a nominal 8,000 or 16,000 bytes—that is 64,000 or 128,000 individual bits. That is an impressive amount of information to be held in a piece of silicon foil about the size of the pupil of your eye. And you may purchase microcomputers with main memories holding a nominal 32,000 or 64,000 bytes, or even 128,000 bytes. Look for designs that offer *add-on* capability, so that you can start small (with 16,000 bytes) and expand capacity later.

Memory add-ons start small, with about 4000 bytes, and run up as high as this 64K memory board from Cromemco. With this particular add-on module, up to 512K bytes of memory are possible in eight banks. Do not take it for granted that any computer you buy will accept memory add-ons, however. The most popular microcomputer chips (8080, 8085, Z-80, 6800, etc.) are inherently limited to 64K of memory or less, unless hardware/software provision has been made in the computer design for memory fan-out.

Courtesy of Cromemco

Random Access

The storage in the heart of the CPU, that we have been discussing, is a **random-access memory**, which the industry predictably calls a **RAM**. In a random-access memory, the "memory search" for a wanted byte is virtually instantaneous. The CPU can go staight to that byte when it is needed.

It is easier to understand a RAM by first considering a non-random memory. A phonograph record is an example of a non-RAM. The phono platter stores music information, a rigid sequence in space and time (along the groove). You cannot instantly call forth a particular note or chord from the record. It is impossible for you to know in advance exactly where to set down the pickup head to catch a favorite hemisemidemiquaver, grace note, or tympani bang. You just have to let the record play "until it gets there." A music tape, of course, operates the same way. So does a computer data tape. To retrieve any one item of data you must let the tape "play" until the item is reached. Records and tapes are **sequential-access memories.**

Your own memory is a random-access memory in the way it usually operates. You can recall any one thing you know without first having to recall everything you learned before you learned the particular thing. Your memory is not as efficient as a computer's RAM. Sometimes you are obliged to go through some sequential searching: "Where did I put my glasses? Now, let's see, I came in from the garage, set the six-packs down on the kitchen counter, went to the hall closet and hung up my coat...." But if the location of your glasses were in the computer's memory, the computer would go straight to that. "Hall table by the telephone" would be displayed in the readout.

In a computer's random-access memory, each word (or each byte, in a typical microcomputer) has a unique *address.* No other word or byte has the same address. The closest analogy to a computer RAM is probably the honeycomb wall of post-office boxes in the lobby of the post office. Each box has a number. To get your mail, you go right to your numbered box. You do not have to search all the boxes sequentially (or randomly!) to find your mail. Likewise, each address in a computer RAM has a number. To retrieve information at that address, the computer invokes the number, and *voila!* — out pops the "mail."

The RAM belongs to a wider class of memories known as read-write memories. You may put information into a RAM ("write" it in) any time and get it back ("read" it out) any time. Your memory is obviously a read-write memory. A magnetic sound tape or data tape is a read-write memory: you can record information on it, "read" the information out again, change the

A 48K-byte RAM card from Vector Graphic.
Courtesy of Vector Graphic Inc.

information you have recorded if you wish, and thus change what you will read out. In contrast, a phonograph record is a "read only" memory. Music information can be "written" onto the record disk just once. You may "read" it back out hundreds of times, but there is no way you can change it without permanently damaging the record: you can only destroy the information.

Your own memory has *non-destructive* read-in and read-out. Your learning a new thing does not force you to forget other things you had learned previously. According to currently accepted psychological theory, your memory still holds everything you have ever experienced, and you can retrieve experiences in complete detail, with total recall, at least in special states such as hypnosis. The human memory seems to have unlimited capacity. (While no one has devised a way to locate its limits, common sense says it must be finite.)

A computer RAM has non-destructive read-out, but *destructive* read-in. Suppose you have an "8K byte" memory in your computer. This means "8000 bytes" and the actual number is 2^{13}, or 8192 bytes. This allows you a nominal 64,000 bits of information (actually, 65,536 bits). But what matters is the 8192 bytes, because the information has to be organized and addressable. Very well. Once you have entered the 8192 bytes you have reached the absolute limit. You cannot enter one more byte.

You cannot even enter one more bit, *without destroying a byte already there.*

Your attempt to add information can only create a new byte. But this has to be at the expense of one of the old bytes, so you still have only 8192 bytes of information. The computer's internal memory or RAM is not like yours; it is strictly limited.

Your computer's RAM, by the way, typically consists of a number of separate chips, though in principle the entire RAM could be accomodated on one chip.

Volatility

One thing you ought to know about the RAM is that it is a *volatile* memory. That is, its contents are lost when the equipment is turned off (or if there is a power failure). Programs and data that were in the RAM before the power went off must be re-entered once the power comes back on. This is the nature of the currently typical *semiconductor* RAM circuits. Like the vacuum-tube memory circuits of the ancient main-frame computers, they only function while they are turned on.

This is no great cause for concern, as will become plain in a moment. It could cause some inconvenience at times.

In principle, there is no reason why a RAM cannot be developed that would retain its contents whether power was on or off. But be patient.

There are two kinds of semiconductor RAM, *static* and *dynamic.* This is supposed to be a nontechnical chapter, and we apologize for inflicting this technical detail on you. But you will be hearing one type or another mentioned, especially when you are talking with a salesman.

In *static RAM,* the "switches" really are transistor switching circuits, and once they are switched either way they stay that way until you do something to change them (or the computer does).

In *dynamic RAM,* the "switched" states are represented by relative levels of charge in tiny capacitor circuits. Capacitors leak; microscopic capacitors leak fast. The memory elements in a dynamic RAM tend to "forget" fast. For this reason, a dynamic RAM needs to be continually *refreshed.* The computer itself will do this, taking time out from other chores every few milliseconds. It will read all the RAM memory positions while they are still readable, and put appropriate new charges on each capacitor. This, of course, slows the computer down. Some dynamic RAM memory circuits include built-in "refresh circuits," to relieve the computer. But this defeats, at least in part, the attractiveness of the dynamic RAM: it can be cheaper than static RAM.

We, the authors, personally favor static RAM on theoretical grounds: there are more chances of error when information has to be constantly rewritten, which is what is happening in a dynamic RAM. But static RAM costs more.

A design engineer has to worry about tradeoffs. A good designer always looks for cost effectiveness. But his boss, the manufacturer, has to worry about what you, the customer, may think is cost-effective. Maybe, he thinks, you won't want it so foolproof; maybe you would just like it cheaper. Any design short of an ideal design involves compromises and agonized judgment.

The ROM, PROM, EPROM Family

Your small computer will contain other semiconductor memory chips known as **ROM**, for *read-only memory*. These have had information permanently written into them at the factory. Unlike RAM chips, they are *non-volatile*. On or off, awake or asleep, they maintain their cargoes of information. Yet like the RAM, the ROM is *random-access,* with discrete addresses and instantly retrievable contents. Only, like the phonograph record, it will only read information out. It cannot take new information in.

Your computer needs some permanent, "instinctive" information, figuratively to enable the computer to know, "I compute, therefore I am." It needs at least a few hints on *how* to compute. Theoretically, you could run a computer on RAM-type memory alone (and that's how it was at the dawn of the computer age) but that would be frightfully inconvenient and slow. So, some of the system programming, the internal operating instruction set, is permanently resident in your microcomputer on ROM chips. Interfaces for I/O devices also involve ROM chips. A ROM can be considered a "hard-wired" memory with its internal switch connections physically set.

You will hear about the ROMs along with the RAM chips in your computer: in the sales talk. You will also hear about PROMs. A **PROM** is a *programmable read-only memory*. It is still a ROM, but its programming was not simultaneous with its manufacture. It contains a light-sensitive surface in which program pathways can be etched by a process akin to photography. So, a computer manufacturer — who is distinct from the semiconductor chip manufacturer — can purchase blank, unprogrammed ROMs in the form of PROMs, and program them for his own purposes. Once the PROM has been programmed, it is sealed into a light-proof package.

That was another technical detail. You don't care how the computer manufacturer programs his ROMs. At least, you don't need to. We apologize, furtively hoping that you at least find it interesting to know how somebody in some other line does something. But there is more.

Inevitably, there has been marketed the **EPROM:** the **erasable programmable read-only memory.** A special ultraviolet lamp erases the old programming paths. An optical system etches in new ones. This is not a convenient way to reprogram anything in the business office. But you will hear about the EPROMs and read about them in blurbs.

The information (programming) in an EPROM chip is erasable by a beam of ultraviolet light. Then the chip can be reprogrammed. The window in this DIP (Intel's 2716) is opaque to the weak ultraviolet components in ordinary light. This chip can be programmed with 16,384 bits (2048 bytes) of data.

Courtesy of Intel Corp.

The **EAROM** may matter. This is rather new as we write; it is the *electrically alterable read-only memory*. It is non-volatile like the ancestor ROM but no ultraviolet optical system is needed to reprogram it. Its contents can be changed by an electrical circuit, amenable to manipulation through a computer keyboard or program. It might conceivably lend itself to some do-it-yourself reprogramming in the business office.

The family of ROM-PROM-EPROM-EAROM devices will probably continue to grow, and you will encounter new acronyms resembling these. They are all read-only memories of some sort, that's all.

A computer salesman may make much of the number of RAM, ROM, and PROM, etc., chips his little wonder box uses. If he does, we suggest that you go through the motions of suppressing a yawn and of contemplating the sheen on your fingernails. Or give whatever couldn't-care-less signal you like. Then politely but implacably demand to know how much information his computer can process how fast; what kinds of **applications software** (discussed later) are available for it; whether the store offers loaner services and has its own repair shop; what his dealer-guarantees cover; what the details of his financing plan are; and how much of a discount is offered on 90 days net. Questions like that. Nitty-gritty.

A FINAL MEMORY

Coming into the stretch: **bubble memories.** These are random-access, read-write memories that use microscopic domains of magnetic polarization in a metal film — rather than the microscopic transistor or capacitor circuits of the semiconductor memory. Magnetic bubble memories should soon offer greater memory capacity than the semiconductor RAM at lower cost. Also, like magnetic tape or ROM, they are *non-volatile*. Their information contents will be there whether the power is turned off or on.

Bubble memories offer a number of technical advantages including partial simplification of the CPU system circuitry, and may achieve marginally lowered cost of the rest of the computer. It is conceivable that removeable (or "plug-in") bubble memories may replace tapes and disks for external storage. *This could mean enormous system savings* since the expensive tape or disk drive mechanisms would not be needed.

As with semiconductor devices, the costs of magnetic bubble devices have been trending downward, and are expected to go sharply lower from year to year. A few computer manufacturers offer early-model bubble memories right now, but not at the invitingly low cost they are expected to have in just a few years.

However, if you can use a computer right now, do not wait for cheaper bubble memories. Your *total system* might not be much cheaper a few years from now even with dime-store priced bubble memory chips. (They'll never really be dime-store priced.) You can always change or upgrade your system later. Remember that analysis of the "computerize now" *vs.* "computerize later" options outlined in Chapter One. What's available NOW does the job you need done NOW.

MASS STORAGE

So much for internal memories. External memories exist; these are called **mass storage.** Unlike a RAM or ROM, with its criss-crossing pulses of electric current, these are not really "memories" but "files." Common examples include:

1. Stacks of Hollerith cards ("IBM cards")
2. Rolls of punched paper tape
3. Magnetic tapes and disks

Suppose we ignore examples 1 and 2, since you will probably use the third types exclusively. If we are mistaken, you can easily find out what you need to know about 1 and 2 elsewhere. As of 1979 no manufacturer we know of was offering card equipment for microcomputers. A few firms were offering Teletype™-style automatic paper tape punches and readers, but really for hobby and experimental use. We envision no business-office uses for punched Teletype™ or "computer" paper tape. Magnetic tapes and disks are so much *faster* and more compact.

Disks

Magnetic-recording storage devices for microcomputers are mainly *dual* tape-cassette drives and *dual* floppy-disk drives. Increasingly, *double dual* disk drives are appearing—capable of handling four disks. But the principles are the same regardless of the number of tapes or disks. The drive mechanisms, by the way, are operated by the computer itself. You would not have to play disk jockey or tape jockey when using your computer.

A small disk drive with connecting cable and "diskettes."
Courtesy Midwest Scientific Instruments

Heathkit's dual-diskette drive with its disk controller (interface) board.
Courtesy of Heath Company

A disk has a magnetized surface, like a tape, and accepts or gives back information the same way—by means of recording and playback heads. Tape drives have the advantage of low cost, plus the ready accessibility of cassettes, which have been around for a long time. But disks have the advantage of being, virtually, random-access memories.

A disk cannot be as fast as a true RAM, because it depends on moving parts. But it spins—and its record and playback heads can move back and forth along a radius. This enables the designer to assign blocks of information to definite parts of the disk. Thus a given byte can have a sort of address on the disk—a true geographical location where it can be quickly found. The disk spins at several hundred RPM, and information retrieval is "instantaneous" in terms of human reflex times.

Different manufacturers have different schemes for distributing information on a disk surface, so that one computer's disk drive may not make sense of another computer's disk, or may not directly interface with some particular CPU. This will probably give you no problems unless you are buying your computer system components one at a time, by mail order, rather than shopping for a complete system.

The Reason for Mass Storage

It's simple. Your CPU's internal, random-access, instant-access memory (RAM) is limited in capacity. It cannot hold all the information you are ever going to work with. What you need your RAM for is to hold instructions (programs) for the job at hand and enough of the data for the instructions to chew on. What's more, the internal memory is volatile—turn the machine off, or have a power failure, and that's that. Instant amnesia. Hence your need for external files.

You want to save space and expense as well as time, so you want *compact* storage. For obvious reasons, you want information stored in a medium that is computer-compatible—a medium that deals in the computer's own currency, electromagnetic impulses. Such a medium lets you move information into and out of the computer with a minimum of fuss. No fuss, in fact, once the disks or cassettes are in their drives and the computer is working with them.

As storage, these magnetic devices indeed are compact. One small floppy disk can carry the equivalent of 160 typewritten sheets of paper. Progress at increasing the density of data stored on disks was rapid in 1978 and 1979. *Small* files on disks will replace bulky files of paper documents for you.

Of course you cannot visually read the information stored on a disk or tape. That is no cause for concern. Assuming decent programming, the computer will print out in concise form whatever you do need to read, at a simple command from you. (And it will display the information on a CRT screen during entry, at various processing steps, or before or during printout.)

You (or your operator: Elsie from Bookkeeping?) will keyboard information *through* the computer onto file disks for immediate or future processing. Display or printout permits monitoring and review of the process. If you should have custom programming done, the programmer will produce a number of sheets of paper covered with columns of typewritten numbers. He or she will expect these numbers to be keyboarded onto a disk or tape. (Most packaged programs that you might buy will be delivered on disk or tape.) Of course the program can be "typed directly" into the computer's memory, but without that storage, more "typing" will be required each time you use the program.

It is easy to see that external mass storage is essential. It saves time and boosts efficiency in countless ways. Now, suppose you have processed a lot of data and need to produce a voluminous report. While the computer is printing that out, it is tied up. Printing is slow. The printer may produce 30 to 300 characters per second, but the computer can handle thousands of *words* per second. You have an option. You may delay printout, storing your data on a disk while the computer does other urgent jobs. When these are finished, the computer can produce the big report from the disk "at leisure."

Chapter 8 describes the new hard or "Winchester" disks, that are not removable but which store millions of bytes on one disk.

Multiple Use

Actually, a computer can do two (or more) jobs "at the same time." At least it seems like the same time to the human operators. This is variously called multiplexing, timesharing, or some other name that translates to one of these. For example, your computer *could* print that big report *while* being used to process other data. How this is done, and a closer look at what is really going on, are matters for the next chapter (and Appendix A). Until recently most microcomputer systems could not do this, but the number is growing. The ability to multiplex is inherent in all true digital computers.

Multiplexing is a software problem, not a hardware problem, and software is what we should be talking about just now.

The same computer can be used to operate all these work stations simultaneously. How many separate users and how well they are served is in large part a function of the system's software. Each of these stations connected to a Cromemco System Three computer also has its own memory (RAM), to augment the computer's main memory. Your office setup may never look quite like this but you get the idea.

Courtesy of Cromemco

Are you kidding? SOFTware?

Don't skip or skim this section, and do give the next chapter your full attention. Software for microcomputers has been a problem, and to some extent still is. We seriously advise you not to buy any hardware unless you have solid assurances about where the appropriate software is going to come from—and how much it will cost. Software is the heart of your data processing system. The hardware (the computer itself) is just the means by which the software does the job.

Software is programs and documentation. A **program** is a set **of instructions given a computer to enable it to do a certain** thing. **Documentation** is instructions for using the programs, along with important related information—it is roughly analogous to the circuit diagrams and other information that enabled the computer itself to be built.

You will have different programs for different jobs (**applications**). There are also internal programs, or sets of programs ("systems") that enable the machine to operate itself and its peripherals. **Operating systems** that are permanently stored on ROM chips, by the way, are called **firmware**. You even want whatever documentation you can get on that. It is best to have a complete description and record of everything that is going on in there.

Software will be discussed in detail in the next chapter (this one is the hardware chapter). Hardware has all the glamor and sex appeal; it's the part you can show your employees and customers and your partner and your spouse. It's the solid, hefty, shiny stuff that you will more or less buy by the pound. But it's really of secondary importance.

Software is your real tool. Computer hardware can be endlessly flexible if it is given the right software. If your hardware breaks down, one excited phone call to your local dealer may get you a replacement module delivered and installed in 20 minutes. If the software is sour, well—that's all for the day (week, month).

"Good" software can be *adequate* or it can be *powerful*. You don't absolutely need to know how your CPU works but you will need a decent understanding of your software. It will not take much of your time to pick up the main lines of what you need to know.

THE OTHER STUFF

A closer look at printers, CRT displays, and so on can wait until you get to Chapter 8. That chapter will also discuss ways of sizing up the dealer.

Chapter Three

THIS THING CALLED SOFTWARE

The hardware gets delivered to your office. Out of the cartons and crates, out from under the sculptured blocks of plastic foam, come the CPU box, the keyboard, the CRT screen, the dual disk drive, and so on. You watch the dealer's technician hook it all up with the connecting cables supplied. What a beautiful assemblage of equipment! And now a hushed moment. You plug the power cable into the wall. You flip the switch to turn it all on.

If it has a little ventilator fan in it somewhere, it goes *hmmm-mmmmmm*. Everybody is impressed: your employees, your accountant, your partner. Even your spouse is impressed. But unlike the snappy little car in the TV commercials of a few years ago, *hmmmmmmmmmm* is all this gorgeous electronic miracle can do. Unless you have the software for it.

Software. A word to reckon with. A *thing* to reckon with. *Talk software, and join the big clique.* "Software," the word on everyone's lips. Roll it around on your tongue: soft-ware. Softly now: *software.*

But who needs it?

You do

But what is it?

Software is programs and documentation. That's all.

Programs are sets of instructions for your computer. **Documentation** is instructions and other information for you.

As a rule, your programs will arrive "packaged" in magnetic disk or tape form, to be run into the computer's memory as needed. These are the **applications programs** — sets of instructions for specific tasks, like inventory control or tax records. In a sense these are "visible" programs. You can see and handle the disks or tapes they are on. Your machine has (*or ought to have*) some "invisible" programs. They may be already installed in the computer. They are on ROM chips (as discussed in Chapter 2). They are permanent. To fall back on ancient computer lingo, they are "hard-wired" in. These internal, permanent programs are called **operating system** programs and are nicknamed **firmware** (because they are permanent).

Very well. The programs are what you are after. The programs of interest to you are the applications programs, that do actual jobs for you. (Those internal, operating-system programs are important, too, as we shall discuss later.) What you want is a **system** that does the work for you. The software is at the heart of that system. The hardware is merely the medium that permits the software to work.

We do not think it possible to state this strongly enough. You must never buy hardware for the sake of hardware. You buy hardware for the sake of the software—those working programs, and the documentation that gets the most out of them. Your focus, then, henceforth and forever, will be on software.

But oh, problems, problems

Software can be a problem. A big problem. Getting the right software can take quite a quest. Until recently, the overwhelming majority of hardware manufacturers did not know where their software was going to come from as they rushed their products to market. The situation has been improving. It is a good deal better than it was when we first started this book project, late in 1977. Then, and on into 1978, we were seeing exciting hardware coming onto the market—but our hearts were in our mouths. Where was the business software? Well, there is a lot of it now, some of it quite good. But we can't honestly say that "the software problem" has been "solved." We shall get into this later on. It's a big subject. We thought we ought to warn you early. But don't worry. Let's look at documentation and a few other things first.

DOCUMENTATION

The documentation is in the form of manuals. They may be thick or thin, depending on the size and nature of the particular programs or of the total system. Your system's documentation may come in one thick bound volume, a loose-leaf binder, a set of small booklets or pamphlets — whatever the purveyor thought would be convenient. (Let's hope he gave that some thought.) You may get a combination of things, ranging from thick books down to shirt-pocket cards for certain frequently run programs or procedures.

The documentation tells you how to use the programs. It should have a booklet or book, or a section of a bigger book, about each specific program. This should be nontechnical. It should tell you in step-by-step form how to load a program into the machine, and then how to work with it. The book should give you adequate examples, including practice problems with their solutions. There should be a listing of commonly made mistakes and how to correct them. The operating instructions should warn you about things not to do. And in each case, it should show you the quickest way out of whatever predicament some little blunder got you into. The instructions should be written from *your* point of view, not from the computer designer's or the programmer's point of view.

Good documentation, in other words, should make the programs easy to use.

The computer itself should have a nontechnical user's manual that tells you — in complete detail, step by step — how to unpack, check, set up, turn on, check out, and operate the equipment. A similar manual should accompany each peripheral. The equipment manuals are part of your total system documentation. You should not have to be sophisticated about computers in order to be able to hook up any peripheral and get it to operate with the computer.

In our opinion, the best manuals get the reader involved with the computer right away, for hands-on experience. We concede that there is more than one good way to write a manual. But all the good ways, we think, use some form of *top-down* presentation. What you need to know first you get to read first. No abstruse technical mazes to wind through before you even get to turn the machine on.

Likewise, software manuals should be written top-down. There should always be nontechnical user's sections (or user's booklets) that get right down to loading and operating the programs. Even if you happen to be technically competent with computers, you don't have time to experiment with software.

A good documentation set has materials of *escalating technicality*. This involves background material that you can master later, once you are familiar with the system. It also involves the maintenance, repair, and programming sections of the documentation. Yes, there should be a concise, nontechnical minor troubleshooting section for you, but there ought to be circuit diagrams and logic diagrams for the repairman. He will need to know the design "philosophy" and other technical matters. Don't depend on the repairman always to have "the book" for your machine. The manufacturer could go out of business, and before you know it, nobody has a manual on your machine! Yet it's a perfectly good machine. If you have your own manual, any competent technician can keep your machine going for you indefinitely.

Avoiding Trouble

This goes in spades for the programming manuals. Sometimes programs need troubleshooting. Some day you may want to have a program modified — you will want it tailored precisely to fit your operation. (There is an overwhelming probability that you will want this on many things.) You may want a program expanded. There are many reasons why you will need *complete* information on your programs: the language, dialect, and even subdialect used; the actual lexicon, grammar, and syntax used; the source coding, everything. A manufacturer's proprietary subdialect can cause great difficulties — unless he has documented it all for you. And the standard dire things can happen: the manufacturer, systems house, or original programming firm can go out of business, disappear, leaving nobody you can call. But if your documentation is complete, any competent programmer can use it to modify, troubleshoot, maintain, and expand your programs.

So, when you are shopping for a system, *look at the manuals*. make the dealer bring out the whole set. Take some time. Study the tables of contents. Zero in on specific sections — do the operating sections seem clear, simple, direct? What about the glossary? The index? Leaf through the entire book or set. Do you begin to encounter stuff that's Greek to you — but you can tell would be useful to a technician or programmer? Go through a kick-the-tires exercise. Even *heft* the manuals. Check their physical quality. Attractive in appearance? Good paper stock? Clear, crisp, high-quality printing? Good, pleasing typography and layout? Lots of big, clear, beautiful drawings? Meaningful photographs? Sturdy binding?

In short, does it look as if the producer took some care with, and pride in, his documentation? If he did, you have reason to believe that he took pains with all else that matters to you — like the programs, and the hardware.

Some companies, like Heathkit, are famous for their excellent manuals and documentation, even on their smallest, simplest systems. Not all companies care so much. The disk and the tape cassette in this photo hold programs, ready to be loaded into the computer.

Courtesy of Heath Company

If the documentation is a sheaf of $8\frac{1}{2}'' \times 11''$ sheets originally produce on an old typewriter (probably with a worn ribbon) and then dimly offset-printed in a quick-print shop, take thought. Maybe you don't want that system. Poorly printed program notes can be *useless*.

Don't worry about somebody trying to dress up shoddy equipment and shoddy programming with sexy-looking manuals. A producer who is careless about the quality of his equipment or programs is likely to be careless about all else. He's cutting corners. He won't spend money on fancy paper.

We do admit that good documentation can be printed in "manuscript" style, with high-quality reproduction of clear typewritten pages on good paper. Then it must feature good writing, good writing *style*, and good graphics. It ought to have a loose-leaf binding or some other binding that makes it convenient to use. We tend to suspect that anyone who rushes a "manuscript" into print is rushing a product into the market — and are the bugs out of it yet? However, some software houses have set a style for themselves of "typewritten" copy in loose-leaf format. If it's well-organized (top-down!), well written, *complete*, and clearly legible, then it's useful and okay.

PROGRAMS

Suppose we look at an applications program — a specific program to do a specific job. We are not going to look inside it. We are just going to see how it interacts with you. Most applications programs that you acquire will be in the **interactive mode**. In that mode, the computer (actually the program) prompts you with clear requests for information or for actions by you. Let's suppose it is a payroll program.

Presumably, your machine has a CRT screen. However, you and the program could interact if you had a printer. Either way, once you have the program in the machine and have commanded it to run, you will see a display like this:

        WHAT DO YOU WANT TO DO?
        1. ADD EMPLOYEES
        2. CHANGE EMPLOYEE INFO
        3. RUN PAYROLL
        4. RUN QUARTERLY REPORT
        5. RUN ANNUAL REPORT
        6. DATA BASE MAINTENANCE
        7. END PROGRAM
        ENTER SELECTION:

You choose an activity by typing in, from the keyboard, the numeral corresponding to your selection. Let's suppose you want to CHANGE EMPLOYEE INFO, so you hit a 2 on the keyboard. The 2 appears on the CRT screen or printout next to ENTER SELECTION. You get to check it and make sure you did indeed hit the key you wanted. The program waits for you to command it to implement your choice. You do that by pressing the CARRIAGE RETURN key (or RETURN or CR: keyboard labelings differ slightly). When you do that, the program responds with:

        WHAT INFORMATION DO YOU WANT TO
        CHANGE?
        1. ADDRESS
        2. DEPARTMENT
        3. JOB DATA
        4. PAYROLL DEDUCTIONS

5. SALARY
6. END CHANGES
ENTER SELECTION:

Again, you choose the activity by entering the numeral next to ENTER SELECTION. Suppose the employee has moved. You enter "1" and again you are prompted for the specific information. This time the screen displays:

ENTER SOCIAL SECURITY NUMBER:
ENTER NEW STREET ADDRESS:
ENTER NEW CITY:
ENTER STATE:
ENTER ZIP:
LAST ENTRY? (Y or N)

A blinking square called a **cursor**, by the way, will show you where whatever you have to type in will go. When you have typed the answer to one question, the cursor will jump to the next.

You enter the employee's Social Security Number. This is a much more convenient way to identify the employee than to have to sorry about spelling — correctly — a complete name to match the spelling in the computer's file. Also, you don't have to worry about whether you remembered to change Virginia Kennedy's name to Virginia Newberry if marriage is the reason she has moved. (The program has a way for you to do that when you want to; in fact, your total system has a **data base** containing all requisite information that you need sometimes but not all the time; at least we recommend a data base as a part of your total computer file system.) After entering all the details of the new address, you tell the program whether this was the final entry. If you type N, the display is repeated. You can make changes for another employee. If you type Y, the program returns to the WHAT INFORMATION DO YOU WANT TO CHANGE? menu and displays it.

If all you wanted to do was to make that one change, you select item 6, END CHANGES, and the program displays the original menu: WHAT DO YOU WANT TO DO? You can make another selection, such as 4. PAYROLL DEDUCTIONS, or you may type in a 7 for END PROGRAM.

Anybody can use this kind of program. When you shop for software, look for good interactive programs that involve the least amount of backing and filling (preferably none) on the operator's part. Then you can confidently assign your bookkeeper or any other staff member to run it. When you shop, *involve your staff*. Bring that bookkeeper along. More about this in Chapter 5.

COMPUTER LANGUAGES

This looks like a forbidding topic, but there isn't much to it. All programs have to be written in some sort of computer language. Communication between a human being and a computer also requires a computer language. This is because a human is ever so much smarter than a computer. Never mind the legends and jokes that have it the other way. Just being able to use what you call "simple English" requires quite a remarkable brain. You have that brain, but no computer has it.

You are aware that a computer "thinks" only in ones and zeros. Everything, whether instructions or data, has to be conveyed to the computer's brain in clusters of ones and zeros called **bytes** (Chapter 2). But you don't think in bytes, and you don't want to. Besides, you haven't got time for bytes.

It is possible to write applications programs for computers in **machine language**. This is a predetermined pattern of bits and bytes that is unique to the particular machine design. The programmer has to learn that design, and learn the language that the design dictates. That is not convenient or easy even for the most dedicated programmer. But a program so written can be very economical of memory space and running time, so such programs do exist. But it is much more convenient, and in other ways economical, to write programs in some language closer to English.

Most programs of interest to you will be written in a **high level language**. Don't let that "high level" scare you. It means a level closer to "human." A high level language is one that is convenient — sometimes even easy — for human beings to use. Machine language is *low-level.*

The user's program in high-level language is translated downward into machine language. Another program, already in the machine, does the translating.

Se habla ALGOL?

You have heard of at least a few high-level computer languages: ALGOL, FORTRAN, COBOL, for example. By now, since you have taken an interest in small computers, you have heard of BASIC.

Those names are acronyms, and acronyms have a tiresome way of being cryptic and arcane. Most might as well be written in hieroglyphics. They not only convey nothing to you, they repel you. But computer-name acronyms make sense. They actually tell you something useful about the language they name. For example,

ALGOL = **Algo**rithmic **L**anguage. This is one of the earliest successful high level languages. It is an algebraic and logical language, designed for scientific and engineering applications.

APL = **A** **P**rogramming **L**anguage. It was one attempt to design a language easy for human beings to use.

COBOL = **Co**mmon **B**usiness **O**riented **L**anguage. An earlyish high-level language, invented once people realized that the computer might have business applications.

FORTRAN = **For**mula **Tran**slation. This, too, was designed for engineers and scientists. Its statements follow the form of algebraic statements—as machine-language statements do not. It is a high-level but highly symbolic language, like the notation ("language") of mathematics.

PL/1 = **P**rogramming **L**anguage **1**. As others have pointed out, this could be condemned as a rather arrogant name. Well over a hundred other languages had been developed before it. PL/1 was an IBM product, and IBM will be IBM sometimes. PL/1 was designed to combine the business capabilities of COBOL with the mathematical properties of FORTRAN.

RPG = **R**eport **P**rogram **G**enerator. It helps a programmer generate programs for reports. Its inventors realized that data-processing was as important as sheer number-crunching, that a computer was really more than a deluxe-model calculator.

BASIC = **B**eginner's **A**ll-Purpose **S**ymbolic **I**nstruction **C**ode. A nice, traditionally awkward acronym, and yet an apt name. Born on a giant computer, BASIC was designed for teaching programming concepts and giving the meek and humble access to the computer. It has come mightily into its own with the advent of the microcomputer and is a highly useful language. Still used on the big fellows, too.

PASCAL = Blaise **Pascal**, 1623-1662, the French philosopher and mathematician. Its inventor wanted to honor Pascal, who at age 19 invented an adding machine for use in his father's tax accounting office. PASCAL was designed for business applications and is an up-and-coming language for microcomputer systems.

There are many other computer languages, but there would be little point to extending this list.

Strings to Your Bow

Not long ago, in the late 1970's, any microcomputer you bought offered only one language, BASIC. Early in 1978, some of the leading ones began to offer BASIC and PASCAL, and by 1979 some were offering BASIC, PASCAL, and FORTRAN. We are speaking of "business" microcomputers. The more languages a microcomputer can handle, the richer the spectrum of software potentially available to it.

A word of caution here. High-level languages are supposed to be "machine-independent." The venerable ones like COBOL and FORTRAN succeeded in being such. With properly designed intermediate programs — for the translating mentioned earlier — any of the old giants by Sperry-Univac or DEC or IBM or whoever could accept any program written in "pure" COBOL or FORTRAN. But BASIC presents a problem. There are many versions, or dialects, of BASIC. A program written in Company A's BASIC would probably not run in Company B's computer. Shopping carelessly for packaged software, you could be bitterly disappointed.

However, all BASICs are similar, and as a rule a program written in one BASIC can be modified into another BASIC with reasonable effort by a competent programmer. A programmer's time costs money, of course. But this may be a viable option for you if some particular program you "must" have exists in the "wrong" BASIC for your machine.

You will hear that the BASIC (or any language) must be "put into the machine." Nowadays you will see systems advertised as *having* a certain BASIC already in the machine. (There are a few "standard" BASICs emerging, like North Star Basic.) If you must "put" the BASIC into the machine, that means you must let it take up room in the machine's internal memory. What really happens is that you run a certain "translating" program into the memory; this translator accepts commands in BASIC and renders them into machine language, in one or two steps. This is disadvantageous. You want as much of that inner memory as possible available for holding two things: (1) complex and versatile applications programs in BASIC; and (2) complex chunks of data to be processed at a given time.

Machines with Souls

If the BASIC (or other language) is "already" in the machine, all of your main memory is available for applications programs and data. This is the random-access memory, or RAM, discussed in Chapter 2. What the manufacturer has done is to add some more memory of the "read-only" kind, on ROM chips (also discussed in Chapter 2). In those ROM chips, he has put the program that will render BASIC commands into machine language. Needless to say, this is a more desirable, higher-quality machine. Yes, it costs more, but not much more. And you have the advantage that *that's settled.* You don't have to cast about for a version of BASIC that you are going to like—a difficult task when you are just getting your feet wet in computers! The leading brands of microcomputer will feature a "good" BASIC and will have software packages written in it. And you can rest assured that independent programmers are familiar with these leading BASICs. The situation improves as we write (and things will be a lot easier for you than they were for us at the beginning).

If you are offered a machine that "has" BASIC and one or two other languages, the ROM treatment has been applied. The more languages "in" the machine, the higher the price of the machine. We need not defend that to businesspeople. What matters to you is, "How much does having a multiple language capability matter to my business?" Talk with your consultant (Chapter 5). You need not pay extra money for a capability you might not want. BASIC alone might serve you very well.

THOSE TRANSLATING PROGRAMS

This may look like a technical detail coming up, but we would advise you to stay with it. It is not difficult, and it will help you to understand some of the problems and limitations of computer software. Without this bit of background, some things that salesmen or programmers might have to tell you would remain pure gobbledook.

A translator program may be either an **assembly program**, a **compiler**, or an **interpreter**.

The next step above a machine-language program is an assembly program, written in an "assembler" language. This is still a fairly low level language, requiring a skilled programmer to implement. It enables the programmer to use mnemonic symbols for writing the program instructions, rather than the machine language's one-and-zero clusters (bytes). It contains a table of the mnemonics and their byte equivalents. The program takes each mnemonic and translates it into machine-language bytes. This can be very powerful and is more economical of memory space than a high level language. But the program is not as easy for you to use, and it takes a skilled programmer to troubleshoot it. You want to work with a high level language, and you want a translator that will work from that level down into the machine language.

For that, your microcomputer will use either a compiler or an interpreter. Where an assembly program provides a one-for-one translation of program instructions, the compiler program gives several for one. One mnemonic instruction in a compiler generates a whole set of machine-language instructions. Have you ever thought about how many little steps you go through to add two or three numbers? The computer does, too. If you command the compiler to "add A and B," it will in effect instruct the machine, "Write down number A, write down number B, add them, write down the result, store the result in the working register and come back for the next instruction." It will generate a barrage of one-and-zero bytes that the machine "understands."

The compiler translates your entire high-level program into machine language as it is read off its disk or tape. Any machine desirable for your purposes has the compiler in ROM — as part of the "hard-wired" system programming, or "firmware." The compiler does its job and gets out of the way.

An interpreter does what a compiler does, but in a different way. The compiler does all its work before execution of the program. The interpreter does it during execution. It, too, generates barrages of bytes for each instruction, but it takes only one high-level instruction at a time. Thus an interpreter must always be active, and it makes for a slower-acting system. But an interpreter offers certain economies in its programming and implementation. (Everything in this game involves tradeoffs.)

BASIC is usually an interpreted language, which means that a program has to work well below its theoretical maximum speed. This does not matter for an interactive program, which is still going to be much faster than the operator. Some compiled versions of BASIC exist and will probably become more common. But at the moment, most applications programs that you will be interested in are written in interpreted BASIC.

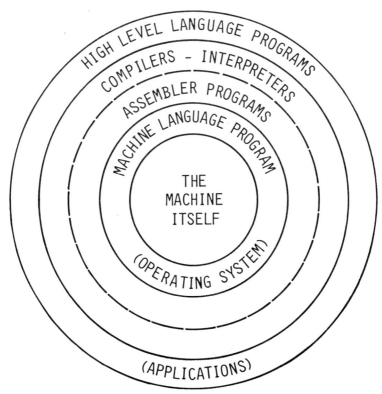

Figure 3-1. A computer system is onion-layered, and most of the layers are software.

WHAT BASIC LOOKS LIKE

How "high level" is a language with a name like BASIC? How close to human thought patterns and habitual modes of procedure is it? Suppose we examine a small sample program that has been "invented" countless times by users of BASIC. It represents an algorithm that you have probably used yourself, "manually." Here is the entire program as it is put into the computer:

```
100  PRINT "PRINCIPAL ($) = " ;
110  INPUT P
120  PRINT "ANNUAL INT. RATE (%) = " ;
130  INPUT I
140  PRINT "TERM (YRS) = " ;
150  INPUT T
160  X = P*I/1200
170  Y = (1 + I/1200)↑(12*T)
180  M = X/(1 - 1/Y)
190  PRINT "MONTHLY PAYMENT ($) = " ;M
200  END
```

Until now you may have known nothing about BASIC. Suddenly you know quite a bit. BASIC is indeed a high-level language. You can read this program. It reads very much "like English" to you. You know what it is the program will compute. You have guessed that the asterisk, *, replaces the conventional × as a multiplication sign. You realize that the computer might have trouble distinguishing the letter X from the multiplication symbol ×. You know that any "interest" problem involves an exponent, so you have guessed that the vertical arrow, ↑, is the exponential sign.

There would be no simple economical way to set things up for the use of a superscript numeral. The only way to express "$3^3 = 27$" in BASIC is to write "3↑3 = 27." The arrow key on the keyboard, by the way, is a **function key**. It automatically signals the machine's system program to do something—here, to take a number to a power.

Take another look at that program. Like high level languages in general, BASIC permits you to proceed with a problem in what you would consider a "logical" or "common-sense" order. To find a monthly mortgage payment, you start with a principal amount, figure in an interest rate, figure in the number of years the mortgage is going to last, and so on. This is how you would proceed with a pencil and scratch pad. And this is how you proceed with a BASIC program.

You could be excused for not guessing that everything on a line following the word PRINT and between quotation marks will be displayed on a CRT screen (or printed out on a printer) but *without* the word PRINT and without the quotation marks or the line numbers. Nor might you have guessed that the instructions *not* preceded by PRINT and *not* enclosed in quotation marks will *not* be displayed. That means, when the program is running, the formulas will not show.

You would run this program by giving the computer a signal to run. You might press a RUN key, or you might type RUN. At first only this appears:

PRINCIPAL ($) = ?

That's funny. Where did the question mark come from? The computer's operating system program, recognizing what you are doing, has added it. Suppose you decide on a house price of $100,000. You would type in 100000 (the computer does not easily deal with commas inside numbers) and the display immediately becomes

PRINCIPAL ($) = 100000
ANNUAL INT. RATE (%) = ?

Let's suppose you decide on 14 percent interest. You merely type in a 14 and the display becomes

PRINCIPAL ($) = 100000
ANNUAL INT. RATE (%) = 14
TERM (YEARS) = ?

You decide on 30 years and type in 30. The moment you type in the 30 the display changes to:

PRINCIPAL ($) = 100000
ANNUAL INT. RATE (%) = 14
TERM (YEARS) = 30
MONTHLY PAYMENT ($) = 1184.87175

That's the final display.

It would be no big thing to write a more elaborate program to scavenge up all those hundred seventy-five thousandths of a cent and add the total (63 cents) to the first payment to make everything come out neatly. But let's keep things simple.

After the program has run, it is still in memory. Give it the RUN command again and the screen will prompt you with PRINCIPAL ($) = ? Answer it how you will.

Those line numbers

What about those numbers to the left of the program lines — 100 through 200? Those are line numbers or instruction numbers. The program "lines" are numbered that way so that the program can be modified or added to without complete rewriting. We can intersperse additional numbered lines. The new numbers have to be "whole numbers" (integers) in most languages. The computer does not recognize "5½" or "9.5" as instruction numbers. (Theoretically it could be made to, but that would complicate the operating software.) If you want to add something you can write a line 101 or 163 and the computer will accept it. The numbers demarcate distinct high level program steps. They do not appear on the display screen (or in the paper printout) while the program is being run. But they are essential to keeping a program organized. And when you give the computer a set of numbered lines, it recognizes that you are building a program.

More easy tricks

Because of this line-numbering convention, it is easy to make the program more versatile. Suppose you wanted to be able to consider another house or another interest rate or term without having to tell the program to RUN each time. Before Line 200, the END, you could add a Line 195. This line would say GO TO 100. This would run the program back to the beginning, and PRINCIPAL ($) = ? would be displayed again. When you got through with that calculation, this beginning prompt would immediately appear again.

However, this puts the program into a **loop**. Left to itself it would repeat "forever," refusing to quit. That means the machine is tied up; you can't do anything with it but satisfy that program. There are loop-breaking steps you could take. But it is preferable to have a loop-breaker built into the program. Our choice would be to add a Line 115, right after Line 110 for INPUT P. Our Line 115 says, IF P = 0 THEN GO TO 200. When you've done your last calculation you just enter a 0 for the principal, P.

With that, the program jumps to 200, the END, and quits. The computer displays a signal, such as READY, that means it is free to do something else.

But what if we had forgotten a house or an interest rate and wanted to bring the program back? Just commanding RUN brings it to life again. The computer holds that program ready to go until we either write in another, read in another off a tape or disk, or call up another that is already in the memory.

How do you make changes?

To add to or modify the program, you first command LIST. The program is printed on the screen, entire—line numbers, quotation marks, the works. And it waits. Suppose we display here what it looked like when we first ran in the modifications:

```
100  PRINT "PRINCIPAL ($) =" ;
110  INPUT P
120  PRINT "ANNUAL INT. RATE (%) =" ;
130  INPUT I
140  PRINT "TERM (YRS) =" ;
150  INPUT T
160  X = P*I/1200
170  Y = (1 + I/1200)(12*T)
180  M = X/(1 - 1/Y)
190  PRINT "MONTHLY PAYMENT ($) =" ;
200  END
195  GO TO 100
115  IF P = Ø THEN GO TO 200
```

WHAT? Put the added instructions after the 200, the END? Won't the computer run through the program and then stop with END before it can read Line 195 or Line 115? No! Not our computer, anyway. The computer is an idiot, but the programmer who wrote the internal operating system was smart. He or she was at least thoughtful. Once the afterthought lines have been added, it is only necessary to command RUN or LIST. The computer will eyeball the whole megillah, shuffle all lines into their correct places, and run or list the program the "proper" way. It is not necessary to "retype" the entire program in the new sequence just to add something. Or to make corrections to a line.

ENOUGH, ALREADY

The foregoing was not a course in "how to program in BASIC." We didn't even start correctly, with the bare-bones basics of BASIC. We shall take you no further with it here.

But now you *know* you understand.

BASIC holds no terrors for you now. Neither should any other high-level language. You have been introduced to the esoteric mysteries. There turns out to be nothing very mysterious. Of course all we gave you was an elementary program. A good BASIC programmer is still worth his healthy hourly fee. But the nagging suspicion at the back of your mind that you could learn to write little utility programs like that one is correct. You could, if you wished, write longer and more complex programs, with fancy loops and branches and other clever stuff—if you learned BASIC, or some other high-level language. *It could suit your convenience some day to do so.*

But you don't have to. Understanding is enough for now. You can hold your own in sessions with dealers and consultants and programmers. If they should decide to go technical on you they couldn't completely snow you (and you could decide to take your business somewhere else).

A final word on languages

Any computer language has a vocabulary, a grammar, and a syntax. So has English or Russian. When you learn any language, human or computer, you learn those three things. BASIC's vocabulary is small and its grammar fairly simple—it's the beginner's language, remember. Its syntax is rather strict, but that's because BASIC lets you "talk" to a stupid computer. When you have to instruct less-than-brilliant human beings you often have to be careful of the order in which you say things. You're used to that.

Yet BASIC, like other high-level computer languages, really offers you *idiom*, just as English does. You can make simple statements that convey a lot of meaning. If you decide to learn BASIC you will find yourself learning a small list of idioms along with that small vocabulary. But BASIC accomplishes much with little. A reasonable analogy is the English alphabet. It has only twenty-six letters, but those few letters can spell hundreds of thousands of words.

NOW, ABOUT THAT PROBLEM...

The problem we mentioned was that good software can be hard to come by. That is, it is by no means as easy to buy the "right" software as it is to buy adequate hardware. Hardware there is aplenty. By mid-1978 we, the authors, counted a couple of hundred firms (most of them new to us) that manufactured, or purported to manufacture, business microcomputer and minicomputer systems. This looked like a population explosion over mid-1977, when there seemed to be a relative handful. In 1979 we saw some houses disappear, while still others appeared on the market. We expect to find that the peak of new "births" of microcomputer lines will have passed as this book goes to press just short of 1980. Indeed, we have formulated Rosa and Rosa's Evolutionary Law of Computerdom: *The fittest will survive, and the fittest will be those manufacturers who succeed at providing turnkey systems.*

We defined "turnkey" earlier. It's a system that lets you turn the key, start up, and drive off, just like at the car dealer's No worries about software: turnkey hardware, by definition, comes with good software. In practical terms, it should at least have a startup package of software that *you* can use.

Some computer makers still don't seem to be terribly concerned about the problem. Their philosophy seems to be that all micro- or minicomputers can, or should, use BASIC, and there are, after all, plenty of people writing programs in BASIC out there. Madness. That way lies extinction. Only a dodo bird thinks that software is *your* problem. Shun the dodo.

But take heart. There is software today; we have watched it proliferate over the past couple of years. There is even business software, assuaging the misgivings that we had when we started this book. Even as the situation improves, some of the software does; there is some good stuff out there. Shop thoughtfully, and you'll find some that's right for you.

There are turnkey systems around, sort of. Primitive turnkey systems; you won't find one that closely fits all or even most of your requirements. But you can get started, with good hardware and adequate software. Now, software can be adequate or it can be *powerful*. (It can also be zilch; watch out.) Your relentless search, in the future, will be for ever more powerful software.

If you thought it would be a foregone conclusion that the undeniably essential software should have evolved concurrently with the small-computer hardware — that's because you do not know much about the history of the computer industry. (Properly so. It wasn't your line.) We shall now fill you in with the briefest sketch of that industry ever written. (If you would like a more complete history of the computer you might enjoy reading *From Dits to Bits: A Personal History of the Electronic Computer*, published by Robotics Press.)

The Reason

There is an ancient tradition that computer hardware should be developed first, and software laboriously developed afterwards. Also that software should be developed for *each* machine, uniquely. Also that years must pass, and sizeable fortunes be spent, before these marvelous machines could actually work. That is, before the software could mature, and produce results. Thirty-odd years ago this nation (and the world) had *one* programmable electronic digital computer. About twenty-five years ago there were *two* such computers. A government study concluded then that this entire country would need only a dozen or so computers to do all conceivable computer work for a nation this size.

Now, in those days, the customer for a new computer was either the government or some large university. Of course, the university's computer project was financed in large part by the government. Money was no object. Neither was time. The computer was being built for some abstruse research project that could wait.

In those days, a smart company like IBM ignored the computer. It already had the last word in data-processing equipment and techniques. (All you needed was stacks and stacks of those cards. . . .) It fell to another company, Sperry, to build the first big computer. A big computer was the only kind you could build in those days, since each required thousands of vacuum tubes, and consumed enough electrical power to run a small city. But Sperry got out of the computer business. ("What? Tool up for only a dozen?") Now Sperry is back, as Sperry-Univac.

Of course, nobody could then write software without specific hardware to write it for. The very concept of software was brand new. Besides, each new machine had a unique machine language. It was necessary to get the machine built, tested, trouble-shot, and rebuilt before that language could become stable enough for a programmer to tackle.

And so, "build the hardware first, worry about the software some time later" became a tradition.

Another tradition was to get hold of the customer's money first, then start development of the hardware, with software on the far horizon. A sensible procedure, in those purely developmental days. The only possible procedure.

Tradition dies hard

The traditions persist, long after there is neither reason nor excuse for them. There is no need for you to part with your money for hardware that does not exist. Your supplier should be able to guarantee a delivery date. Yet you still may be asked to put your money into a blind hole, and wait indefinitely. Don't!

Nowadays, small computers are being turned out by the thousands. You could buy a kit and put one together on your kitchen table. (You probably won't. This book is being written for people whose motto is, "I'm a businessman, not one of those computer freaks.") In principle, "there is no reason why" *software* should not be available for every make and model of small computer.

"In principle." In theory, shall we say. Yet there is a practical reason why all systems are not yet turnkey systems.

That bottom line...

That reason is expense. It takes time to write a good program. It can take many months, or a whole year, to write a reliable applications package for one make and model of small computer. The computer programmer has an expensively acquired skill. Like the composer of a Broadway musical (or the author of a book), the programmer is usually an independent contractor who may be on the beach a lot. Like you, he has a family and a mortgage and all the rest. He can't afford to work for shoeclerk hourly rates. His wife and kids like to live in the suburbs, just like yours. (Or, *her* husband and kids need to see *her* well rewarded.) So, the programmer may charge $25,000, $30,000, or more to write that package. And it may be just a basic BASIC package, a handful of generalized programs to enable the computer user to get started.

We need hardly describe the manufacturer's dilemma to you. Let's say the manufacturer is willing to pass the program along at cost. He decides to sell his hardware with the software thrown in as a "free" dividend. He will have to add a little to the price of each computer he sells, to defray the programmer's fee. If he raises his price by $10 he need only sell 3000 computers to get his investment back. Of course, he's new in the game (just about everybody is) and he is not at all certain he will sell 3000 computers.

Now, right down the street in Santa Clara is a competitor who makes a virtually identical machine at virtually identical cost. The natural tendency is to find ways to shave dollars off list prices so as to get a competitive edge. The firm that *adds* a few dollars to its price relieves its competitors of the necessity for taking dollars off. The competitor, then, gets to sell more computers — at a greater profit.

Besides, until somebody came along and asked, "Could I use your small computer in my small business," no manufacturer had to worry about software. Until only a couple of years ago most microcomputer manufacturers were aiming for a hobbyist market, not a business market. The hobbyist was (and is) hardware-oriented, often for the sake of owning the hardware. The hobbyist had unlimited time and unlimited interest in the computer *qua* computer. He could acquire books and subscribe to magazines about computers, join a computer club, and learn to program his shiny new gadget to do something — if only to turn itself off whenever he turned it on. From some publication or some friend he could acquire a program for blackjack or *Star Trek* games. He had time for laboriously modifying and converting that program — written for some other microcomputer — to work on his machine. From the hobbyist's point of view, who needed software?

From the businessman's point of view, who needs all that hassle? For the hobbyist, the hassle is part of the fun. But there is a lot of ready-made software around these days even for hobbyists. The microcomputer industry has come a long, long way in just a couple of years.

A couple of years is not a long time. Especially considering the time it takes to develop good programs or good packages. Part of the software problem is generated by the newness of the industry — or the tardiness of some computer houses in realizing that they needed good software in order to sell their hardware.

The awakening has come. The more solid microcomputer firms realize that if they sell a machine to a business firm, and "it doesn't work" simply because it lacks software, they get bad-mouthed. They get bad-mouthed on the golf course and they get bad-mouthed at the Rotary Club luncheon and they get bad-mouthed at the Annual Anodized Wing-Nut Jobbers' Convention. So now, they are in there trying.

Here and there the trying has paid off quite well, at least with some things. Here and there it has not. We have watched the makers of good hardware fling software onto the market in its "first draft" stage, not really fully developed, not completely debugged. We know one firm that acquired a nice, compact little accounting program. It just fit into the available RAM space on their original machine, which had an 8K memory. It was a rather rudimentary accounting program that required some side-jotting on the part of the user (so that results attained in one part of the program could be used as input data to another part) but it could serve as business software for an 8K machine. (You may recall from Chapter 2 that we recommend 16K as the bare minimum for a "business" machine.) However, the company brass decided that the program should flash the company logo and a brief patent-and-copyright warning on the CRT screen before it got down to business. Programming for that was added. The result, as you can guess, was that the tail end of the accounting program was effectively lost; it just could not go into the memory. So there you were, running equation after equation and jotting result after result, and when it came time for the grand finale, the computer just quit.

Surely, you say, they didn't try to sell that program? Yes, they did. There was a general hysteria on at that time, inside and outside that company, to fer-Chrissake-get-some-software-into-the-field. They were brought up short by a pair of reviewers (us) and by screams from the first few customers. Now, this was not a dishonest company. It's just that haste—*panic*—causes oversights. The oversight has been corrected. The company has also released several models of its computer with bigger memories. But that kind of thing happens. In lots of companies. Including ones that make fine hardware.

We mentioned a patent-and-copyright notice. Another problem the manufacturer has, or had, with software was plagiarism. He could spend thousands getting a program developed, only to find that it could work, with minor or even trivial modifications, on some competitor's machine. The competitor was likely to be alert to that. The same problem beset independent programmers and systems houses. In the old giant-computer days, each new computer was unique — not merely as a design or a model but as an *entity*. Learning its machine language for purposes of plagiarism would have involved a massive and delicate job of industrial espionage. But programming for microcomputers requires no such thing. Anybody who programs for a computer using the famous 8080 microprocessor chip pretty much knows the machine language for all 8080-based machines. The same goes for the Z-80 chip, the 6800 chip, and so on. Plagiarism can be fairly simple.

Lately, software producers (from independent programmers to manufacturers of hardware) have been copyrighting their software. How well these copyrights might hold up in court remains to be seen. But the *threat* is there; a plaintiff could get an injunction to hold up sales of a defendant's software until a suit was settled. And good programmers could conceal subtle, hard-to-find (and thus hard to eliminate) "signatures" or "trademarks" in a complex program, that would win suits. As a result of this, a set of ethics is evolving by consensus.

Ethics bring order. Order emboldens the workman. Software development now proceeds. All is not "perfect" yet, so beware — but don't despair. Shop carefully. Get everything demonstrated, especially software. Firms with good software will require you to sign a user's agreement that is pretty liberal as to how you use the software, but includes a noose to hang you with if you market it as your own or abet anyone else in doing that.

Big outfits get stung

Environmental organizations are "big" these days, and not just figuratively. One of the most prominent of them had a membership explosion in the early and mid-1970s. This meant a paperwork explosion. The need for a computer was discerned. A shaky systems house sold them a "system" according to some fine old traditions. It sort of brokered somebody else's expensive hardware, took a commission, and then undertook to start ginning up software for the customer. Only it wasn't too well established, or experienced, in the software business. And it ran into cash flow problems. One thing led to another, and the supplier defaulted on the contract, went belly-up, disappeared. The environmental outfit was left with half a jillion bucks' worth of hardware and just enough software to print mailing labels.

Solution? Sell the hardware and start over, right? But who wants to buy a massive computer that "won't work"? Who can use partly developed "ecology club" software? Who needs an expensive semi-maxi computer just to print mailing labels?

The people who run the organization are bright but not computer-oriented. Their "computer problem" is low on their list of priorities. They do not see the way out of their expensive dilemma. They tend—like their quarter-million members who are victims of the "computer situation"—to curse the computer and be bitterly thankful that it prints mailing labels.

Their way out, of course, is to find a software house that understands their machine and can write them some applications programs that will really put the system to work.

Nothing like that need happen to you. HORSE before the cart. Software first. As later chapters show you, you must (1) Analyze your business. (2) Decide on exactly what you want the computer to do for you. (3) Translate that into a definition of your software needs. (4) Shop for a complete system. (5) Avoid, abhor, eschew the "traditional" approach that says, "Let's acquire some hardware, and then figure out a way to program it." Remember: before you have a firm idea of the dimensions of your software, you don't even know what size memory your computer should have.

ACQUIRING THE STUFF

There are several ways to acquire software. They are not necessarily obvious.

1. It comes with the machine. At least, a general startup package does. Not "perfect" for you, but a manufacturer or a systems house (or "OEM," see Chapter 2) has made an honest attempt to come up with a system.

2. You go to a systems house or independent programmer, with an analysis of what you need the software for: the specific tasks. You can do that *first*; they'll help you find the "right" hardware for it. A dealer or even a manufacturer may even advise you, "We haven't got much that meets your specific needs, but XYZ Associates has been writing some pretty good stuff for our machines."

3. You acquire the hardware, and retain a programmer to generate custom software from scratch. Expensive and

necessarily slow. But you may want that programmer part-
time even if you go the route of (1) or (2).

4. You write the software yourself. Unless you are already involved with computers, and are savvy about languages and
programming, this is a slow and difficult way to go. It can
pay off (remember our plumbing contractor of Chapter 1)
but you are probably not ready for that. You might even
want to try adapting some else's software to your needs.
This is tricky at best. If you think you want to try this
approach, you will want to read *Nailing Jelly to a Tree: A
Guide to Making Software Work* (dilithium Press).

All of those ways work; you may use any one of them, or two
or more in combination. As for (4), it probably will suit your
interest and convenience some day to learn something about
programming. (It would do you no harm to start now.) Some
day, at least, you are going to want somebody on your staff who
understands programming, and who can generate spot utility
programs, or even entire packages and systems.

Don't worry.We have done your worrying for you. Proceed
with reasonable caution. That's already typical of you, or you
would not be a successful businessman (so successful you now
need a computer to help you keep up with yourself). But do proceed with your customary confidence. You'll learn the ropes
quickly.

This has been a long chapter, but we hardly need tell you now
that software is your most important consideration.

Chapter Four

DATA PROCESSING AND WORD PROCESSING

To reiterate, what everyone calls a "computer" is really a data processor. The distinction is not a technicality or a bit of pedantry. After all, the term "compute" translates in everyone's mind as "calculate," and a computer can do much more than that. Your pocket calculator "computes" in that narrow sense, but it is not a "computer" because it is not a data processor. Your computer can do things that *you* can do: it can make records, and combine them into files, and then retrieve and read the records and files, update or otherwise change them, copy or duplicate them, and also make direct use of the filed information. The files may be sources of numbers that your computer may calculate with, but the computer, like you, can go far beyond calculation in manipulating the file data.

Those who enjoy semantic niceties raise the question of the programmable calculator. It doesn't take much reflection to realize that the programmable calculator is still not a computer. It is superficially similar to a computer in that it can accept a set of instructions—a program—and it will carry out a limited sequence of calculations for you. Fine. But the calculator cannot fetch the file for Smith & Co., add Smith's most recent transactions to the file, examine the history of Smith's account since he last paid your bill, remember to give Smith discounts on certain items, pass the old file data to the archives and retain an updated file, then *calculate*, and then print out an itemized bill for Smith & Co.; going right on, if you wish, to Sportstrend Golf & Ski Shop's file to repeat the process. Your computer can.

Industrial Process Control

Not only that, your computer could control the mixture of ingredients going into your frankfurter-making machines, and monitor the output by weight, batch by batch. Yes, it could count individual weenies (sorry! you probably don't call them weenies) and even check their color. If you insisted, it could weigh them individually, too. For these applications your computer would have input and output devices that the "typical" small business computer lacks, but they can be had. So can software: programs already exist for meat-mixing.

No, you can't run down to the nearest Byte Shop or Computerland Store and pick them up off the counter. But they can be had. Our point here is that the computer can do things no calculator, however elaborate, can do. Give the computer some cogent input and it will treat it as *data* to be processed; it can do something meaningful with the data. It can relieve human beings of taxing jobs that involve that data.

The data might include temperature readings from a freezer room and its anteroom. Also, readings on whether the freezer room door is open or shut at a given time, and a count of how many times the door is opened per hour, and so on. With these and similar data items—automatically entered as input—the computer can control everything from the freezer mechanism itself to your building's heating and air conditioning. At the same time, it can monitor all the doors and windows in your plant, to guard against unauthorized entry.

This book is about office computers; readers who want process control ought to consult local dealers and systems consultants (see Chapter 5). Of course one obvious question now dangles in the air: can the same small computer run the meat mixer and also run your payroll and accounts receivables? There is no technical reason why not. It's a matter of interfacing and software.

As a practical matter we think that you would be better off with two computer systems, one running the machinery and one doing the office chores. Unless, of course, you are a *very* small frankfurter-maker, who finds it no problem to make the franks *and* do the paperwork. (In that case you may be too small to need a computer for anything.) If you have several disparate needs for a computer's services you may as well have more than one computer. Maybe some day you can link them together (that's feasible, too) but having more than one computer gives you one or more spares. Centralization is probably not the way to go in small-business data processing.

Simplicity

Small businessmen have tended to flinch at the mere mention of electronic data processing (or "using a computer") because of prior experience with it in a larger firm, back in one's apprentice days. Not very long ago, data processing seemed to be a matter of endless *keypunching* — with all data being minutely formatted to fit on Hollerith cards ("IBM cards"), and some "girl" sitting there all day at a job that seemed (and was) inhuman. It's still done that way here and there, in some outfits using big computers.

Tradition dies hard

No such agony is in the cards for you: the cards are out. You or your operator will "type" data directly into the computer. What you "type" in is immediately displayed on the CRT screen. If you wish, it is immediately printed out on paper as well. But either way, it goes directly into the computer's memory. It can simultaneously be recorded in a storage medium, such as a disk. If you make a mistake while entering data, it is instantly correctable, by simple strikeover. (If a keypunch girl put a hole in the wrong place in a card, well, correcting that took some work.) And what about computation, about data processing itself? That occurs the moment you are satisfied with what you have typed in.

In those bad old days, "data processing" seemed to be an endless matter of processing *cards*. Little human slaves scurried about with stacks of cards and reels of tape. All kinds of machinery had to go clickety-clack and zippety-zap and whirr-whirr before the computer was ready to compute. Or rather, before the data were ready for the computer itself to work with. And every line — every picayune instruction — of a program took a separate "IBM" card.

"A punched card is a device for holding holes apart." **— Anon.**

Nowadays, you and your computer are in rapid, easy dialogue through an interactive program. You have your bulk data on disks, and the program operates the disk drive, feeding itself data as it needs to. The programs themselves are on disk or tape, and take only a couple of minutes to load into the main memory. To change a disk or tape, you just pop out the old one and pop in the new one: no fuss.

Today's microcomputer is simply an office machine. A sophisticated office machine—but you just use it, the way you just use any other office machine. There will be no aura of worship around your computer facility. There will be no doubt, either, about who is boss. It's you, not the machine.

THE NATURE OF DATA PROCESSING

Your computer can handle *numeric* data and it can handle *alphameric* data. It can manipulate numbers you put into it, and also letters or words, punctuation marks, mathematical symbols, anything that your keyboard is set up to give it. In every case, the number, letter, or symbol from the keyboard key will be converted into a code consisting of "ones and zeros." In practical terms down inside the computer, a one or a zero means a voltage is present or absent at some point in some circuit. As far as the computer "knows," it is only handling those ones and zeros—those present and absent voltages. It handles them according to instructions in a program—and the program, inside the computer, consists only of more ones and zeros! Hence you can trick the computer into doing "anything" with your data. It will add, subtract, multiply, and divide your numbers, yes. But it will, indifferently, accept your letters, words, spaces, and punctuation marks and as indifferently process those, according to program. For this reason, the computer can accomplish **word processing**; more about that later.

Analog-to-Digital Conversion

For industrial process control, various kinds of information about the process are converted into those ones and zeros. This is called **analog-to-digital** conversion. Sometimes this is quite a simple matter. Let's say you have a laser that is turned on only after cooling water has been provided. The water system is equipped with a pressure switch. The switch is thrown by the pressure of water in the system. In the simplest system, that switch, on closing, would permit a signal to run along a wire to the computer. This signal is at a certain voltage which the computer interprets as "one." The program is set up to turn on power to the laser when it receives that "one" from the switch.

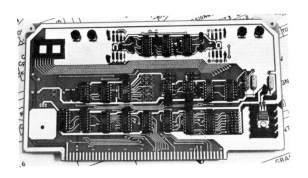

An analog-to-digital interface (for input).
Courtesy of Vector Graphic Inc.

Suppose, however, you have a valve somewhere, and it is important to know whether that valve is shut, one-quarter open, half open, three-quarters open, or wide open. Then the valve would be equipped with sensors that would detect its position, and send coded signals to the computer. In the crudest case, these could be 0000, 001, 0010, 0011, and 0100, which are the numbers Zero through Four as expressed in binary rather than decimal notation. This would involve some gadgetry a bit more complicated than a pressure-operated switch, but no big engineering problem.

Suppose the valve had a 360-degree rotation and it was necessary to know its position exactly, to the degree? This, too, can be done. The valve could be mechanically linked to a potentiometer, which is a varying electrical resistor. (The volume control on your radio is a potentiometer.) At one extreme position, the potentiometer has a very high resistance; only a low voltage can come out of it. At the other extreme it has a low resistance, and a high voltage can come out of it. Proportional voltages come from other positions. A sensitive voltage-measuring circuit can thus be used to sense the positions of the valve. The different voltages, representing degree-by-degree changes of position, can be translated into digital code. Just how this is done need not concern us. It is only necessary to realize that the computer will receive groups of zero-and-one combinations that will inform it of the exact position of the valve.

Your industrial process control might make use of other analog variables, such as temperature, humidity, time, weight, the depth of liquid in a tank, or the depth a drill had penetrated a material. To control that depth, or any other parameter, your computer system would use **digital-to-analog** conversion, so that digital information from the computer can be translated into "real world" outside values.

Data Processing "Solutions"

The computer, as we have remarked earlier, is an idiot, a simpleton with no common sense at all. A human being has to tell it to do everything, to take every little step. The computer can take no unconscious or "intuitive" steps. Somebody has to spell it all out, tediously. But just once. The result is a computer program, and equipped with that, the computer works like a genius. (Only, the programmer was the "genius.") Thomas Edison used to say that "Genius is one percent inspiration and 99 percent perspiration." Defining a problem, analyzing the problem, charting a solution, *programming* the solution, debugging the program, and documenting the entire process looks like a lot of sweat. It is. But with a computer, you sweat just once no matter how many times the particular solution has to be implemented.

Existing Solutions

The sweating has already been done for you, for various routine office jobs. Countless programmers have worked up microcomputer software for a respectable variety of tasks. This is starter-package software, that package that will make the system you buy a quasi-turnkey system. Little of it may be perfect for your needs, but it gives you a start. You can modify and tailor it later.

Here is a partial listing of programs and packages available now from the various software suppliers:

Accounts Payable	Order Entry and Invoicing
Accounts Receivable	Payroll
Apartment Management	Purchase Order Processing
Automotive Sales	Real Estate
Engineering Entry	Realty Expense Analysis
Financial Planning	Refund Processing

General Ledger   Sales Analysis
Inventory Planning   Sales Processing
Inventory Control   Shipping Pattern Analysis
Labor Costing   Word Processing
Mailing Lists   Work-In-Process Costing
Medical/Dental Accounts   Work Order Launching
  Receivable

These programs or packages are of course very general. Again, they were not tailored to your own business, even though you find software for your *kind* of business. Using any of them as-is may involve some inconvenience for you, some alteration of your procedures "to suit the computer."

The brevity of the package titles can be misleading: there is often *more* in a package than you might guess. For example, a General Ledger package may include means for handling and updating accounts receivable, cost of sale, sale amount, sales tax payable, shipping cost, and inventory asset value. A Medical/Dental Accounts Payable package may include appointment scheduling, standard procedure codes and charges, Medicare forms processing, daily balancing, family billing, and refund processing. The better business packages have *audit trail* features; these are invaluable if you can get them.

Look for the integrated packages that actually do several jobs —with programs that can update several files (**data base** software). You or your operator may have to keep changing disks so that the program can do everything it was designed to do, but you would have to change them anyway if you used punier programs that could handle only one kind of file per run. (If you have the more expensive hard disks, you may not have to change disks. See Chapter 8.)

Use the same set of data, of course, to test each vendor's software. This insures "fair test" conditions—fair to you. As you run these tests, you will get a feel for how much work the program does as against how much work the human operator does. Programs work faster than people do. Or they should.

Don't forget to make some deliberate mistakes, slip the program a little jabberwocky, fail to follow some instructions exactly. How does the program handle your gaffes? A good program will give you an error message at a minimum. The error message itself may stand as a cryptic instruction for correcting the error. At any rate, the program should take mistakes in stride: it should be easy for you to get back on the track.

Maintain some tolerance, however. Remember it is possible to bug just about any program with some unforeseeable configuration of inputs. If you try hard you can bring almost any program down, paralyze the computer. That's not your aim. You just want to see how tolerant of mistakes one program is relative to another. If it takes several minutes to get the computer back up and running after each mistake (and the dealer must work frantically each time) the program is undesirable. If the program feeds you a question mark and says "PLEASE REPEAT" or "PLEASE START AGAIN AT STEP 3" you've got one you can live with. If it says "SYNTAX ERROR IN 26" and you have to look that up in the manual to see what it means and what to do about it, you probably still have a program you can live with. But it shouldn't signal a syntax error down in the machine-language jungle if all you did was type in a letter or a mathematical symbol where you were supposed to type in a numeral.

Fields, records and files

This is an optional technical detail that you may skip, but it is here for future reference if you should need it.

In your encounters with computer literature and with computer vendors you will hear of fields, records, and files, with even "files" obviously having a special connotation. These may be of secondary interest to you unless you are programming. In programming, these terms have special meanings. But there is nothing difficult about those meanings.

A **field** is simply a unit of information. It consists of one or more values (which may or may not be numerical values for the user, but will be taken as such by the computer). A field is also an area in a record or file set aside for a given kind of information. When computer inputs and outputs used to involve Hollerith cards, each column of holes was reserved for a specific category of information and was called a field. Nowadays we have largely dispensed with the punched card, but virtual fields are still there for the computer; they are a good way of handling information.

A **record** is a convenient collection of fields, a meaningful combination of data items. A file number, employee name, his accrued wage, and the date last paid would be a record consisting of four fields.

A **file** is a cogent collection of records. All those employee identifiers, names, balances, and payment dates would amount to a payroll file. The file is organized in some way inside the comuter, and it may be a random file, a sequential file, or an indexed file. In a *random* file, you may enter and read out records in any order; you can retrieve the information by specifying the record number (such as the customer identifier or the employee Social Security number). In a *sequential* file—always used in tape-based storage systems—new records can only be added at the end, and the entire file must be read in sequence before the last-entered item can be reached. An *indexed* file involves two (or possibly more) subfiles: a master subfile and a key subfile. The master subfile contains all the records in a complete form, usually entered randomly. The key subfile contains simply a matching identifier for each record in the master file (such as customer number or name). This is called a "key." The key subfile also contains each record's real record number in the master file. Here, that record number is a "pointer." It tells the computer where to go in the master file to get the record.

Files have names, just as the paper files in your filing cabinets have names. Often, the names are abbreviated for computer use, for your convenience as well as the computer's: you don't have to type out the complete, formal name Concrete Loads Delivered to State of Massachusetts Projects File on the keyboard, and the computer doesn't have to run that impossible name through all its registers just to get at the file. (You've probably got it abbreviated in your paper files, too.)

So now you know a little about how information is organized inside a computer system. Conceivably, you might have to discuss with a programmer or vendor just how many fields may be used in a record, and how many records a file can hold, for some particular data-processing requirement of yours. Or a salesman may dwell on something like this in an attempt—conscious or unconscious—to snow you. Now he can't snow you. You get his drift.

Forecasting and Planning

Suppose it's July and business is great and the guys on the shipping platform are really sweating, pushing those orders out. You are eyeballing the invoices day by day, week by week—maybe you're even reading your computer's daily and weekly reports. And your eyes are lighting up with dollar signs. This is really livin'; This is what being in business is all about.

One fly in the gazpacho. You're paying everything up to the minute: your weekly payroll, quarterly taxes, and 30 days on all your bills. Even ten days, to get discounts. But an alarming number of your customers hold out for 90 days. Some of them accept the carrying charge and go to 120 days, 150, 180. Your product is going out, your *money* is going out, but not much money is coming in. Oh, along about November it's going to be great. But.

But. Are you going to be critically short of cash by October? Maybe even by September?

You step to the computer keyboard and tickle in a little quick-ratio problem. The ratio of cash on hand to cash due to go out by the end of July is 1.2 to 1. Good. Your head is above water. But you knit your brows over the cash flow, mull over a couple of reports, try a projected quick ratio for August. Less than 1.1 to 1. If it dips below 1 to 1 in September or October you're in trouble. And it probably will; in September you'll be paying off the current advertising campaign.

Maybe you can stretch out the cash. But intuitively you know that the ratio will be perhaps 0.95 to 1 by October. Bad. But at least you have a clue! You have the option of alerting your bank and your friendlier creditors. You can take steps. But you wish you had thought about this back in June.

Doing the quick-ratios ahead was a good step, but a crude one. The figures you used weren't precise enough. Of course if you gave your accountant all the relevant data she could come up with a more precise cash-flow projection. But that would take her some time, and it would cost you. If only there were some economical way of making continuous cash-flow projections, of knowing at any time what the cash situation is likely to be in a month, two months, three months, even six....

Well, there is. There are such things as cash-flow projection programs. If you can't find a satisfactory one in the stock of ready-made programs, you an have one written. You'll want to go over the problem with your accountant to see how much of what kinds of information you will need. Once you know that, you have accomplished Steps 1 and 2. You will have defined the problem, and worked out a procedure for solving it. The next step is to hire the programmer.

With the computer always keeping track of cash flow for you, you need never be shriveled by a sudden drought of cash. You will always know where the cash is going and where it is going to go. You will be able to see more clearly, too, what makes for sudden drains on cash.

The computer can help in planning for the future. You will need some "modeling" programs, so you can test out options against changes in vendor prices to you, and in interest rates, tax rates, inflation rates, and your prices to customers. You can test the effects of increases and decreases in the size of the market, and the cost effectiveness of advertising and promotional campaigns, given reasonable estimates of response rates. You can fictionally try out owning your own building *vs.* staying in the rented quarters. All this involves data you have on hand or can easily obtain. All you need is a program to process it so as to give you forecasts and projections that you can use as planning tools.

When you are using your computer for purposes like these, you will certainly have much more than a fancy calculator there.

What about your inventory? Customers are displeased and may turn away if you have to back-order. Is overstocking a valid solution? Overstocks tie up money and space that you could put to better use. They subject you to overt and hidden carrying costs and to increased inventory taxes. A computer can help you analyze your inventory turnover, showing you when certain items move and when they stagnate on your shelves. The computer can be programmed to remind you when to reorder, allowing for typical delivery time for each item. (If you have no records or clear memory of some delivery times, the computer can obviously help you accumulate and collate that kind of information.) The computer can also alert you to frequent changes in your acquisition costs for each item — a useful thing for realistic pricing.

The graphics option

As mentioned in Chapter 1, some microcomputer systems offer graphics capability. This involves both software and hardware (an extra printed circuit board full of chips, to be plugged into the computer's innards). The better systems will draw up comparison graphs (bars or curves, filled or unfilled), and even circuit diagrams or other engineering drawings. A **light pen** is offered with some systems for making changes by "drawing" on the face of the CRT display. Specialized printers are offered for rendering graphics in hard-copy form. Some systems offer color capability — either integral to the system, as in Tektronix's Color Graphics Terminal, or by use of an external color TV set, as in Cromemco's Dazzler series. Vector Graphic (whose main lines are small business systems and word processors) offers an option for reproducing photographic material on the CRT screen with remarkable resolution, even though the CRT picture is made of up picture elements — "pixels" — which are somewhat coarser than the elements of a standard television picture.

Graphics capability is much more than a curiosity, especially considering that the graphic material can be stored on disk like any other data.

Graphics can be produced on a small computer system and can be preserved as hard copy with the special printout device at right. To the right of the computer, on the desk, is a "joystick," an analog input device for drawing lines in any direction on the screen. This Tektronix computer works by itself ("stand-alone" mode) or may share data with a "host" computer, for which it becomes an intelligent terminal.

Courtesy of Tektronix, Inc.

However, computer graphics systems vary in quality and versatility. The ones mentioned here are impressive. Less "serious" systems may offer selections of squares, triangles, line segments and so on from which a business office might or might not be

Reproduction of photographic materials on a computer's CRT screen, by means of a Vector Graphic High Resolution Graphics board, compatible with computers using the S-100 bus (Chapter 2). A sample of the picture-element "pixels" is at right. The same board permits drawing original displays by X-Y plotting or generating alphanumeric characters.

Courtesy of Vector Graphic Inc.

able to assemble useful graphs or "drawings." If you need graphics, check out every system you can find that offers them.

The Report Generator

Computer programs exist, or can be tailor-made for you, to enable you to obtain special reports *not already provided for* in your routine programming. Report generators can retrieve and format information that lies buried in your files (your disk or other computer storage media, that is). Perhaps you have had every customer or supplier listed alphabetically, or under inventory stock number, or under some other normally adequate scheme. But now you want to put out a bulk mailing and need everyone relisted according to ZIP code. Or you need to extract all accounts that gave you more than or less than a certain amount of business last year. (Or all customers who customarily take more than 90 days to pay!) The report generator simplifies this kind of thing immensely. Usually a report generator works interactively, querying the operator and instructing him or her in the procedural steps. You or anyone you designate, not a computer specialist, can manipulate the files and produce an easy-to-understand report.

Let's say you have 52 major items or classes of data. And suppose the value of each item or class is enhanced if the data is presented in relation to three other classes. Value is enhanced even more if the data is presented in certain "winning" combinations. With good data processing techniques and a well-programmed computer, you can stack the deck to have straights, four-of-a-kind, straight flushes and royal flushes any time you want.

THE NATURE OF WORD PROCESSING

Just as a computer doesn't care (or know!) whether it is doing your inventory or mixing your sausage meat, it doesn't care whether it is writing an inventory list or writing out a contract. It doesn't know an itemized bill from a personalized form letter, but given the right software it will generate either one for you. That's **word processing**.

This is an exciting application for the small computer. All it consists of really, is writing or typing a text, editing it, and producing it in a final form. But with a difference. The difference is in the efficiency of computerized word processing.

A compact word processing system. The keyboard includes a numeric pad and word processor function keys. The computer and its disk drives are in the desk pedestal. The printer's output resembles fine typing. The system can be used for data processing by changing programs.

Courtesy of Vector Graphic Inc.

There is no magic to it. The document produced is a human creation. The computer is used in lieu of a pen or typewriter. But, for large documents or repeated runs of small ones, or for any document for which absolute perfection is a must, the human's work becomes more efficient: easier, faster, more accurate, if the computer is used.

The computer offers a radical change in method. With *manual* word processing, all corrections and modifications must be done on a physical copy on paper — **hard copy**. A succession of modified manual versions means a succession of hard copies. Correcting one little typing mistake could mean the production of an entire new page. With computerized word processing, all correcting, editing, and modifying are done in the machine's memory. Typing and other small corrections are a matter of simple command. Nothing need be committed to paper until the operator is satisfied that the document is perfect. The document can be examined repeatedly on the computer's display screen before the command is given to print out. The production of a page of hard copy then takes a minute or so — which is several times as fast as the best human typist could do it.

Unquestionably you can do all your own word processing manually. That's probably how you are doing it now. Even if you can't type, your secretary can. Either of you can check, edit, revise, or rearrange, and the secretary will patiently retype. But we defy you to turn out a typographically correct document of 500 pages manually! And how long does your manual method take you? How much does it cost you?

Any business with a considerable volume of correspondence, contracts, proposals, direct-mail advertising, product manuals or other documentation can benefit from computerized word processing. There are so many things it can do, so many costs it can cut.

Writing a mailing list may be considered either data processing or word processing — hence the computer can indifferently do it. A list is similar to an invoice; an invoice resembles a report; a report is one step from a letter, circular, or flyer; these differ in length only from a contract, proposal, or massive technical manual. Word processing can streamline the production of all of them.

Ringing the Changes

Proposals and contracts involve boilerplate, but there are advantages to varying the boilerplate for particular applications. A word processing system can allow you to go into the boilerplate for quick surgery, cutting out inapplicable words, phrases, sentences, and paragraphs and substituting others at will. No need to retype the entire document and individualize it. When you have made the changes you want, the computer will print out an "original" in just the shape you want it in. The skeleton boilerplate, still intact, resides on a disk; you may use it to write a proposal or contract for Baker Company either identical to or differing from the proposal you just wrote for Able Corporation. A good word processing program lets you fill in blanks — even create blanks where you need them — but the finished document shows no signs of blanks.

Formerly, computerized word processing was available only to large corporations that could afford a large outlay of money. The microcomputer has made it available to almost any small business that wants it. Now you can have "letter-perfect" correspondence, all the time. Goodbye to correction fluids and lift-off tapes. You can produce a hundred circular letters in a matter of minutes, each of them perfect — or produce one perfect camera-ready original for offset printing.

The advantages to lawyers, or to any firm that has typists pounding away all the time, are obvious. So are the advantages to companies that produce technical documentation, whether it's a one-page instruction sheet for assembling a wheelbarrow or the maintenance manual for a television transmitter, since much editing and revision has to go into any manual before it is published.

Certain documents must — for legal reasons — be absolutely perfect even if they are one-of-a-kind. The most obvious example is the Last Will and Testament. In most states, a will is invalidated if its text is found to exhibit any changes whatever, including innocent corrections of typing errors. This means every signed copy must come out of the typewriter perfect, in one pass. An expensive, time-consuming job for manual word processing. A quick routine printout for computerized word processing.

Of course, if your correspondence or document text editing needs are minimal, computerized word processing might be an expensive luxury. A good office typewriter is much cheaper than a word processor. But assuming you have any volume to handle, word processing could be a highly economical tool. If you are acquiring a computer anyway, you might as well weigh the costs and benefits of having the additional software for word processing. (You could get away with as little as $1500 extra, at 1979-1980 prices.) As suggested in Chapter 1, being able to sell a word processing service to other small businesses could bring you extra revenue even if your own business has little need for the service.

A system can use a teleprinter as a terminal. The CRT display and the computer-disk drive cabinet may be mounted anywhere convenient. This system is also a general business system.

Courtesy of MicroDaSys

Capabilities

The simplest word processing systems allow you to type text, correct typographical errors, store the document as it appears on your display, and then automatically type it out in its corrected form. You will probably want more than that. You can have capabilities for automatic page numbering, automatic formatting of lists and tables (and reformatting in response to simple keyboard commands), and document page formatting: length, number, and spacing of lines; indentation or other paragraphing; and perhaps margin justification. (For justifying lines of type, so that both margins are clean and straight, the program must be able to "think ahead," spacing words so that all lines have uniform length.) You will certainly want the ability to alter, delete, or add individual words or lines anywhere in the text on command.

For extensive editing and revision of large documents, the ability to rearrange entire blocks of text (the **cut and paste** capability) is essential.

Capabilities can go on and on. In large computers, entire lexicons of words have been stored, so that the program could automatically check spelling. It could also check where words may properly be broken for splitting at the ends of lines. (In some cases, the program embodies the general rules for word-breaking, but each rule has endless exceptions.) This kind of thing can go further: if a word is a proper noun, the program may recognize it as such and give it an initial capital letter. Such capabilities make it possible for near-illiterates to use the computer for word processing. In principle, all this can be provided for microcomputers.

However, that kind of thing is expensive. It is also a voracious eater of internal memory space. "A computer that can spell" is a fine idea for large corporations staffed mainly with klutzes at the clerical level. You're a small business and you can't afford to hire klutzes. For the small business, a good secretary who can spell (or even a so-so secretary) backed up by an up-to-date dictionary is plainly more cost-effective than some over-fancy program.

Now, a *good* word-processing system does most of the work, so that the operator is free to make decisions and issue commands. The operator should not be involved in intricate procedures unless he or she is *doing* something intricate. If the operator has to work too hard, the programmer has not worked hard enough. The harder the programmer has worked, the more expensive the program is likely to be. But you get what you pay for. Would a primitive, puny word-processing program be cost-effective, even though "least expensive," if it required the operator to put in almost as much time and effort as for manual word processing?

So, you will test word processing software just as you will test data processing software. What works best? What is quickest, smoothest, simplest? What is really going to do the job for *you*?

A good word-processing system could cost as much as a good secretary's annual wage, or at least a major portion thereof. This applies, of course, to a complete system, both hardware and software. But even just adding word processing software to your data processing system can cost a respectable bundle — that $1500 estimated minimum. The payoff is, a good word processing system can enhance your secretary's efficiency and output by 20 to 200 percent, depending on the kind of material being worked with. And the over-all quality is consistently high.

Take the matter of correct spelling. You will have composed and stored, on disk or tape, many different "form" items, ranging from actual report and invoice forms, and brief form letters, to major boilerplate blocks for contracts and proposals — indeed, entire standard contracts and model proposals — plus perhaps extensive technical or legal documentation. Once stored, these can be "played back" repeatedly for minute checking of spelling, grammar, syntax, and style. Once you are sure you have them right, they stay right forever. Every time they are printed out, they will be printed correctly. With manual word processing, you and your secretary are always checking for errors (and frequently missing a few).

Have you ever costed out one brief letter dictated to your secretary? An interesting exercise, with possibly dismaying results. We shall come back to this later.

What do you need?

As with all microcomputer system purchases, the success of the purchase depends on your thoroughness in analyzing your needs. Obviously, if your requirements run to a moderate amount of brief correspondence, occasional form letters, and some long document now and then, the less elaborate, less expensive software will do for you. If your output is heavy, varied, and frequently consists of long, complex documents, the more capable but more expensive software will ultimately be more cost effective.

You will need the same categories of hardware for data processing and word processing, beginning with that CPU (Chapter 2). For any business purpose, the minimum recommended memory capacity is 16K bytes anyway; if you can afford more memory, it will enhance your word-processing capability. You will need, of course, a good keyboard, or a reasonable substitute such as Writehander™ (Chapter 8). Word processing systems exist *without* CRT or other display screens, but the CRT is essential unless you plan to dedicate a specially trained operator to word processing. (Without a CRT or plasma display, the operator must work blind to put corrections or changes into the memory.) Disk storage is to be preferred to tape cassette storage unless all your documents are brief. The most critical item is going to be your printer or printers.

The most common utility printer for a microcomputer system is the dot matrix printer. It is relatively inexpensive and relatively fast—up to 900 characters, or about 11 "typewritten" lines, per minute.

```
THIS IS DOT-MATRIX PRINTING.  IT IS FINE FOR
YOUR IN-HOUSE COMMUNICATIONS, AND YOU CAN GET
BY WITH IT FOR THE NUMBERS ON YOUR BILLS AND
INVOICES.
```

There was a vogue some years back for sending out everything in dot-matrix print, to proclaim LOOK AT US: WE'RE REALLY MODERN 'CAUSE WE'RE USING A COMPUTER but you will probably agree that this practice is no longer even cute.

For "outside" communications, you need this. This looks like a good typewriter's output, doesn't it? And you can get modified electric typewriters to use as computer output devices. However, what you see here was produced by a daisy-wheel printer.

The daisy wheel is much faster than a typewriter, and (equally important) a good daisy wheel apparatus will go for hundreds and hundreds of hours without needing adjustment or repair. Your electric typewriter will break down frequently in heavy duty word processing service. We would not recommend using a typewriter as an output device unless your word processing load is rather light.

This different type face results from the changing of the print wheel or "daisy" used on the daisy head. Bold-faced type is achieved through an automatic double- or triple-striking process that shifts the print head a few millimeters to the right for repeated strokes. Underscoring is also available: the printing head will sweep back to accomplish this on any word or phrase or passage desired.

Daisy wheels cost more (typically) than dot matrix printers and are not as fast—although they are three or more times as fast as the best electric typewriters. Some dot matrix printers are coming out that produce a form of serif type that perhaps passably resembles daisy-wheel, typewriter, or typesetting type like what you see here. If you see it, judge it for yourself.

A new development: In 1979 NEC (Nippon Electric Corporation) introduced a variation on the daisy-wheel theme, employing a cup-shaped "thimble" in place of the flat "daisy" printing head, on its *Spinwriter* printer series. Everything this book has to say about daisy wheels applies equally well to the NEC thimble machines.

An equally important consideration is *friction feed* or *sprocket feed*? Friction feed is satisfactory if you always use ordinary blank paper, or blank-paper rolls, for your printouts. Preprinted forms, including checks, bills, and invoices, require sprocket feed. If a feed error is "only a hair"—say five-one hundredths of a line, it only takes 20 bills to put it one whole line off; at 40 bills it's two lines off, and pretty soon you may as well not be using a preprinted form. You can imagine what a disaster this would be if you were running a month's checks through the printer. Friction feed cannot maintain accurate alignment; there is always some slippage. Sprocket-feed forms, of course, have extra margins with precisely spaced holes for engaging precisely spaced sprocket teeth. The forms are pulled a precise distance for each line-feed movement.

Learning how

Almost all microcomputer word processing systems are easy to use, assuming decent quality in the software. You *can* use a word processor even if you can't type, though your input would be slower. While it takes several years to make a good typist, you can learn to operate a word processing system in one afternoon. You can become quite proficient within a few days, and an expert in a month or so. True, you probably don't want to bother, yourself. But whichever member of your staff winds up using the computer every day will become proficient very quickly. There is no real training problem.

Vendors of word-processing systems (and even of data-processing systems) may offer training courses as part of the over-all package. Some of the training may take place at the dealer's, but usually at least some of it will take place on your premises. By all means accept this option if offered. It will help eradicate the fear that your employees will inevitably have because of the new computer. (This is discussed more fully in Chapter 5.)

Making like Hemingway

Remember, the software is (or should be!) error-tolerant. The computer will not recognize a typing error but the operator should, and the system will permit immediate strikeover correction. However, *there is no law that says you must correct as you go.* You (or your operator) may wish to compose Hemingway-style, flinging everything down "on paper," or rather into the computer's memory, disregarding typing errors, disregarding "wrong" words, disregarding poor sentences or clumsy syntax, not worrying about whether you are forgetting something—*just running at top speed.* This will work just fine.

When you think you are through, and you "play it back" on the display screen, there it is, errors and all. But now, like Hemingway, you may correct, add, delete, and amend at leisure. That lean, spare, powerful style of Hemingway's seldom showed up on a first draft, so why should you worry? You may just say what you want to say, and then consider afterwards whether you have said it right, or "correctly." It won't take you long to polish it up.

If you are not impetuous like Hemingway, but an orderly, methodical, meticulous person who will be bothered by having left an error in the memory for even a few seconds, you may take your time. The computer has infinite patience. It will wait while you correct spelling immediately, and while you ponder the right word or turn of phrase. It will also wait while you experiment with the "best" way to format a report, list, invoice, or bill. If you have the time, take the time.

Either way, the computer will help you come up with a perfect document.

What if, next day, that document doesn't appear to be so "perfect?" (Every writer has that experience: a creation is best judged after it has cooled off for a day or two. Every page of this book was rewritten several times.) No problem. You have the entire document in magnetic storage. Just put the disk or tape back in the drive, run the text back into the computer, and make whatever improvements you think are needed.

Word processing software usually involves two programs, a Text Editor and a Word Processor. They may be combined in a package. A diagram of a word-processing system might look like this:

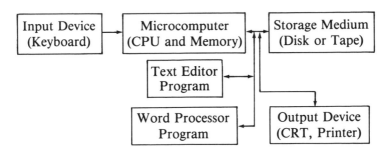

The text and commands are entered together, so that the entire typed output for a short letter would look like this on the CRT screen:

.1s   *(This tells the program to*
                             single-space.)

.in40   *(This tells the program to*
                             indent 40 spaces.)

November 10, 1979

.un   *(This tells the program not to*
                             indent any more.)

.sp4   *("Skip 4 lines.")*

Mr. Jeremy Watson
1901 Camellia Terrace
Stamford, Connecticut 06902

.sp   *("Skip a line.")*

Dear Mr. Watson:

.sp   *("Skip a line.")*

We are happy to inform you that your credit application has been approved and that we have inaugurated your account with us. As you requested, your credit limit is $5000.00. We look forward to a long and happy association with you.

.sp4	*("Skip 4 spaces.")*
.in40	*("Indent 40 spaces.")*
Sincerely yours,	
.sp5	*("Skip 5 spaces.")*
William Holmes	
Credit Manager	
.e	*("End of document.")*

This example assumed that the program has already taken into account the printed matter at the top of the company letterhead, so that the first line, the date, will appear at a predetermined place on the paper. Once the text has been run through the word processing program and printed out, it looks like this:

November 10, 1979

```
Mr. Jeremy Watson
1901 Camellia Terrace
Stamford, Connecticut 06902

Dear Mr. Watson:

We are happy to inform you that your credit appli-
cation has been approved and that we have
inaugurated your account with us.  As you requested,
your credit limit is $5000.00.  We look forward
to a long and happy association with you.


                                  Sincerely yours,



                                  William Holmes
                                  Credit Manager
```

Does that look like a lot of work for one short letter? Of course it is. But what you have stored on disk or on a tape cassette is the *form* of this letter. If your program allows for variables, the next time you need to send a letter like this you need only enter the new date, new customer's name, and credit limit amount. You could have a program that would automatically type an entire batch of these letters, pulling names, addresses, and corresponding credit limits form a separate file disk or tape, or prompting an operator to "fill in the blanks" at a keyboard.

With a program permitting variables, your form letter as typed in would have something like "&1 &2" for the recipient's name, and the salutation would be "Dear Mr. &2." Or it could be "&1 &2 &3" to allow for a middle name or initial. The file would be set up so that each real name, and its address, would be substituted for "&1 &2 &3."

Each letter would have the appearance and tone of a personal letter, not a form letter.

Economies

It costs you several dollars to produce one letter manually, counting dictating and transcribing time, checking and correcting time, and the time taken to address the envelope. But as the same letter is machine-repeated, the cost per letter goes down. Even if you did only four of the letters of the kind addressed here to Mr. Jeremy Watson, you would have saved a chunk of money greater than your "daily" payment on the computer.

Each successive letter takes a minute or two to print out, depending on its length. Our Jeremy Watson letter would go through a good daisy wheel printer in seconds. Each letter has no mistakes. Each appears to be "personally" typed. The envelopes can be addressed from a similar program. The system can print directly on the envelopes or produce self-sticking address labels. (The latter is a great boon, of course, for circulars and other promotionals; staff time invested per piece is cut radically.) Whenever an addressee moves, the file can easily be edited to reflect the change.

Longer Documents

Producing a long document is cheaper by word processing than by hand because you can correct and revise without going through successive hard-copy versions. (Paper itself, a "minor" expense only a few years ago, is now a high-priced item.) All production of paper versions can be deferred until everything is perfect in the file (on the disk or tape). This can be verified simply by inspecting the document on the CRT screen. All copy will appear "instantly" on the screen.

All good word processing programs have a **scroll-up, scroll-down** feature. This stands in lieu of turning hard-copy pages. The operator can scroll back any distance to re-read something, or scroll ahead any distance. The scrolling rate can be set so that a document can be comfortably read from beginning to end. The scrolling can be instantly stopped so that editing, additions, and emendations can commence.

This facilitates making boilerplate changes in contracts or proposals, or in updating technical manuals to incorporate design and operating changes. As mentioned before, good programs will have a cut-and-paste capability, to permit the operator to delete, move, or copy entire blocks of text (as well as single sentences or lines, or individual words).

One program does cut-and-paste like this. The Text Editor program is used to locate the beginning line of text that is to be moved. The operator selects where on that line to begin, and types the command BEGIN. He then searches the screen (scrolling up, if necessary) to find the end of the passage, and he commands END. Scrolling again, the operator locates the place where the block to be moved is to go. He sets the screen's blinking cursor symbol at that spot (using the cursor key). He types MOVE, and everything between BEGIN and END is automatically moved to that spot.

Suppose the operator wanted to repeat the text block in a new place, without deleting it from its old place? Then, instead of MOVE, he would command DUP for "duplicate." With simple further editing commands he could vary the wording and emphasis of the duplicated passage, deleting or adding words, deleting or changing whole clauses or sentences.

Suppose you had a 100-page document to which you could not avoid adding six lines on page nine? With manual word processing, this could mean laboriously retyping up to *92* pages. The computer word processor will take over that chore, automatically shifting everything by six lines, while maintaining automatic page numeration and maintaining 26 or 27 lines per page (or whatever line value was chosen by the operator). Suppose page 1 originally carried only 14 lines, ending a section, with the next section starting on page 22? A good program could stop the printing after having typed twenty $(14 + 6)$ lines on page 21.

Of course, adding lines anywhere would affect the location of figures, tables, charts, section headings, and so on farther along in the document. Dealing with this would require some operator intervention. But this would be required with manual word processing, and the whole operation would still be easier and faster with machine word processing. Besides, it is no great trick for your editor or operator to skim through (scrolling) looking for places where a line or two can be picked up, by eliminating a superfluous word here and there, or by restating something more briefly. If all six lines can be picked up before the next figure or table is reached, the day is won.

Machine word processing saves time and effort. It leaves your secretary or operator (or you) fresh, for handling another document. Or it leaves them free to do something else. There is that famous one of Parkinson's Laws, "Work expands to fill the time." You might be tempted to come up with busywork projects to fill up computer time and "justify" either the computer's cost or the operator's salary. Or you could step down the hall or across the street and sell word processing or other computer services to some other business. That's justification with a vengeance, a sweet, money-in-the-bank vengeance.

CHOOSING A SYSTEM

Choosing a word processor system is like buying any other small business microcomputer. The first thing you do is analyze your needs. Second, you survey the word-processing systems available. (These may be dedicated hardware-software combinations, or special software to add to your data processing system; you will also look closely at printers.) Third, you compare and evelute the physical equipment: its cost, reliability, printing quality and speed. Fourth—but by no means last—you compare and evaluate word processing software. How well does it work? How easy is it to use for your purposes? What does it cost?

You will need to ask yourself questions like these:

What kinds of documents will I want typed?

How long are the documents I must frequently process?

How much revision will have to be done on typical documents?

How important is printing quality? (Daisy wheel *vs.* dot matrix.)

How important is printing speed? (Dot matrix *vs.* daisy wheel.)

How heavily will the system be used?

How long will I want my documents stored?

How easy or difficult is the system to learn?

How much money can I afford to spend?

Exactly how will a word processing system save me money?

Storage and memory are important considerations. For manuals, long proposals, or heavy legal documents, you might find hard disks preferable to floppy disks. Hard disks systems for microcomputers are new and they cost more ($1500 to $4500 more, at 1980 prices). But a hard disk can hold hundreds — or even thousands — of typewritten page equivalents. A floppy diskette (5 inch diameter) may hold up to 60 pages, and an 8-inch floppy a hundred or so. You should always aim to store a complete document on a single disk or other storage unit. Otherwise, data manipulation becomes difficult and tricky: scrolling is no longer a simple matter; nor is cut-and-paste. For quite short documents, you might find data cassettes economical; a cassette holds about 15 pages. Cassettes are slower than disks in data input and output; the time tradeoff might or might not be economical for you.

Of course one disk, even a 5-inch diskette, is the equivalent of quite a few tape cassettes. Any disk might hold more than one document; you could keep all "short" items on a single disk. Disks are widely judged to be preferable to cassettes for business office purposes, unless the computer itself is very lightly used.

Disks have another advantage over cassettes or any other tape medium, and that is virtual random access. Data can be read from its place on a disk, or stored in a domain on a disk, very rapidly, at eyeblink speed. Any tape medium has sequential access, and that's slow.

All tape and most disk media are easily removable and offer no serious off-computer storage problems. Most hard disks are not removable, but each permanent disk stores much more data than a removable disk. You will weigh disk-type capacities and costs against your storage needs and your budget.

Related to external storage is the question of the size of your computer's random-access (RAM) memory. This governs how large a portion of a text can be brought into the memory for processing. It also governs how large and elaborate a program can be for your word processing. Except for brief-letters-only processing, an 8K-byte memory (or even a 16K-byte memory) could be inadequate. On the other hand, you would not want to pay a premium for a large memory (64K, 128K) that you would not use to its fullest.

Every letter, numeral, punctuation mark or other character that you type into a computer's memory costs you at least one byte of memory space. A *space* in your typing costs a byte. Assuming 80 characters per line and a 26-line double-spaced typewritten page, one page costs you an absolute minimum of 2080 bytes. A small memory might not have much room for storing text data once the programs have been run in. A good program would allow for constant disk-reading for scrolling purposes, but good programs are likely to assume a memory of better than 8K bytes.

Dedicated systems

Complete small-computer systems are now offered as word processors. These typically have a quality printer and a modified keyboard. The keyboard would have function keys that are not present, or not used the same way, in a straight data-processing system. There are advantages to a system designed for a single application, by people whose forte is that one application. The word processing software is likely to be quite powerful and highly developed if it is the primary software for the machine, and not a sort of afterthought.

Yet, the machine is still in every way a microcomputer, and it *can* run data-processing software written for it. For some time data-processor manufacturers have been offering word-processor software as an added enticement. Now, the word-processor manufacturers are beginning to offer data processing software as an accessory.

Again, your choice of software is the key to the hardware you will buy. If you are a lawyer, or have some other endeavor in which the computer's main load will be words rather than numerical data, your shopping emphasis will be on word-

This dedicated word processing system has no numeric pad on its keyboard; all "non-typewriter" keys command word processing functions: deleting or inserting characters, deleting or inserting text blocks, scrolling, etc. The system can also be used for general business purposes.

Courtesy of Alpha Professional Systems Inc.

processing software, and you may as well buy hardware designed to make the most of its capabilities.

Any computer "brand" that has been around, *and doing well*, for a long time (and remember, in the microcomputer field, "a long time" may be three or four years) will probably have both data processing and word processing software highly developed. You may be able to acquire a single system that will serve you very well in both departments.

However, as you make increasing use of your computer over time, you could encounter internal competition problems. Your numbers people and your words people might both want to use that computer all the time. You might soon wind up acquiring two systems, each specialized for a primary application.

Or, if your system has a big enough internal memory (or easy add-on capability) and your supplier has the software for it, you could modify it into a multi-user system. You can now acquire a multi-user microcomputer at the outset if you wish. Such a system has more than one keyboard, more than one CRT or other display (that is, more than one terminal), and could have more than one set of disk drives or tape drives. Multiplexed or "time-shared" in this way, the computer gives each user the illusion of having a separate computer at his or her command. Multiplexing is really a software problem, not a hardware problem, and some of the leading manufacturers have produced the software and are touting this capability. It probably offers economies.

On the other hand, having separate dual systems offers you spares — provided that they are software-compatible, so that you can run your billing on the word-processing computer, or can write the annual report on the accounting computer, if either of them breaks down.

This whole matter is full of ifs, and buts, and tradeoffs. You will have to study your needs and make your own decisions. Such decisions are best made after you have had solid hands-on experience with at least a single-user microcomputer.

Is there no good word to say for those "memory typewriters" and similar word-processing devices that are not billed as computers? (Never mind that some of them may be microprocessor-based.) Yes. They are just fine, provided you are willing to employ specially trained people to use them and leave their use restricted to those people. The crucial thing is that they lack a CRT or equivalent display; once again, the operator works blind. Needless to say, the nonspecialist, like your secretary or yourself, could find them difficult or impossible to use. The typical and leading "memory typewriter" is the IBM Mag Card™ system, certainly a quality machine: but each magnetized plastic "card" holds rather few pages of text. It wouldn't let you scroll a long document, and "cut-and-paste" requires some skill. It has no inherent data-processing capability. And *you* can't play Hemingway on it, leaving your mistakes for your secretary to clean up tomorrow.

We admit a strong prejudice in favor of the full-fledged microcomputer, because it is versatile, and because anybody can use it.

Chapter Five

HOW TO SHAPE YOUR COMPUTER SYSTEM
(What Does Your Business Need?)

Before you go out to buy your computer hardware and software, you will need to have developed a strategy. Just what do you plan to use your computer for? Now? In the near future (six months, one year)? In the foreseeable farther future? How is your computer going to be used? Who on your staff—probably more than one person—will need it most? Just what tasks can a computer take over from you and your staff?

Right now something is making you think about computerizing. It isn't routine stuff that you adequately cope with by manual means. There is something in your operation, some troublesome, urgent item, that may be keeping you awake nights, and getting you thinking about computers.

What is that item? What is that problem? What is it that keeps getting out of hand? Are orders getting lost? Back orders neglected? Inventory turnover running faster than your staff can maintain status reports? Billing errors? We can't imagine what your problem is. Only you know—only you and your beleaguered staff.

All right, what's the *shape* of the problem? What kind of information is getting lost—or lagging too far behind the events? Don't just name it. Write yourself a detailed report about it. This may require one page of handwritten scrawls on a yellow tablet—or it may run to 20 or 30 typewritten pages. You may need the aid of your key staff people in order to really get into what is wrong.

Now you have a start. Just having the shape and dimensions of the problem down on paper will begin giving you a leg up on

it. The clearer picture may help you alleviate the problem somewhat even before you bring a computer aboard.

However, you may still find that massive amounts of information have to be processed, and filed in easily retrievable
form. You still have a need for week-by-week, day-by-day,
hour-by-hour and perhaps even random, *right now* status
reports. This the computer can do for you, provided you format
the information and the reports intelligently. You have to
distinguish what you need, say, in an on-the-spot report from
what you need in a weekly report.

However, you are beginning to know specifically what you
need the computer for. You must continue to map out *what you
need to know* in the problem area. A computer can't tell you
that — it can only help you once you know what you need. When
and how often do you need to know a particular thing? To what
depth of detail do you need some monthly, weekly, daily, or
hourly report? What *kinds* of information have to be processed,
for whom? (Bookkeeping? Quality Control?) Once you have
that kind of insight, a total computer system can be designed for
you.

Needless to say, you can't be bothered with reading reams and
reams of computer printout to find some crucial item each time.
This is why we have you sorting out categories of information.
The small computer can give you instant reports on even one
obscure item, provided you have worked out the desired formats and provided you obtain the proper programming.

That software problem

There's the rub. Once you have your particular business
nightmare measured and described, you probably won't find the
"correct" software for it right off the bat. You are unlikely to
find a canned program package ready to attack your problem
and straighten it out. Your business is unique — but all the available software is either very general or is really tailored to someone else's problem. (See Chapter 3.)

This is no reason to despair. You may be able to find software
that partially fills the bill for you, alleviates the problem somewhat. Certainly, if you have made a good buy of your computer
system, you will have bought sideline application packages that
make do for the moment with payroll or accounts receivable

and all else that you do that is pretty standard anyway. (By now, your accountant has surely forced you into some standardized procedures.) But once you have a complete system you will probably want to go for some customized software.

Mapping and detailing the one big problem area won't be enough. The moment you introduce the computer, all kinds of things are going to have to change. Not because the computer is Procrustean, bound to demand that everything and everybody fit its "bed." It's just that, if you are going to make the most efficient and economical use of your computer, you are going to have to upgrade your operation all along the line. Yes, you can do it piecemeal, but you can't afford to dawdle. This means *you are really going to have to analyze your business*. You are going to have to spell out, for yourself and your computer, just how your business operates.

You may be a fiscal genius, and you may fly your business by the seat of your pants. But the computer is no genius. It is a talented idiot. It is dull, literal-minded, and passive. It needs meticulous instructions, so it needs myriad nit-picky facts. Sorry, but you are going to have to accept this unpalatable chore and turn your "art" of doing business into a "science" for that stupid computer.

GETTING INTO IT

In the course of your analysis you are going to get to know more about your business than you ever knew before. Or rather, than you thought you knew before, although there may be a few real if minor surprises. You will have new perspective. Facts long overlooked will stand out clearly against the new background. And, in your consultation with your staff (and your accountant) you are going to receive some criticisms, friendly and otherwise, at least by implication.

It may take a few weeks for all your knowledge to jell. Then you will wake up some morning with *satori*. Enlightenment. Revelation. You are going to see new, more efficient ways of doing business. You are going to see changes to make, with or without a computer. And you are going to see ways in which a computer might help you even more than you had thought. (Check those ways out—don't rush out and buy just yet.)

Flow Charting

Let us hope you are going to do some *flow charting*. We don't mean the formal flow charting, using esoteric symbols, that a programmer or a computer systems analyst would do. We just mean the setting-down-on-paper of what goes where, when, and what next happens *in your business*. Just what does happen when an incoming shipment arrives on your receiving platform? What are the steps through which the shipment is unpacked, broken down, moved to stock, delivered within the plant or store? Who first receives the shipping invoice and routes which copies to whom? When? What happens to *each* of these copies? (Check with staff members every step of the way to make sure of what *really* happens, regardless of "official" procedure.) And so on. As you develop informal charts of what really happens, you can concurrently develop ghost charts of what, according to your judgment and preferences, ought to be happening.

During this process, you will develop firmer ideas of what kinds of reports the computer should generate for you, and how detailed. You'll know which details you want. You will judge how often you will need a given item of information. You will be better able to decide what you want to see instantly on a CRT screen and what can wait for deferred archival printouts.

Once you get these informal charts done, you will pore over them alone, and then with Charlie from Shipping and Receiving, Elsie from Bookkeeping, and George from the Sales Floor. Then you will revise them. That done, you will start acting on them, even though your computer purchase is still in the future. Once you have them just so, *save those charts*. They may turn out to be just what your custom programmer will need when you get into gear on programming. They will save him time in his formal flow charting, expensive time (expensive to you).

And remember, you are probably going to need a custom program for that one crucial matter that impels you toward acquiring a computer. And at some time, you will have the programmer modify packaged applications programs so that the routine things — payroll, accounts payable, and so on — are done in the way *you* and your staff (and your accountant) need and want to have them done. You will be that computer's master, not its servant.

In the course of all this you will be developing a picture of what all your software should be like. You will be able to specify what each of your applications programs should do. Knowing that, you will have indispensable knowledge to help you choose the hardware that your programs are going to run on.

With a small enough business you may need only to consult your staff in a token way. With a larger business you will need to consult your accountant about your data processing needs— for "now" and also for "when we get the computer." But with a big enough business—or hairy enough problems—you ought to engage a computer consultant. This will be a *systems consultant* (defined later).

USING THE CONSULTANT

The consultant may be an independent, or he may be an employee or associate of the outfit from which you are planning to buy the computer. (Choosing that outfit requires a process that we shall go into later in this chapter.) Either way, the consultant is going to have to know certain things. What things? Everything. Just like your accountant, this guy gets to know all about your business.

Some readers will shy or bridle about that, but consultants can be checked out as to reputation for character, reliability, and so on. A qualified consultant is not an industrial espionage agent, itching to sell your business secrets to your competitors. He is a professional who exercises the discretion of a lawyer or accountant or banker. He doesn't discuss your business affairs with anyone unauthorized by you, and, if you wish it, will not let anyone else know you are his client.

The consultant is going to take you over the same ground you took yourself over when you were analyzing your business and drawing up flow charts. But this will not be "duplication."

The consultant will ask a lot of questions. Probably hundreds of them. Be patient—and don't "save time" by volunteering too much information. Don't reply at greater length than his simpler or briefer questions seem to call for. Let him "coax" the information out of you, one item at a time. Give him time to take his notes and to ponder. Let him work his canopener strategy on you.

We are not implying that you ought to be secretive or perverse or coy. It's just that a consultant worth his fee should know all the right questions to ask. If you keep blurting out answers to questions he hasn't asked, he may fail to ask certain collateral questions that will give him a truer picture of your situation and needs. He must have his answers in a context that *he* is generating.

If you let him ask all his questions, you will soon be able to size him up: Does he know his business? That is, does he know how to get to know yours? If he asks far fewer questions than you have already found answers for, you need a different consultant. He should be able to ask questions you never thought of. Running a business is your forte — and analyzing a business is his.

An important part of the consultant's value to you is his fresh, disinterested perspective. You are in the habit of making numerous unconscious assumptions about your business. The consultant will ask about matters you take for granted. He will require you to examine things which you haven't noticed but which could be crucial. (At least, crucial to a successful computerizing.) His process of questioning you will cause you to learn still more about your business.

As the consultant interviews you — and this will probably take several sessions — you should have, on your desk slide and in your lap (and figuratively at your fingertips) most of the information he wants. You will have done your own preliminary analysis. You and your staff will have written various reports and memoranda. You will have notes to yourself on what the hell your "flow charts" mean. You will have summarized much of the information, and reviewed your summaries before the consultant's each and every visit. It's perfectly proper to say, "I think I can lay my hands on that, just a moment," and riffle through your papers. But you should make sure it's all there, organized so that you can retrieve particular facts easily. Remember, you're paying for the consultant's time at $$$ bucks a day. Your secretary can help you get your information organized in concise form.

The consultant is going to ask you to list the number and kinds of transactions for all types of functions, function by function. He'll want to know the number of customers you have, the number of vendors you buy from, the number and kinds of products, the number of invoices written per month, the number of each kind of invoice, for each class of product or service, the numbers and kinds of checks you write per month, and so on. He will want details of how you pay your people, details of the kinds of credit you enjoy from each vendor, and of the kinds of credit you extend, and so on and so on. We said there would be hundreds of questions—and some answers will prompt subquestions.

The client-consultant relationship

At various times, the consultant will probably get politely hard-nosed with you. This will happen at the outset, during, and toward the end of his relationship with you. He will want to settle how much, and according to what schedule, you are going to pay him. This will be a function of exactly what he is going to do for you. He will undoubtedly want some money up front, then one or more performance payments as interim and final reports are delivered. There will be several stages in his work; he will need to outline, for himself as well as for you, just what he will deliver at the end of each stage. To what depth, at each stage, should he do up plans for your computer system? He will want to tell you how much latitude he can allow, at each stage, for changing plans on your part.

Why will the consultant try to dictate how much latitude you can have for changing plans? He will want to head off one dire eventuality. After some days or weeks of working with him, you may *again* wake up with satori, enlightenment, revelation. And just when he's two-thirds or nine-tenths finished with the planning of your computer system, you call up all excited, with a revolutionary plan for the complete overhaul of your business. You're "going to do everything different," and more or less expect him (almost finished with the job) to "do everything different." Consultants of many kinds, including the authors of books, proposals, technical manuals, etc., have had many a hungry month when a client has radically changed plans when most of the real work was already done.

But if the consultant can't be flexible along with you, what good is he? Yes, he can be flexible, but you will have to extend his time (and fees). You can't expect him to rewrite his product in a hurry once you've played switcheroo—or even to catch up on all your changes overnight. Certainly he will not be able to give you the same quality and completeness if you turn his careful work into a crash project.

Now, you may be one of the significant segment that takes pride in being a hardheaded, unsentimental, *ruthless* businessman; you might figure that a consultant's problem is not your worry. It isn't, so long as the problem isn't you. The consultant is a professional, and playing switcheroo is not the most efficient, effective way to make use of him.

Remember, what you want out of the consultant is *the optimum plan for computering your operations*, not the ego-stroke of having achieved a coup at his expense. (Or, as a *Newsweek* feature story once put it, having been "not the man who gets ulcers but the man who gives ulcers.") Cooperate with your computer consultant as you do with your accountant, lawyer, and physician. Otherwise, he could just quit; he doesn't want to be the eaten dog.

FINDING THE CONSULTANT

How to find a good consultant? In some cities, computer consultants may be listed in the Yellow Pages. (Make sure that you have reached a consultant for *microcomputer* systems.) Even so, your best course is probably to ask your accountant.

The larger accounting firms usually have a management information systems staff that can help you. Even a small local accountant, however, should know, or can find out, who is worth his fee in the systems consulting profession. Most important, your accountant can probably locate a consultant who is familiar with your line of business.

Computer vendors—especially the larger, better established software vendors—often employ staff consultants, or have independent consultants as associates, as indicated earlier. The computer vendor may first want to send you a salesman, who will listen to your description of your needs and write you a preliminary proposal. (He should, of course, ask you some consultant-style questions.) As things move toward (but not yet *to*) the "let's do it" stage he will show up again with a consultant.

Obviously there can be pitfalls in dealing with a consultant who is associated with (or employed by) a vendor. Your accountant may have some knowledge of who is objective and reliable in the way of vendor-associated consultants. However, as you contact each vendor, you are going to ask (aren't you?) for the names and addresses of prior customers. You can ask those customers what they thought of his associated consultants. Of course you will get in touch with those customers right away, before you have any "commitment" with the vendor or anyone associated with him.

A vendor may simply refer you to a small list of independent consultants. You can check around easily as to how independent they are. Even an "associated" consultant may really be an independent. This will be obvious if his or her name appears on several vendors' lists.

Consultants and consultants

What we have been discussing here is the *systems consultant*. At some time you may have need of a *programming consultant* (to be distinguished from a *programmer*). In some instances, these consultants could be the same person. However, the functional distinction is real. Both of them know computers—but the systems consultant knows business, while the programming consultant knows programming. The latter will want the kinds of inputs that the former generates. The systems person tells you what needs to be programmed up; the programming consultant tells you how best to get it done for your computer.

The systems consultant may enable a small business to bypass the programming consultant. Once your business' software needs have been analyzed, the consultant may be able to refer you to good programmers. He or she may have been able to generate *specific* task flow charts that will be just the inputs a programmer needs for your special requirements. It all depends on how complex your business and your problems are. The consultant may guide you to some canned or packaged software that might (at least roughly) meet your needs—provided your worst problem is not terribly complicated and isn't uniquely yours, and that you could safely adjust your methods to the existing software rather than require it to be tailored to you.

If a programmer does turn out to be needed (and that will probably be the case for your special requirements) the consultant should be able to steer you to one who can work with your kinds of problems. The programmer is, typically, a peculiar kind of virtuoso whom you may not enjoy working with too closely. His questions might bug you as a consultant's would not. But if he has no questions, he will produce a sort of Work of Art that may be a programming masterpiece but probably won't meet your needs. Supply him with *answers*. The more inputs you have ready for that programmer, the more comfortable you will be. The load will be off your shoulders. The programmer can just follow the consultant's guidelines and charts, the "answers" to questions he might or might not think to ask.

Don't sweat about fees. If your business is so small you have to sweat, your accountant may be the only "consultant" you will need. So ring him or her in. If you are that small, your software needs should be fairly small. Run your own analysis, straighten out your own kinks, use the computer for the straightforward but time-consuming routine things (payroll, billing, and so forth) and put the human talent on your staff on any bottleneck you may have. This will increase your efficiency, increase net revenue. After a time you will be able to afford to computerize any bottleneck item, too, and thus — to use a software term — you will **bootstrap** yourself into gravy country.

What about that programming consultant? When might you need him or her? Whenever you might have a complex, sweeping custom-programming job that covers all or most of your needs. The programming consultant may be the same individual or firm that did your systems consulting, or someone else. The need or lack of need for one will become apparent in the analysis of your business. Now, to reiterate an offhand remark from Chapter 3, your software can be *adequate* or it can be *powerful*. The programming consultant can set things up so that your programming will be powerful, making best use of your hardware system's capabilities. Any programming firm you engage may want to have some consulting sessions with you before they start writing your programs. These sessions can be brief and inexpensive if you have the systems consultant's results available to them. (The lone moonlighting freelancer may just plunge in and start writing programs for you, without bothering to develop the "big picture." That would not be cost effective.)

FINDING THE VENDOR

Concurrently with your business analysis you will have been visiting the computer stores and the "systems houses" offices and showrooms. You will have been collecting brochures and looking over equipment. You will have been pulled into inter-actions with dealers and salesmen, eager to demonstrate. Very well. While you're there, *run their sample programs*. If they tell you they have five separate business programs in the applica-tions package, make them let you try all five — on a machine like the one you think you will probably use. Don't let anyone get away with cute things like demonstrating "You can write programs in BASIC – just follow our book." Bring dummy data (or obsolete data, whose results you already have) to be fed into their existing programs.

Don't stand around watching while a salesman operates the console or terminal. Sit at that keyboard yourself, keying in your own data. The program will probably be interactive (Chapter 3) and will ask you for data items step by step. Better yet, bring Elsie the bookkeeper and whoever else will use your computer, and let them have a go at the machine and programs.

You will be finding out what the various vendors' programs can do with your kinds of data. You will get to know the vendors, get a feel for their attitudes toward your needs and problems. You will develop firm impressions about whether this or that vendor can provide or help obtain good custom software for you. Your employees, meanwhile, will be treating their fear of this new beast by patting it and making it do tricks. (More about this later.)

How tender the vendor?

For a *mini*computer (expensive – $18K to $100K) you would be dealing with the old established mainframe manufacturers whose names are more or less household words – IBM, DEC, Wang, Hewlett-Packard. For *micro*computers, the names will probably be obscure to you, and you will probably look to local dealers, or to "OEMs" or "systems houses." Now, "OEM" is an acronym for Original Equipment Manufacturer, and in this Alice-in-Computerland world an OEM may or not actually be a manufacturer. Many OEMs put systems together from components made by various true manufacturers. Even your dealer may be an OEM in this sense, putting out his own "brand" of computer though he has no factory. (It's like Safeway having its own store brands.) This happens in the minicomputer and mainframe fields, too. You can acquire a Tymshare "Tymcom 370" system that is, of course, a relabeled IBM 370, assuming you can afford a big computer.

There is nothing wrong with this "OEM" approach. Nor is there anything wrong with the "systems house," which will sell you or write you a batch of software and also purvey the hardware to run it on. The crucial question is, *how well established, stable, and solvent* is the vendor – regardless of whether he is actually a manufacturer, a secondary source, or frankly a local dealer?

Stability and solvency count, because you will need to have some sort of reasonable guarantee that servicing and support will always be available for every crucial component. This matters for software perhaps even more than for hardware. We deluged you with caveats about this in Chapters 2 and 3.

You should get in touch with several vendors. Visit dealers in your area; write for the brochures from OEMs whose advertising you spot. Let the salesmen call when you are ready. Invest some time discussing your needs with several dealers and several salesmen. (Be firm, at this stage, about your just-shopping-around status.) Your judgment will tell you which of these is best attuned to your problems. (There may be two or three to choose from later.)

Again, get the names and address of prior customers. Check with them at the outset on how well everything is working — and how responsive the vendor is to service requests or other SOS calls. Check out your selected vendors' financial stability and solvency before you get closely involved. (Remember, seemingly *big* outfits that sold big computers, or Rolls-Royce level components and peripherals, have come and gone with breathtaking suddenness. This turnover is bound to be repeated in the micro-computer field.)

GET IT ALL IN WRITING

Whether you settle on a local dealer or some OEM, we cannot stress too strongly the principle of getting everything in writing. It may be okay that the proposal or contract simply lists the standard or routine items that may need no explication, like the DOS (disk operating system) software for your disk drive. But every special requirement of yours should not merely be listed but adequately described. True, you would be wasting the vendor's time and yours if you made him write down all the technical minutiae of how he is going to meet your needs (so that the contract becomes your documentation!). But you must require him to provide some reasonable depth of detail, so that you can be assured that you will get what you pay for — and you will have a legal leg to stand on if you don't. Get delivery times nailed down, too. (You should be able to get delivery on micro-computers and their components in a matter of weeks. Custom software can take months, of course; consult your consultant on what to expect.)

INVOLVING YOUR STAFF

In Chapter 3 we mentioned involving your staff in your thinking and planning. If your staff is more than one or two people, some of them, not you, are going to be the actual users of the computer. In any case they are all going to be affected by the computer — and you can bet your total equity that they are already scared. You will need their acceptance and cooperation or the computer just won't work. The staff has to see it as a tool *for them* or they won't use it properly. You won't get the results you want.

The computer is, after all, ultimately going to replace some staff. You may not be planning to fire anybody — the "replacement" may amount to not having to hire additional clerical people. But your workers will sense that the computer could replace somebody. With the typical insecurity of the hired hand, they are all going to be a little paranoid at first. "Maybe this machine is going to replace *me*." They have all seen the movie *2001* and other future-fantasies in which a computer is a downright sinister character. The public is just plain nervous about computers.

All you want is to increase efficiency, reduce costs, increase revenue, help your staff to work more effectively and — perhaps more than incidentally — relieve some of them of certain wearying tasks. But somebody on your staff has enough of a business head to figure out that the computer will probably cost you less than the salary of one or two clerks. And he or she won't be able to resist whispering that around. The moment "computer" is mentioned on your premises you will have a morale problem a-building. (The moment somebody spots this book on your desk, the problem is born.)

Prepare the staff. Confide in them that you are considering a computer purchase. Let them know it will be a tool for them, to lighten their load and enable the entire firm to move ahead efficiently. Tell them that they are going to use the computer; it will be their servant. Don't just assure them they will be shown how. Let them know that you are interested in what they feel they need from a computer "assistant." Of course, you won't make any rash promises. But let it be known that you intend to acquire a system that they can live with. Stress subtly that it will be a microcomputer, a little one, harmless. Get rid of the malevolent HAL-from-*2001* phantasm. Let them think of the computer as just a sort of extended calculator and compact filing system.

As suggested earlier, take key members of your staff to computer demonstrations. Let them sit at the console, "typing" information in on the keyboard and "conversing" with the computer *via* the CRT. If the demonstrations are on your own premises, let everyone who can be free gather 'round.

The systems consultant will want to talk with your staff. You may wince at that, but it won't hurt you. The consultant will want to smell out your staff's attitude — especially if some fancy custom programming is in prospect. He knows that if your staff is afraid of the computer (or "hates it") they just won't work with it, *or* with him, *or* with the programmer. They may put the vendor's training instructors into polite Coventry. Just passive resistance — but unconsciously, they will sabotage your computer system. No, of course they won't damage the hardware. They will just keep goofing up and giving you the old Garbage In, Garbage Out routine that once gave computers a bad name.

Why should the consultant care? Isn't that your problem? Isn't it up to you to dragoon, if necessary, your people into accepting your computer? Well, yes, one might suppose so. The only thing is, if the consultant finds your staff too hostile he might decide to give up on you.

If he's independent he could just throw up his hands and bow out. As one consultant explained to us, he doesn't want to be associated with a system that "won't work." An executive of one vendor told us that their consultants sometimes advise them not to pursue a deal with a customer who staff is judged to be "too negative."

Why should they? Would you? After all, new prospects check with old customers. Somebody will check with you. The vendors' reputation matters to them just as yours does to you. They don't want you saying that their system doesn't work well. Also, they won't want their programmers and their training people forever revisiting your premises, "solving problems" that arise because an uptight Susan won't learn to hit "Carriage Return" to make a program run. You can't just fire Susan. Think of what you have already invested in training her.

You intend to acquire that computer to solve problems, not to make them. Deal the staff in, from the start. Let them look forward to "when we get the computer." Not, with dread, to "when The Boss gets the computer."

THE HAPPY OUTCOME

All this might look like more trouble than it's worth. On the contrary, it isn't as much trouble as it might now appear. This chapter has actually been on how to avoid trouble: on how not to make false moves. You will probably find the exercise of really getting acquainted with your business exhilarating (as well as profitable). And you will have the satisfaction of being able to make wise decisions in your acquisition of a computer system, unmoved by the blandishments of salespeople. You will know your business *and* computers the way you now know your business *and* your dumptrucks, plastic-molding machines, or whatever your prime tools are.

Now as you settle back and dream of the day when you will turn the business over to a son or daughter, you will realize that he or she will not experience this gestation-and-birthing process in regard to a computer system. He or she will have cut his business teeth on the small business computer — on the perfect little computing system that Dad (or Mom) conceived, created, provided.

The small home-and-hobby computer is a teaching machine, about computers or anything else. It will make our entire society more computer-savvy, and will accelerate the trend, now apparent in small business systems, toward completely user-oriented systems. This one uses the home TV set as a CRT terminal.

Courtesy of Atari Inc.

Of course, in their time, computers will be like any other home or business appliance. Computers will come with complete, flexible and versatile all-purpose business programs, permanently committed to massive internal memory. They will probably have true English-in, English-out interaction. The machine may respond to spoken commands or requests. (That exists in rudimentary form *now*, even for microcomputers. The requisite software and hardware exist. But remember, it's rudimentary — your cheapest, most efficient option remains that versatile keyboard.)

Much of this happy contretemps may be only a few years away (well, true English-in, English-out may take a little longer). Things should certainly be simpler, two or three years hence, should you want to upgrade or update your system. But don't wait. We'll say it again: if acquiring a computer will save or make money for you now, you will never recoup the money you will have lost by waiting.

The only "drawback" is that you need to be computer-wise. But you have this book. This book even steers you toward additional sources of information and perspective. And you have the intelligence and shrewdness that have made you a businessman. You can become computer-wise with a great deal less effort (and in far less time!) than it took you to become business-wise. Grab that scratch-pad and sharpen those pencils. Now, how many invoices do you usually process in a month?...

Chapter Six

BUYING SERVICES INSTEAD

The small business that needs the services of a computer has more than one option. So far in this book we have concentrated on the acquisition of an in-house computer. But other options exist: service bureaus and time-sharing. These are companies that own large computers, and which sell computer services (or time, or both) to other businesses.

Businesses differ, and there is no single solution to any problem that applies to all businesses. We confess a bias in favor of the small-in-house computer. We think our bias is well-justified. It is not an *a priori* bias but an "after-the-fact" bias. But maybe the answer *for you* is an outside service.

You can buy computer services of just two kinds: service bureaus and timesharing. Any thing else is a variation of one of these, or some combination. You send your service bureau your raw data in batches. They return it to you in batches, processed —within 24 hours for the better bureaus (given jobs of reasonable size). With timesharing, a remote terminal is installed in your office. This gives you a connection, *via* a telephone line, with the timesharing company's big mainframe computer, somewhere within your telephone Area Code area if not right in town. With your terminal "on line," actively connected with the computer, you have the illusion of having the computer to yourself. (Well, almost, or maybe most of the time.)

It's worth noting that quite commonly, a business that acquired its own computer has used service bureaus, timesharing, or both, and then dropped them and opted for the in-house computer. They found they needed absolute control of the system, unrestricted, non-competitive access, immediate processing, and absolute security of their data. For the most part these were larger firms than yours, and they bought maxis or big-name minis — but until very recently firms like yours weren't using computers at all, in-house or out-of-house. The bigger fellows' experience counts for you, however.

In fairness, we do know of instances in which a company had a computer, but gave it up and turned to timesharing or service bureaus. We tend to suspect that such a company did not know how to make the most of its computer. It found itself floundering. It was better off in the hands of someone who knew computers. Also, it may have made the wrong purchase. Overbuying is a big temptation. You are less likely to overbuy a service, and you can rectify the mistake easily if you do.

SERVICE BUREAUS

Service bureaus come in two main kinds: the "package" bureau and the "custom" bureau. The package bureau has generalized software that in theory should be able to do anybody's payroll, general ledger, or whatever. The business that insists on being exceptional is simply not accepted (or is let go) as a customer. Generalized software has the polite nickname of "vanilla" software; it's not supposed to offend anybody but sends very few into ecstasy. You've got the one flavor; you adapt your "business taste" to that. Sufficient businesses are willing to do that, can live with that, so that packaged bureaus stay in business. And they perform valuable services.

The custom bureau tries to be more flexible. It will modify or adapt software to particular clients' needs; it may develop virgin custom software on demand. Of course that costs more. And it takes time. But the custom bureau is trying "to do what the client would do if he owned the computer." The client, as a rule, does not quite know what he can do with the computer, or how to do it — if he owned it, he might not get the most out of it. The good custom bureau does know, and is a genuine help.

With either kind of service bureau, you are stuck with batch processing. Perhaps that's okay for the kind of business you run. Most small businesses, we think, require instant-response, fast-reflex processing, and the ability to retrieve specific items of information quickly. The typical small businessman always wants to be on top of the situation. He feels he is at a disadvantage if he must wait, even a day or two, for certain "answers" (buried in a voluminous printout). He wants control of the software, the whole process.

If you've got any use for a **point-of-sale terminal**, you probably need day-to-day, or hour-to-hour, processing and reports, and specifics, not batches. But if you don't have that, don't have to invoice every day (or week) and can operate with periodic summaries, batch processing may be for you.

Once your "batch" is delivered, the computer usually forgets it, except for what's being accumulated for your annual reports. But any printout you receive contains data that is *no longer in a computer-compatible form.* It's on paper now. If you want to refigure something, it all may have to be keyed back into a computer. You usually can't ask to have what *was* run re-run on a different program to give you a different kind of report. Not immediately, anyway. (Some bureaus do save your data on disks until you give the okay to kill it, or for some set period.)

You have no control over that remote, alien computer or its operators. You have no recourse in the case of "computer error." That's *human* error: somebody keyed in your data wrong, left something out, ran it on the wrong program, mixed it up with somebody else's data. Computers, unlike Homer, don't nod; they don't get tired; they don't get absent-minded; they don't get distracted; they don't commit bloopers. Human error. You won't even know about a "computer error" until your printout gets back (if then—if you spot it).

If the computer crashes, "goes down," you won't know that, until and unless your batch of data comes back late. Of course, if your business can use batch processing, it probably isn't critical most of the time just when the reports get back. But perhaps sometimes it is.

Errors can be made in shuffling the printouts, pulling out and addressing everybody's output, so you may find yourself with pages of data belonging to United Fast Screw and Bolt Company. Or they may have some of yours. These things happen. Of course any decent service bureau is, for obvious reasons of self-preservation, careful about that.

So much for our objections. But, if your data processing situation is such that you don't need the services of a computer often, and then only for a few hours, you certainly don't require interactive modes, instant processing—you don't need to own a computer or to use timesharing. A few hours a month of processing everything and getting one big archival report may be just the thing you need. Then, service bureaus are the solution for you.

TIMESHARING

With timesharing, you actually rent the big computer. The terminal installed in your office puts you in direct communication with it. It's as if you were in the computer room, or the computer were installed in your building. It's a prestigious computer, with lots of well developed software. And a good timesharing company can help you make the most of the computer, given the software they've got. Or they'll generate custom programs for you.

You are connected with the computer by means of a telephone line. Your terminal may have a built-in modem, or a separate **modem** may be supplied. If you are going to use an ordinary voice line, the modem will have a pair of rubber-lined holes that accept the mouthpiece and receiver of an ordinary telephone handset. You may wish to dedicate a line to the computer, or anybody's desk phone will do. Data transmission both ways is rather slow with a voice line. That won't matter to you while you're typing data in—you can't type fast enough even to keep up with what a voice line could deliver. Return printout will seem impressively fast.

With a more elaborate setup, you could ask the phone company for a **data line**. No telephone handset involved there; your modem gets physically connected to the phone system. This will handle many more bits per second (**bauds**) than a voice line can. But oh, a data line costs. Yes, "if you have to ask how much, you can't afford one."

The cheapest terminal will be a semi-portable (or even portable) keyboard-printer combination. The printer will be of the dot matrix type. You could rent more substantial printers. But even this "basic model" costs at least $125 a month. You could go to $250 a month.

Pay a little more, and you get a CRT display terminal. You'll probably still get a printer, too, for indispensible hard copy, but the CRT is convenient. Things get "written" on a CRT face much faster than they can be printed out on a printer of reasonable complexity and cost. (The sky's the limit. Your local timesharing outfit can probably rent you the most impressive and costly printers IBM or DEC or Hewlett-Packard have ever built. But you're a *small* business.) Most important, the CRT saves you from fussing with bales of paper when paper is not what you want.

Okay, now where are you? As with the service bureaus, you probably have a choice: vanilla-flavored, all-purpose software, or custom software. You might adapt your business methods to suit the vanilla programs. Or, you pay extra for the custom stuff. But you wind up only renting your custom software; *they* own it.

You've been accumulating some costs. Between $125 and $250 monthly for a terminal, with CRT in the upper ranges; a telephone connection at least $1.00 an hour; a "connect" cost of several dollars a day for connection to the computer; and computer time at $5.00 to $7.00 an hour, most likely the higher figure. Your phone bill could run up to $500 a month just for the computer usage. Even at a dollar an hour, for only four hours a day, basic telephone cost would be $80-plus a month. Data storage on the timesharing system may cost only about $.50 or $.75 per 1000 characters per month, but suppose you must store even one floppy disk's worth—500,000 characters? Your *total* bill for 40 hours of computer use a month could be as high as $900 or $1000, all things considered, incuding software charges if you don't like vanilla.

For that kind of money you could be paying off your own computer system, and fast! Not only that, you would be amortizing or depreciating the computer. When that was done, the computer would have some salvage value if you decided to (a) abandon self-computerization, or (b) get into a bigger and better in-house computer system. You can't amortize or depreciate a service you merely rent. If you get sore at the timesharing house, or want to terminate for any other reason, there's no salvage value.

To be sure, the telephone bills and direct "computer" bills represent a cost of doing business, and that cost gives you a tax break. We do not claim in the remotest way to be tax experts. Go over the matter minutely with your accountant: what is the best tax strategy, or the best over-all strategy with taxes taken into account, among buying computer services like timesharing, leasing a computer, or buying a small computer?

You can buy or lease a typical microcomputer-based system for under $500 a month. The system, remember, will cost about the price of a new car. How much do you pay for your car, assuming you drive something bigger than a Honda? Even according to the president of one successful service bureau, "the cost of a computer on a five-year lease is about equivalent to half an employee—a part-time person coming in 20 hours a week." (Gary Mokotoff, President, Data Universal, Teaneck, New Jersey—in *Small Business Computers* for March 1978.) Small computers have continued to more than hold their own against inflation—and Mr. Mokotoff may have had a bigger computer in mind than the microcomputer system we envision.

Dumb, smart, intelligent

The CRT terminal you rent may be a dumb terminal, a smart terminal, or an intelligent terminal. A dumb terminal merely enables you to communicate with the computer. A smart terminal offers some data-processing capability. However, this capability serves the computer's convenience, not yours. It has some limited software that enables you to format and condense your data before transmission to the computer. An intelligent terminal has stand-alone computing capability. It has or can have quite a variety of programs, any or all of them tailored specifically for your purposes. It can be equipped with local disk or cassette storage. It can do endless spot jobs that you needn't bother the big computer with, or for which the big computer is inappropriate. Dumb, smart, or intelligent, you pay accordingly.

That intelligent terminal certainly looks attractive. It looks like the equivalent of an in-house microcomputer. That's because it is a microcomputer. We won't labor the implication.

One advantage to the timesharing outfit's intelligent-terminal approach: they have, or ought to have, software for it, so you should have a sort of turnkey system the moment they install it. They should have programmers on their staff who can come up with custom programming within a reasonable time. A good timesharing outfit can be your computer consultant, systems analyst, programming analyst, and programming source all rolled into one. You don't have to search around. That's no guarantee you'll be satisfied with their service, but they should be able to offer a complete service. Even if you dropped the service later, you would have had experience at computerizing your operation.

Buzz, Buzz, Crash!

With timesharing, you are vulnerable to electrical noise on the phone line. Annoying when you're trying to call across town. Devastating when you're trying to put data through the line. The computer will keep sending you error signals, and could give up on you. All you're giving it is a scramble. You could pay the premium for a data line and have guaranteed low-noise transmission (nobody can guarantee *no-noise* transmission) but then you're really paying through the nose. Or, as a New York-bred friend of ours used to say, it costs you a nominal egg. (Say that aloud a few times.)

And finally, you have to cope with the temperament of a *remote* remote computer that doesn't know you and can't love you. You are just one of a horde of users yammering for its attention. And they might cause it to "crash," or "go down." They might, all together, cause some unforeseen combination of inputs that will just blow its mind.

When that happens, you're stuck. You can phone the time-sharing company, and if you get through, they'll route your call to Miss Smith. She takes complaints. Her job is to keep you mollified, to put you off with a vanilla explanation. All she knows is that the computer just went down like the *Titanic*. (She can't possibly know why. *They* don't know why yet — if they did, they'd fix it right away. And *they* don't want Miss Smith bugging them, any more than they want you bugging them.) She tells you that they expect to have the trouble fixed "soon." What else can the poor kid say? The computer may come back up in minutes or seconds, or it may take hours.

Sometimes the computer's okay, but you'll get bumped. It's just overloaded. Maybe there's priority traffic (refer to the time-sharing company's customer manual to find out what constitutes traffic that has a greater priority than yours). Maybe the computer is just screaming "Enough, already!" and is cutting out users on some eeny-meeny-miney-moe basis. Maybe it has to put everybody on hold for some seconds or minutes while it tangoes through a really abstruse mathematical function. Maybe the real disk that part of your "virtual disk" is on just had a motor failure, so your program takes a break for want of meaningful input.

You may be typing along, interacting with the computer, which seems to be "conversing" with you in a truly intelligent way, and suddenly it prints out, or flashes on your screen, "Please log on." Now, you *were* logged on. Logging on is part of your initialization procedure, part of what you did to get this electronic genie out of its bottle. Whatever you do next, the computer may (a) ignore you, or (b) repeat "Please log on." We were once involved with a timesharing computer that seemingly had been trained to frustrate your first half-dozen attempts to log on (again). That weeded out the faint-hearted. The persistent or stubborn (like us) were eventually rewarded with polite printout messages to the effect that the host program for our program would not be available until, say, Saturday night at 2330 hours.

That kind of message is most likely to appear on a Friday afternoon or evening, when "everybody" is logging on and trying to get some serious computing done—on the reasonable assumption that "everybody else" has just flown off to Las Vegas or Atlantic City for the weekend. You needn't take it seriously. Wait till Saturday morning, when the computer has had a chance to catch its breath, and it will probably let you log on again and continue with what you were doing. Meanwhile, just nurse your ulcer.

Granted, computer overloads that bad are not necessarily frequent. They just seem that way.

Needless to say, failures and overloads can occur in your own in-house computer system. But you get to take action. If the computer suddenly goes down, you can review with Sam or Elsie just what the hell they were doing with the program sequence when it happened. You can backtrack and get the program up and running again. You're the only user, that's the only program. If it's a true failure, electronic or mechanical, you can plug in the spares, and call the dealer's service shop. You aren't just left with a suddenly *dumb* terminal. Being able to take some action is a great relief for your stomach lining, blood pressure, and heart.

Dialing in, logging on, and logging off can get to be a pain somewhere after a time, even if all usually goes well. It is a positive pleasure to switch on your own computer, and after a brief pause see that CRT displaying, "READY. 15,236 BYTES AVAILABLE."

Comic relief

If you are intimately involved with a computer, crashes can be a rueful sort of fun. You get philosophical, and find amusement in finding out what went wrong this time. In the 1960's we were involved with the development of an industrial testing system that had a really fine computer at its heart. One elaborate program would trip itself up at about the same computing step every time. The assigned programmer, a close-mouthed, anti-social troll, would take it back, mull it around for a couple of days, and throw it back at you. Then it would hang up on the *next* step. Or the one *before*. The coding used in this program was such that certain data could appear, to the computer, as program instructions. These "instructions" would then scramble part of the memory—usually destroying the next few real instructions.

The programmer finally caught on and cured that. He came up with a version that got to its sticking point and attacked the computer's operating system. The computer became an idiot that couldn't even gibber. We awarded the fellow the Psychedelic Plastic Cup for that year. *In absentia.*

Our picture of the dire consequences of computer crashes and overloads may seem a bit overdrawn. Timesharing outfits are still thriving. The good ones do their job superbly. But it's not all truffles and caviar. Timesharing is the ideal way to go for the few—but not, we think, for the many. Most small businesses belong to the many.

Who's got the key?

We—and others—have some misgivings about the security of your data, sitting there on the disks of somebody else's computer (whether timesharing or service bureau). You can probably trust the companies themselves, but can you trust every single employee of those companies—the great majority of whom you don't even know? Such companies employ numerous highly qualified computer experts, including experts who for one reason or another aren't recognized as such. Even outside the computer companies, an expert with a terminal—or his own computer and a modem—could dial in, and get past the electronic security. You can't do that, we can't do that, but a creative *expert* can. There is no room here for anecdotes about "computer thefts." But many have been sensational. And *big*.

Suppose you are a psychiatrist, with your patient list and salient notes on each patient committed to disk somewhere? Or just the patient list alone? But not on your disk. A computer company's disk. Not locked up in your office. Maybe our paranoia is showing, Doctor, but do you feel at ease about that?

Then there's the CIA, the FBI, IRS, and various other government agencies. What has their track record been like lately with Constitutional rights?

Perhaps you have nothing to hide. No risk to anyone if some unauthorized person learns who buys anodized wing nuts from you, and how many per month. But most businesses have at least confidential data.

Never mind encryption. Whatsoever hath been encrypted can be uncrypted. Especially with the aid of a computer. A good code-cracker might even add insult to injury and use the computer whose encryption he is cracking. (We admit to a sneaking admiration for that sort of crook....) Besides, if your service bureau or timesharing house encrypts your stuff, they'll probably charge for *that*.

Warm toes, cold bottle...

With your data on your own disks and locked in your own firesafe, you can toast your toes at your own cozy fireside and relax with your Pouilly-Fuissé, knowing that the Computer Phantom isn't even aware you exist, and besides, he's probably not a Second Story Man. (Or she's not a Second Story Person.)

WHITHER TIMESHARING?

Obviously, we believe the age of the small in-house computer has irrevocably dawned. Are timesharing houses and service bureaus on their way out?

We doubt it. They perform necessary services — services that will continue to be needed for the same reasons they were always needed. And these houses have ways of competing with the small computer for the small business, for example, by renting you an intelligent terminal. But mainly, they are going to go on serving the kinds of customers they have traditionally served. For the most part, those customers have been somewhat bigger than you are. (Or even a lot bigger — for example, the U.S. Government.)

What kind of business needs timesharing? Suppose your operation is widespread, and you need data from several or many remote locations, plus central processing and a large data base. (Let's say you're a restaurant chain.) You could go through the expense of acquiring one or more big computers, a flotilla of battleship-sized disk drives, a large flock of terminals of whatever IQ, and of renting all those data lines from Ma Bell. Then you've got to have the software ginned up, and so on — not to mention *staff*. It represents a scary investment — and for some time to come, all that hardware will be underutilized. The bare minimum that you need in the way of hardware and software gives you more data-processing capability than you can immediately use.

Now, a good timesharing company already has all that stuff. It has your network essentially in place. It has permanent data trunks, and it's no trick to pick up a data line to Missoula if they haven't already got one. And they can rent you the whole works, *for as few* or for as many hours as you need it, for a lot less money than you could buy it. Software? They've got plenty in the vanilla bucket to get you started, and they've got the people who can write you custom programs. They have had long experience with maintaining a complex, scattered network, with crashes, with data lines going out, with all kinds of geographically near and distant disasters that could shut you down for a day or two — but not them. They'll keep you running, and in close touch with your remote branches.

Electronic mail

In fact, you can communicate with your remote branches through the timesharing computer. It's called **electronic mail**. Computer outfits aren't supposed to be in the communications business (well, Ma Bell and IBM have been in litigation for years over that issue) but if you send a message to your manager in Missoula by electronic mail, he'll receive it on his terminal. There's no technical *or legal* reason why he can't type his reply right back. We, ourselves, have enjoyed essentially two-way, real-time communication between California and New York, sending and receiving electronic mail "letters" almost as fast as they could be typed in the timesharing terminals at each end.

What about growth?

"All well and good," you say, "but my restaurant chain is getting so big that my advisors say I will need an IBM-370, or something in its class, all to myself—to handle all that traffic from and to my branches." A well established timesharing company can rent you that, and probably at lower cost than it would take to buy it. And they are set up with software and staff for it. We are long acquainted with a venerable and reliable and great national timesharing concern, Tymshare, Inc., of Cupertino, California. Tymshare can provide you with a "Tymcom 370" and everything you need. Other big houses can do the equivalent.

How can they do it "cheaply"? We have not pried into their business secrets, but we can offer a plausible guess. There are always tax breaks in income-producing property. For a big computer system, the tax break is probably pretty good. That makes it possible for Tymshare to rent you the 370 system "at cost" (or perhaps "lower than cost") and still come out ahead. Besides, they'll be selling you their services, renting you their established network.

Tymshare uses a great many 370-class computer systems, complete to battleship peripherals. Maybe they buy them in bulk. They must make some kind of "fleet" deal. They can buy more cheaply than you can. Besides, if you only use it part-time, they rent it to you part-time.

Various timesharing outfits and service bureaus got started because, "rightly or wrongly," they had acquired sizeable computer capacity and found it underutilized. (We suspect this happened with General Electric, whose Information Services Business Division is, in essence, a timesharing firm. And once they got that started, they had to install more equipment and develop more software to meet the demand, and so on. Tymshare, Inc., of course, started out in the 1960's with faith that there would be a healthy market for timesharing services.) Many "non-computer" companies that have computers for their own purposes sell computer time or services to at least one other company.

Elsewhere in this book, we have urged you to sell computer services to other businesses down the hall or down the street— not let your system be underutilized. Pay it off faster, make it produce revenue directly. What the big fellows can do with their big computers, you can do with your small computer.

Into the sunset...

There will always be a place for the service bureaus and the timesharing houses. Businesses that have voluminous data but no need for continuous processing or immediate response will continue to use service bureaus. They would grossly underutilize an in-house computer; the service bureau is cost-effective for them. Businesses that need continual processing of data from several or many remote sources, and a big common data base, will continue to use timesharing houses, probably with intelligent terminals for local spot processing. Again, most such businesses are probably larger than you are.

The timesharing outfits also have options besides selling computer time for data processing (or word processing—you can use a timesharing system for that, too). For example, Tymshare, Inc., recently bought out TRW's Telecredit network; a logical acquisition. That's another vital service they can sell you. And Tymshare, Inc., has a subsidiary, Tymnet, Inc., which specializes in electronic-mail and other communications.

AMEN, AMEN

It is interesting to us that in large firms having large computers, departmental managers (or at least division heads) are purchasing microcomputers, more or less on the sneak, for "local" data processing. The company has a big lollapalooza of main frame somewhere, but the departmental or divisional manager has one of two headaches. One headache is batch processing down at the Corporate Computer Center, which may be off-site. Data must be carried down there physically, as hard copy. There, it disappears. There's a wait until the data gets keypunched. Then it gets scheduled on the computer. Then it gets run on the computer. Then there is the wait for printouts to be sorted, batched up, and physically delivered back to the office. And parts of printouts (or sometimes entire printouts) do get lost. They get misdelivered, and that poor junior clerk in the deliveree's office has no idea how to get them readdressed to their proper recipients. Or doesn't even know that he should. Or doesn't recognize them as "wrong."

Maybe the department has in-house timesharing. It has a terminal. Now comes waiting in queue for priority traffic to get done before the Computer Center's computer is available. Now come transmission-line troubles—the computer keeps sending back error messages. Then comes the "computer going down" syndrome — the system has *many* simultaneous users, and together they have sent the computer that fatal combination of inputs.

What the astute manager does, if he can't honestly acquire a small computer, is to demand an intelligent terminal. If he gets it, well — now the department *has* a microcomputer! All kinds of data can be locally and immediately processed. If they won't let the department have an intelligent terminal, the department head finds a way to scrounge a microcomputer out of the typewriter-desk-chair-filing cabinet budget. This is happening.

Maybe it's not happening everywhere, but it happens. We obviously regard the hapless department, oppressed by its Procrustes of a big corporate computer, as a paradigm for the small business getting involved with a big remote computer system.

That big computer, with its Computer Center, its priorities and its schedules, suits the purposes of Corporate Headquarters. The microcomputer, right there on the department or branch floor, suits the purposes of the department — that is, of the *people* who need to interpret data every day or on demand. As a small businessman you need to be in command of your data situation. The out-of-house big computer is "Corporate Headquarters" and it's not even your corporation.

Chapter Seven

THE MINICOMPUTER

You may comment to yourself at this point, "I thought this was a book about microcomputers!" Well, it is. The problem is that it is virtually impossible to know where microcomputers end and **minicomputers** begin. At computer conferences you are likely to hear numerous definitions of what a microcomputer is and of what a minicomputer is. Many people use the criterion of whether the CPU is contained in a microprocessor chip. Those people are behind the times. Just try to find a new computer of any size without microprocessor chips! Some people say that it has to do with computing speed. But microprocessor chips are as fast as any other practical CPU device. Others use capability, which is related to speed and internal memory capacity, as a criterion. Still others go for an external criterion such as physical size or price. This last is more or less valid when looked at in combination with the others.

The real point of this book, however, is to look at small computers of any kind that a small businessman might be interested in using. The IBM 5110 and several other computers put out by the larger, better-known computer companies are in a range that many small businessmen can afford. For our purposes, we'll call a computer a minicomputer if it has somewhat greater computer capacity, and a somewhat higher price than the other computers mentioned in this book. It is likely to be produced by a "main frame" firm, and be software-compatible (in part) with its ancestral main frames. We shall also consider it a minicomputer if that is how it is generally referred to.

While microcomputers run in price from about $6,000 to around $30,000, minicomputers run from a low of $15,000 up

A compact minicomputer that cannot be distinguished at a glance from a microcomputer. Like the latter it requires no "computer room" and ordinary people can operate it. This is the DEC Datasystem 308.
Courtesy of Digital Equipment Corp.

to about $70,000 or even $100,000. When you consider a micro-computer for your business, the choice is usually between having a portion of your business computerized and no computerization at all. Often, when you consider a minicomputer, the choice is between an in-house computer of your own and a time-sharing arrangement.

Many small businesses turn to minicomputers after having a disappointing experience with the time-sharing companies. This is not to say that there is anything wrong with time-sharing in itself. But sometimes a time-sharing company cannot provide the customer with the exact programs he wants. Sometimes customers find that their usage becomes too heavy for the time-sharing environment, and their needs too specialized. Most important today, the cost of owning a computer — micro- or mini-, is now competitive with (or lower than) the cost of timesharing services.

Other small businesses decide upon a minicomputer rather than a microcomputer because they want to computerize a large number of their operations, or because their inventory or accounting needs are large. Some businessmen plan to increase their usage of their computer and decide to buy one with all the capability they will need for the future, when the system is fully expanded. This may not be the wisest decision because of the way computer capability is increasing in relation to price. You

A "traditional" minicomputer, which, by golly, looks like a computer. This is Ohio Scientific's Challenger Series C-3B, a very capable machine, backed by a wide selection of peripherals and software.

Courtesy of Ohio Scientific

may be better off to buy a microcomputer now and when you are ready to expand, buy a minicomputer and either sell the microcomputer, upgrade it, or move it to a peripheral area within the company.

Another appeal of the minicomputer is the manufacturer's name, reputation, and clout. Everybody has heard of IBM or of Wang, or of Digital Equipment Corporation ("DEC") or of Hewlett-Packard. The names of microcomputer companies are still for the most part obscure. But there is more to the big company than the name. There is the service it is able to offer. And there is the completeness of its systems. No hunting for software when you buy a small system from a big-name firm. They have had programmers on their staffs for years. Once they finally decided to develop small systems, they were able to develop software concurrently. Reliable turnkey systems are, or at least appear, more likely.

The big-name firm can usually offer a variety of peripherals (input-output devices) that reliably operate with its CPU circuitry. No need to worry about interfacing; that's all built in, either into the computer or into the given peripheral. The big-name firm offers a complete equipment package. [In fairness, the leading microcomputer firms, such as Cromemco, Logical Machine (ADAM), Altos, Northwest, North Star, Radio Shack (TRS-80), and others, are doing the same, though perhaps not yet to the same extent.]

Small machines are certainly in vogue: witness Hewlett-Packard's HP 300 (left) and its HP 3000 Series 33 minicomputer systems. As with most other minis they are supported by a venerable firm's service network.

Courtesy of Hewlett-Packard

Lastly, the big old firms have far-flung servicing networks and can offer service contracts. They can give you hard (or ostensibly hard) estimates as to how long it will take their field technician to get to your office, and how long to repair a particular breakdown (printer, CRT, etc.).

The name itself of a big firm gives the businessman a feeling of security. The big firms have been around for decades. It is a reasonable presumption they will be around for decades to come. "There will always be somebody to service my equipment. The guarantees won't be invalid tomorrow because this outfit suddenly went out of business." The big companies confidently make promises far out into the future. "We won't stop servicing your model of IBM computer without first giving you five years' notice," says IBM. In the late 1970's IBM was still servicing computers it sold in the late 1950's.

Again, in fairness, the better microcomputer manufacturers are trying to offer the same things. Equipment packages are there, some good software is there, the equipment guarantees are there; attempts are being made and implemented to work out servicing arrangements with local dealers. That feeling of security is the hardest thing for a microcomputer company to impart. No company that has been in business for only two or three years can forcefully convince any customer that it will still be in existence ten or twenty years from now. But you can bet that the leading microcomputer companies hope to be. Some people may have gone into building microcomputers the way others take a flyer in novelties — but the leading microcomputer makers are serious, and expect to be in business forever.

A look at the beast

Before we continue with our discussion of minicomputers we should take a look at one. Most of the large, established main frame manufacturers such as IBM, DEC and Hewlett-Packard, have entered the minicomputer field and are actively competing against the growing numbers of small computer manufacturers. One of the newest minicomputers in the race for the small businessman's dollar is the IBM 5110. This computer can be had for about $18,000 with the standard peripherals and up to $32,000 for a more sophisticated system. Other manufacturers have similar machines in a similar price range.

The IBM 5110 has its CPU housed in a self-contained unit that also includes a small CRT screen, a keyboard, a numeric pad, and, optionally, a cassette tape unit. This compact unit sits on a table beside which is placed a diskette unit and a printer or other output device. The 5110 is compatible with most IBM peripherals, but you have to be careful about using other brands of peripherals. Not all are compatible with IBM equipment.

The screen on the 5110 is small. A larger screen monitor can be plugged into the computer and placed on top of it. Most people adjust to the small screen, however. For many people, the large screen must be placed farther back to be read comfortably, and that placement makes its optical size about the same as for the closer-in small screen.

You have the choice of two languages when you buy a 5110: BASIC or APL (actually, you can have both if you want).

A very interesting feature is provided for those who want to do their own programming. The tops of the keys on the keyboard are imprinted with the standard typewriter letters and numbers. The sides of the keys are imprinted with BASIC or APL commands so that when you are programming in BASIC, for instance, you don't have to spell out the words PRINT or GO TO, you simply press the keys with the desired commands imprinted on their sides (simultaneously with a CONTROL key). You can imagine the time that would save once you got used to it.

The system provides upper- and lower-case printing ability, which has not always been available in microcomputer systems except for word processing applications. The hardware and software provisions for this are already part of the system. (However, leading micro brands have been coming on strong with this feature.)

Independent programming firms may now write for IBM equipment, and they can be induced to. The IBM user is not likely to junk his equipment and subscribe to Tymshare and cancel a program contract.

IBM supplies many special features, such as sort routines, at additional cost. Other specials provided with the system enable you to copy from one medium to another, manage data files, and initialize your diskettes. For microcomputers, it may be necessary to buy these functions separately. Some of them are not yet available for *all* microcomputers. Bear in mind, though, if you don't need all these functions, it doesn't matter whether they are available on microcomputers or on any other kind of computers.

IBM had several application programs for the 5110 when they introduced it in 1978. Among them are a meat blending program (imagine that!), a general ledger system, accounts payable, and a payroll/labor costing system. IBM expects to come up with new application programs as time goes by. Many software companies write application programs for various minicomputers. These programs are of the canned variety, but you can hire a consultant to modify the programs to your specifications or to write a custom program for you. The programs from the software houses cost from $500 to $1500 per application.

A note of caution: now that small computers are within the financial reach of the small businessman, installation time is lagging. With installation comes the decision of whether to buy a service contract or to have the computer repaired on a time and materials basis.

A service contract for the 5110 costs about $120 per month. If you buy the service contract, you will probably spend more than if you have the computer repaired on a time-and-materials basis. On the other hand, if you decide to go the time and materials basis and you develop a rare technical problem, you can end up with a serious financial problem as well. Another thing to consider: if you buy the service contract, you are likely to keep your computer and its peripherals in top-notch shape since it doesn't cost anything extra to have someone come out and look at the computer whenever the slightest thing goes wrong.

BUT ANYWAY...

However, we are not completely reassured by the existence of long-established service networks operated by the mini-maxi makers, and by the terms of the service contract. Everything depends on the qualifications of the technician who is sent out —and on whether he has a replacement with him for a component that may be doing something more than hiccupping. *Computer Decisions* magazine has more than once warned its readers about the "green rabbit" syndrome. "Rabbit" is the industry term for a junior or lightly trained technician, "...sometimes dispatched so that the specified time limit for maintenance response is met. The green, or inexperienced, rabbit goes through the motions of diagnosing the problem until a senior technician can be located and sent to the scene." (*Computer Decisions*, October 1979.) The same article points out that use of computers "is expanding into remoter areas, but the comprehensive maintenance facilities aren't following."

You will probably buy a microcomputer from a *local* dealer, and with a micro, you will have your service contract with, or your guarantees from, that *dealer*. Has the dealer a good service shop? Will he have the technician put a spare printer on the truck when you call up to complain that your printer is stuttering? That way, you can be back in the printout business immediately, while your ailing printer goes back to the shop. Remember, you aren't likely to have much in the way of electronics troubles, at least, not after a two-hundred-hour factory burn-in. Your CRT, like a color TV's picture tube, might burn out. A good dealer can cope with that easily—even without a service contract. Also, the electronics in the better microcomputers is in modular form—each distinct circuit is on a separate printed circuit board, or "card," that plugs into the motherboard or "bus." This simplifies troubleshooting; even a "green rabbit" can try PC-board substitution.

The big computer companies are big, and might be tempted to push you around, make you subservient to them in some way for service. You know, having their computer is a prestige thing for you, so they're doing you a favor, right? Your dealer, in contrast, is local and small. He doesn't expect you to be thankful or to tug your forelock because he has done business with you. We know our prejudice in favor of the micro is showing, but.... You are a *big* business to that local dealer, who deals mainly or entirely with small businesses. He can't afford to slight you. Perhaps one of the reasons you are successful is because you provide better service than a large company. He is in the same position you are.

We are not insisting that you will get poor service from big-computer companies and invariably good service from small local dealers. But we honestly do not see that the big companies really have much more to offer than a good, well-established micro dealer has.

ACQUISITION NOTES

You may buy or lease your minicomputer from most makers and systems houses that handle their brands (or from OEM's). Originally you had to buy a microcomputer outright, but nowadays you can lease microcomputer systems, too. The larger mini outfits usually handle the leasing arrangements themselves. Somewhat smaller houses have you lease through a financial organization. A lease/purchase plan usually employs a ratio of $\frac{1}{50}$th of the total price of the equipment for a monthly cost.

Buying or leasing computers (or earth-moving equipment) or whatever involves changes in tax strategy for you, so you will want to consult your accountant before making a decision.

AGAIN, WHAT'S A MINI?

When we started this book project (some two years before publication) the distinction between micros and minis, while not clear, was "clearer." Now, it's really hard to say.

Recently, we stood in a room that had a rack-and-panel mounted microcomputer serving something like thirty work stations, each with its CRT-and-keyboard terminal, with everybody working as if he or she had the entire computing system to himself. As with other leading micro-makers, this brand's add-on (or first-option) memory capability keeps going through the roof and then through the next roof, and their software gets even more refined and versatile. What, we asked ourselves, does any mini system have that this micro system doesn't have?

Equally recently, we have been involved with a computer-using company that has one of the famous minis at the heart of its special operation. We were shown how to wake the computer up by loading its Non-Shift-Register Bootstrap Loader program by little more than the pushing of a couple of buttons. Fine. Great. No need to throw a week's worth of switches on a front panel. Next, we loaded in the Absolute Loader (which is capable of loading any applications program) by means of punched paper tape. Then, with another paper tape, we loaded in the applications program. It all only took a few minutes. The enthusiastic users told us that a disk contraption was coming along in a few months that would enable them to load the whole works by the push of a button or two.

Great, but the microcomputer *we* have automatically bootstraps itself and sets up its "absolute" loader when we turn it on, and, with a simple keyboard command, the chosen applications program loads in (*zip!*) from a disk. That microcomputer already is where the famous old household-word mini is *going* to be soon.

Paper tape, like punched cards, is a device for holding holes apart. It's cheaper than disk, true, but not as convenient, not as *fast*, not as liberating of involvement with the computer as the disk is. It represents older technology.

We asked these people what their famous mini could do that our obscure micro couldn't do, given a memory of the same size (which we could have, as an option). The answer was a lecture on the glorious history of that particular minicomputer design, and of the Great Old Name that made it. (All of which we already knew).

You know, when open-hearth steel-making came in, the little companies that used it got big fast, and rich fast. They didn't know much about the classical Bessemer Conversion process and didn't know what they *couldn't* do. So they made good steel by this "naive" (and cheap!) open-hearth process and ran the older, Bessemer-based giants ragged. *They didn't have a commitment to obsolescent technology.* The microcomputer system designers likewise lacked a commitment to ancient technology. They skipped over punched cards, they skipped over punched tape, and were off and running with the most advanced design concepts, that were easier on the *user*.

Don't minis use disks, too? Oh, yes. But so what?

So what's a mini? What's a micro? The only criteria left are *price*, and *who makes it.*

One good feature the *older* minis have is **magnetic-core memory**. This is at least theoretically a non-volatile memory, although we've never seen one that didn't cause its users concern in the event of a momentary power failure (and everybody tends to reload his applications program every morning "just in case"). A magnetic core memory is horrendously expensive to produce. It consists of a collection of near-microscopic ferrite alloy "doughnuts"—one doughnut for every *bit* of memory capacity. Three thinner-than-hair insulated wires run through each doughnut ("core") and a very ticklish hand-assembly is involved. Microcomputers use semiconductor memories, which are volatile but vastly cheaper. Potentially the cheapest memory device known is the magnetic *bubble* memory which will probably be standard in a few years. The bubble memory is non-volatile. Your micro-maker will probably offer a retrofit bubble memory board once he has time-proven bubble memory chips available. Any "edge" that core memory can given the mini-computer is probably ephemeral, and can you—with your *small* business—afford the core memory?

Datasystem 325 *Courtesy of Digital Equipment Corp.*

MAKING A DECISION

Here, as in programming, the services of a consultant may be a good investment for you. The consultant questions you and learns "all about" your business. You and he together establish what your computer needs are *now* and what they will be in the future: a year from now, three years from now, or some time before the end of your amortization period. You and the consultant may decide that a microcomputer would bail you out of some immediate difficulties, but within a very short time you are going to some wider capability that a microcomputer cannot now provide. Then the question becomes, acquiring a minicomputer or subscribing to a time-sharing plan. The time-sharing company already uses large computers, "all the capability you need." But not all that capability is instantly available to you. Furthermore, time-sharing schemes tend to be Procrustean: your business methods have to fit their formats. Time-sharing companies cannot offer you flexibility and ideally tailored service except, perhaps, at some cost that would make owning or leasing a minicomputer (or buying a microcomputer) more attractive.

THE CLOUDY CRYSTAL BALL

It seems to us that most new minicomputers coming onto the market today are the big old main-frame builders' "answer" to the threat of the microcomputer. It was probably hoped when the decision was made to compete with the micro that you, the customer, could be locked in to the vendor's whole universe: his software, his programming languages (which, not long ago, only his people really understood), his peripherals, his servicing and support and so on. Yet much of that universe had already been surrendered: any computer user can now get IBM-compatible, DEC-compatible, Hewlett-Packard-compatible software and peripherals from independents.

Aside from the spectrum of currently available peripherals and programs, an expensive mini really does not have, at bottom, more flexibility or versatility than a good micro — especially for the *small* business. The micro makers and vendors are coming on fast with a variety of peripherals and a variety of applications programs — and we have seen more than a few micros that now offer FORTRAN or APL capability in addition to the BASIC or PASCAL or other "micro-tailored" (BASIC-based) languages that were all they had and "all they could have" at the beginning of 1978 — an eye-blink of time ago. By mid-1978, Data General Corporation, long a sales leader in the mini field, had brought out a $14,000 *micro* system using COBOL, a powerful and venerable business-use language.

Even looking at a well engineered micro system and at any mini near its price range doesn't show you much difference. They look alike; the micro takes up only slightly less floor space; they perform about the same functions for *small* business. The difference is hard to discern until you reach over and flip the price tags into view.

Certainly they will be about as reliable. The minis use the same or similar CPU and other chips as the micros. All semiconductor devices are inherently reliable — they have no moving parts, and they run cool. Certainly, peripherals may go sour: your fast printer can throw a rod, so to speak, just as your expensive car can. The mini maker usually has that advantage of an established service and repair network that can be to your computer as Triple-A is to your car. But the solid micro makers, OEMs (Chapter 5) and even dealers are developing their own "Triple A" networks.

For us, the one selling point of the better minis is greater computing capacitor or "power," which works out as a function of memory size. But you pay a premium for the minis' bigger memories. And the micros are already out with memory options ranging up to 128K bytes (Chapter 2, Chapter 8). The micro-inspired CP/M programming system makes at least one of the mini's (or main frame's) "exclusive" peripherals, the large, hard disk with its vast storage capacity, available to micros. During 1979, the "Winchester" hard disks exploded onto the market in many brands, and most of them were compatible with various micro systems. In a few years, bubble or other advanced memories may even replace hard disks.

It goes without saying that we, the authors, tend to place our bets on the microcomputer. The mini-makers are really soon becoming micro-makers almost pure and simple; they will surely try to use their vast wealth and clout in competing with less well-financed and not-well-known microcomputer pioneers. But the latter tend to be resourceful as scientists, engineers, and businessmen. They are giving the old giants a run for their money now, and we expect a number of them to have sledge-hammer endurance. It will be quite a marathon and it will redound to the customer's benefit. (*Competition*, by golly, just like in our hallowed economic theory.)

That the giants see the handwriting on the wall (or on the CRT display) is evidenced not only by the current rear-guard action of the minis, but by the sudden return to the computer field of old electronics colossi that had been in it and gotten out — *e.g.*, RCA, which now offers *small* computing systems.

But what about me?

"Very well," you may say, "but suppose I buy a microcomputer now, and a few years from now the manufacturer gets forced out of business by IBM and the other giants because they can market their micros better?" We think you have nothing to fear, even if that might be the destiny of your micro-maker. By the time it happened, if it happened, everything would be compatible. You would still be able to buy peripherals for your old CPU, or a new CPU (perhaps made by one of the giants) for your old peripherals. There would be old and new software aplenty for you. There would be so many micros around, all very much alive despite the extinction of some of their makers, that there would still be outfits that could service them. Just as you can get your oldest, longest-amortized typewriters serviced today. (Or your antique car!)

The leading microcomputer manufacturers are in excellent health, for the most part. We knew Cromemco back in those exciting old pioneering days when they were small. That was early 1977. On our first visit to the Cromemco plant, the current production-line output was lined up just outside the office door of the president of the company. We visited Cromemco again in mid-1979. It had moved down the street — to a vast new building, covering acres. It was already crowded, and another vast building was going up for Cromemco in the former orchard next door. We had a similar experience with the facilities for Commodore's PET and CBM computers. We've watched one company after another take off with its microcomputers. Vector-Graphic started in an engineer's garage, and look at it now.

The point is, microcomputers themselves are now big business, and the leading microcomputer companies, while not as well known (as yet) as the household names that have been around for decades, got to be respectably big companies before the old giants could even react.

Your computerizing now will help you grow. Your growth will stimulate, in turn, some growth in your computerization. Unless you remain quite static, this is likely to occur, especially since new applications are bound to develop. So, you will be upgrading through the years any system you buy today. That system may eventually become just an intelligent terminal for a broader system that you will develop. Don't worry about what might happen, if, years hence, that other "small" businessman from whom you bought your computer gets crushed by the old giants. The only thing you have to worry about is whether he is at least as solvent and stable *today* as you are. What about you? Do you expect to be crushed by a giant competitor?

What's more likely to happen is that your micro-maker merges with or is bought out by a larger micro-maker. This has already happened a few times. It had no effect on the users of the bought-out line.

THE ONRUSHING DAWN

Think small. "Small is beautiful," said the late E.F. Schumacher. Now and then an industry learns to think small and thus gets big. Automobiles were a rare luxury item (costing

$10,000 apiece in early-1900's dollars) until a small-thinker named Henry Ford decided to try mass-producing them and selling small cars to little people at a small price. And look at Volkswagen, Datsun, and Toyota today.

According to Government figures there are something over 13,000,000 small businesses in this country, most of which cannot afford a big main-frame manufacturer's version of a small computer, but almost all of which could use a computer nevertheless. This small-computer market has hardly been touched (hence this book). Henry J. Kaiser's motto was "find a need and fill it," and that is what the microcomputer industry has done.

Besides, there are at least two vast parallel markets for small computers that the main-frame and mini-makers have so far perforce ignored, *but which gave the micro-makers their first opportunity*, and in which they have the lead. That is the hobby computer market, and its twin, the home computer market. The hobby computer market is expected to surge to a sharp peak in the next couple of years and then nosedive—but the home computer market ought to surge past it and attain a plateau. Besides, the home computer will be usable as a hobby computer even while it tends the furnace and the air conditioner, minds the cookies in the oven, waters the lawn, guards against intruders, does the supermarket budget, helps the kids with their math, science, and other homework, gives the slow reader a course in fast reading, challenges the family math whiz with courses in accounting and computer programming—all the while it is serving as everyone's date and appointment calendar, plays video and audio games with anybody, and helps Dad with the small mail-order or cabinetry business he runs from the garage. No doubt there will be applications not yet thought of. What is needed to make this market flower is a proliferation of suitable software (a bare beginning now exists) and a wider spectrum of cheap peripherals—especially little sensor-and-control devices for the oven, furnace, lawn sprinkler and so on.

These are coming. Heathkit and Radio Shack are in the small computer business now. They have always been sharp at predicting what will sell, what long-term markets will exist. Their very presence in the market helps alert the public to the existence and potential of the small, inexpensive computer. And that fabled bubble memory will really give the home computer its boost: the enhanced memory capacity will afford the home computer the versatility it needs. And at lower cost than disk drives, even the best-sealed of which are vulnerable to the family's screwdriver maniac.

We, the authors, are working with our third hands on another book, *The Small Computer Revolution*, that will go into more things in more depth. If enough of you small businessmen will buy *this* book, and talk it up down at the Lions Club so that even more businessmen buy this book, and you all keep your eye out for the second book, we'll have some nice chunks of investment money to put where our mouth is.

There may be talk of recession, talk of depression, talk of runaway inflation and all kinds of dire destinies for the American economy, but there is one thing we know: millions upon millions of small businesses will survive and continue to operate, and they will need and want the *money-saving, revenue-enhancing* features of the *small* business computer. And they will find a way to buy.

This perhaps is the dawning of the Age of Appropriate Technology that a number of seers have called for. The small computer is the morning star of that age.

Chapter Eight

SHOPPING FOR YOUR HARDWARE

It makes sense to look for some degree of turnkey capability in your initial installation. Chapter One defined a turnkey system as one in which the hardware and the software that you need are obtained together. You plug in the hardware, throw the switch, run in the programs, and begin processing your data.

In the old maxi and even mini days, it was customary to install the computer hardware and then begin a long, laborious effort to get the bugs out of it, and to write and test the software. That seems hardly the way to go for small systems, especially after thirty or thirty-five years of experience with digital computers in our society.

Does that still happen? Indeed it does. But it needn't. So beware.

Unless your needs are extremely simple (very small business) and your methods close to ideally standard, no off-the-shelf system will be completely "turnkey" for you. Your business is unique. You do some things no other business does. At least, no other business does them in quite your way. The goods and services you sell are not quite identical with even your closest competitor's. You can comfortably change some things in order to accommodate "a computer's way" but not all. You will buy standard hardware items, but you will want to have some of your software tailored. (See Chapter 5.)

Don't buy hardware that isn't yet developed. If it isn't available for demonstration, forget it. That *almost* goes for software: the exception is when you are having unique programs developed for your particular needs.

Please don't bridle at what appears to be a gratuitous piece of advice. It has been a custom in the computer industry, dating from the maxi-only days, to take the customer's money for a product to be delivered months or years later. Why months or years? Because it didn't exist yet. The customer's money was used to finance its development. This practice was understandable when digital computers were new, few, *immense*, and rather futuristic as a concept. In those days, the customer was likely to be the Government or some well-endowed institution. It was even ethical, because the customer understood that he was paying the developmental costs.

The custom continued as the newfangled minicomputers arrived in the 1960's — and it continues now, in the day and field of the microcomputer. Here and now, the ethics are questionable. So is the need. In the old days, the customer who put up large amounts of money knew he had to take risks. But it was with the Government's or some philanthropist's money. If the new gadget didn't work, well, "back to the drawing board," and back to the Appropriations Committee.

That won't do for you, obviously. There is no reason today why you should take risks and pay developmental costs in advance. Perfectly good microprocessor CPUs exist, and so do keyboards, CRT displays, disk drives, printers, and other conventional peripherals for them. So do complete hardware systems. If the producer needs financing he can go to banks, partners, stockholders or kindly aunts, just as you did.

Is this to say you should never pay a developmental cost? Of course not: we have already mentioned the software exception. When you hire a programmer to work out some tricky program for *your* unique purposes, the risk that he or she might have time and cost overruns, or might even fail, is legitimately yours. But then, the programmer's product is legally yours. You get the benefits, so you take the risks. But the risks are really quite small, given a competent programmer and given a small-business purpose that isn't too utterly hairy.

With all the good microcomputer hardware available right now, there is no need to take risks on hardware.

True, a vendor may have to keep you waiting some weeks for delivery. Demand is growing so fast that it is difficult for manufacturers to tool up for ever-larger production runs to meet it. Even gigantic IBM, in mid-1978, warned customers that it could be months before they got delivery on its hot new 5110 mini-computer. (It is now a matter of weeks.) But all right, IBM doesn't take your money until the 5110 is delivered. Likewise, the good manufacturers, dealers, and systems houses don't take your money for microcomputers until they deliver, either. Certainly, reasonable deposits on a to-be-delivered computer are ethical. In your business, you may offer some sort of layaway plan for a million cubic yards of concrete. But don't let anybody tell you he needs the total price for a microcomputer system he is not going to deliver until months after he gets paid.

HOW MUCH TO BUY?

The conventional wisdom for the purchase of the pioneer-days maxis ("main frames") and even the later minis was to buy all the excess capability you could afford, and then some. Your system would then have greater flexibility so as to meet unforeseen needs later — or to compensate if you had underestimated your data-processing needs or the difficulty of filling them. The immediate result was usually a greater data-processing capacity than immediately needed, but it did allow for future growth in computer applications. The idea was to buy as big a system as you could promote, and then let Parkinson's Law take over: your computerizing would grow to fit the system.

In buying the microcomputer, you should probably stand the conventional wisdom on its head. *Buy only what you know you need.* If the programs needed for your business purposes do not call for more than 16K bytes of internal memory space, the premium you would pay for 32K or 64K might be money ill spent. The frugality principle applies even more in the case of peripherals. Adding on and upgrading later will be easy and cheap. In a few years, expanded memories will be cheaper than today's memories, and tomorrow's CPU will work with your old peripherals. The falling-cost trend may continue for some important peripherals, too. With the wildfire growth of the small computer market, new mass production economies will be realized.

Therefore, allowing for inflation, it is probably going to be cheaper for you to add on tomorrow than to buy an over-complete system today. The temptation and pressure to over-invest may be strong, especially as an entire small system may be cheaper than a new car. (But a big new car, not a Honda.)

A new "conventional wisdom" has been suggested for micro-computer users: buy two of everything. If you can afford to overinvest, it makes sense to have two adequate systems rather than one overadequate system. Breakdowns do occur, especially in electromechanical gadgets such as printers, keyboards, and typewriters.

What breakdowns cost you is time — and time is what you are buying when you invest in a computer system. Having spare components on hand is one way to protect that investment. If you can isolate the trouble yourself ("keyboard seems okay, CPU seems okay, CRT display is okay, but printer seems jammed") you can just plug in the spare unit. In one case we know about, a system was down right after having been moved from one place in the room to another. It turned out that somebody had stepped on and damaged one of the interconnecting cables. The owner had presence of mind to try substituting cables.

THE DOUBLE SYSTEM

Of course, if you have two of everything, you have two complete systems. It will occur to you to make use of both of them rather than to let one sit around as spare parts. Why not? Something more than Parkinson's Law will have you computerizing more and more of your operation anyway. Whatever your data processing load, you may find that you have frequent, or constant, use for a word processor (see Chapter Four). One of your systems can be doing that, while the other handles data and computation.

With two small systems, you need not even swap components from one to the other in case of a breakdown. Just swap programs. You can bump your secretary off the word processor if the billing must go through. Just grab the billing program disk and run that program into her machine.

Two complete systems may cost something like two new cars, but are still likely to be cheaper than the cost of outside computing services (for which you must *wait*!)

SYSTEM IN ONE CABINET?

In shopping around you will see small computer systems in which everything appears to be all one piece: keyboard, CRT display, even a printer in one molded-plastic cabinet. Such a system is compact, and perhaps even cheaper than the aggregate cost of separate components. Some fine small systems do exist in this form.

In considering such a system, it is important to ask about its options for adding on peripherals. What about disk drives? (Or, if it comes with an integral disk drive, what about printers?) How many different outboard I/O devices will it accept, and what, *precisely*, are they?

A computer-in-one box, the CBM. But there is nothing in this box but electronics, and electronics failures rarely occur (especially after factory burn-in). The CBM's printers, disk drives, and all else with moving parts that might fail are separate peripherals.

Courtesy of Commodore Business Machines, Inc.

Remember, however, that if anything in a one-cabinet system breaks down, the entire system may be down, because the entire unit must be opened up for repair. That could entail carrying the entire system to the service shop. With separate components, you can just yank out the faulty black box and replace it with a spare while the faulty unit goes to the shop. (The repairman may bring a substitute component when he comes to pick up the faulty one.)

Of course, if the trouble is with an electronic circuit in the one-piece unit, the visiting serviceman can just unbutton the cabinet, pull out the faulty PC board and plug in another one. But if, say, the printer has gone down, he will probably want to take the whole thing back to the shop. So, carefully check out ease of repair on one-piece systems. It should be "one-piece" on the outside, *modular* on the inside.

One-cabinet systems might have specialized uses around the plant or warehouse or store. You may want to let the boys in the stock room have one, for keeping track of their inventory. You may even network this one with the main computer in your office — in which case, the little remote computer becomes a *terminal*. Connecting devices exist, and some one-piece computers are sold as **intelligent terminals**, designed to work alone or in communication with a master computer, as required. Some day you might have several small computers in your operation, whether networked together or not.

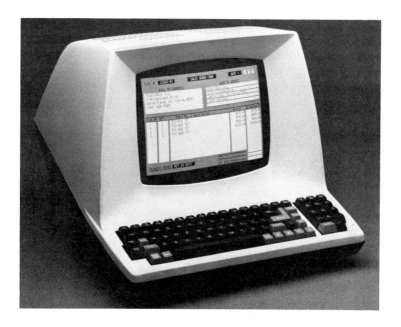

A "smart" terminal by Televideo, capable of some stand-alone data processing, and able to work with a host computer, or with peripherals. A microcomputer has more capability and would be "intelligent" if used with a host.

Courtesy of Televideo, Inc.

Our misgivings about the possible drawbacks of a one-piece system ought not to intimidate you. If after shopping and comparing capabilities and values, you conclude that a particular one-piece computer is for you, that it most closely meets your requirements, by all means acquire it.

In 1979, *portable* microcomputers appeared, complete to plasma or CRT display, diskette drive, even very small printers, all in a case the size of a small suitcase — for the traveling sales rep or field engineer in any kind of industry. But as a rule, an entire business operation will not depend on a portable system. For its obvious applications, the portable looks like a good idea.

MEMORY OPTIONS

Power in a computer is the resultant of two things: memory capacity and processing speed. Actually it's mainly a function of speed, but memory counts, as we shall see. Down inside the CPU, speeds are in nanoseconds (billionths of a second) for retrieving data bits, and microseconds (millionths) for operations on the data. Thus any good computer, including a microcomputer, can accomplish a processing step before you can name it. The standard microprocessors at the hearts of today's leading CPU's all have comparable speeds, so that leaves memory for "the racer's edge."

If a salesman brags to you about how many watts or kilowatts his "powerful" computer uses, just remember that excess watts do not necessarily mean extra computer power. If his machine really uses more watts than his competitors', then all you get is a bigger electric bill. You want capacity, speed, flexibility.

Computer internal memories are installed in increments of 8,000 bytes (Chapter 2) which, again, means a nominal 8,000 8-bit words. The actual number is 8,192 bytes, which is 2^{13} bytes. The number 8,000 is frequently expressed as "8K" in this field. At higher prices, memories are available in 16K, 32K, and 64K options (16,384, 32,768, and 65,536 actual bytes). A few systems are offering 128K-byte options. For business purposes you should consider a minimum memory of 16K bytes.

The more internal memory your computer has, the more fast-acting RAM you have (Chapter 2). And therefore the more "powerful" your computer. You are less dependent on the comparatively slow and cumbersome sequential-access memories (tapes, disks). Also, you can have more complex and versatile programs.

The value of bigger (32K, 64K) memory to you depends, of course, on the volume of data your business needs to process — or on the complexity of your operation. That complexity will be reflected in the complexity of your programs. You have to run a program into that CPU memory before you can run data into it. A program takes up memory space.

While prices on microcomputers increase as memory sizes go from 8K to 16K to 32K and beyond, they *do not* double, quadruple, etc. The total price increment is more like fifteen percent (15%) for each doubling. Therefore it may be okay for you to buy "a little bigger" in contemplation of future expansion of your data processing load. However, some of the leading microcomputer brands now offer *add-on* memory capability.

WHERE TO BUY

Go to a well established dealer, of course. Now, this entire microcomputer field is so new that a "well established dealer" may only have been in business for a couple of years. But there are ways, nevertheless, for distinguishing well established dealers from the shakier ones. The dealer can offer you services that the manufacturer can't or won't. (He is not set up for that — does Detroit service your car?) Manufacturers usually do not care to compete with dealers and will not, as a rule, offer you a better price than the dealer's. And remember, even if everything you buy has factory warranties (and it had better), the factory may be far away. When you need service you need it right now. A reliable local dealer is your logical choice.

What are the signs of the well established microcomputer dealer? First, he is obviously *not* a small, shoestring-financed hobby computer shop (though he will carry lines of hobby stuff; no matter). It costs about $100,000 to set up a good computer store, with an adequate selection of merchandise and a decent service shop. Your business sense will tell you whether or not something like $100K went into the capitalization of a store.

Don't hesitate to investigate the store. Find out who capitalized it and for how much, where it does its banking and so on. In your initial dealings with the store, get the names of several past customers and check with them. Maybe they like their computers and maybe they don't but they can give you an idea of what it is like to deal with the store itself.

GUARANTEES

Does the dealer guarantee everything—not leaving you to depend on factory warranties? What kind of repair service does he offer? Will he come out with loaners or swap-replacements if something goes wrong? Some computer stores are offering *takeover data-processing services* in case your system goes seriously down. This is usually in cooperation with an experienced secretarial service or accounting firm (one of the store's customers, now computerized!). Your work goes on getting done while your equipment is being repaired. Takeover service may be a part of the dealer's over-all guarantee, or it may not. Ask about it. A good dealer arranges for it if he can. When a manufacturer lets you down, he lets the dealer down, too. A responsible dealer wants to keep your custom and goodwill.

Electronics failures usually occur within the first two hundred (200) hours of use; thereafter, practically never. Does the manufacturer or the dealer certify a 200-hour factory burn-in?

Most equipment failures occur in peripheral devices such as printers and keyboards, rather than in the electronics. But

A good dealer has a service shop whose people can repair or adjust his lines of equipment quickly. You should not have to send things back to the factory, or wait while the dealer does.

Courtesy of Heath Company

whatever fails can tie you up. A good dealer will back you up in some meaningful way.

Is the dealer or his manager a "computer person," a dedicated hobbyist if not a professional? At first glance, the dealer's being a hobbyist may seem like a frivolous consideration, and it could suggest to you that the dealer himself is frivolous. Far from it. You don't want to be up against a narrow-focused general entrepreneur who is taking a flyer in the computer market, whose eye is only on the balance sheet, and who plans to get out of this business and back into microwave ovens or lawn furniture as soon as he can sell out. You want your dealer to be somebody who knows and loves small computers, is fascinated by them, is a walking encyclopedia on *applications*, including yours, who knows what and where the best software is, who understands your data processing problems, and — rationally or irrationally — *cares* about your computer.

NOTES ON I/O DEVICES

Change and progress are rapid. We cannot really hope to guide you to actual purchases here. We can only sketch out what is available. Go to the computer store. (Go to several of them.) Talk to the owner or manager. Get demonstrations. Read specs. Insist on clear-cut, plain-English explanations. Proceed as if you are buying another dump truck or buttonhole machine. Consult the glossary and explanatory materials in this book and elsewhere, often, but especially ahead of time. Salesmen and dealers will inevitably use some jargon. Know what it means. And go to the computer shows, look, listen, pick up the literature and compare.

And now, the machines:

KEYBOARDS

The simplest input device of interest to you is an electrical keyboard. This looks exactly like a typewriter keyboard, featuring the QWERTY arrangement of characters, but there is no typewriter. The keyboard just feeds coded electrical signals, representing letters, numbers, and so on, into the CPU. (To see what you are typing in, you will have a CRT display unit or a printout device described later in this section.)

Look for keyboards that have an accessory "calculator" key pad alongside the alphanumeric or "typewriter" key arrangement. This is essential for business purposes, since you will be entering large amounts of numerical data, and even using the computer at times as a calculator.

Of course, a keyboard may be an integral part of some particular computer you are considering buying. That, however, does not mean that you are excused from thinking about keyboards.

A keyboard consists of a set of electrical switches. These switches will receive heavier use than any other hand switches you have ever used. *Quality* in these switches is essential. All switches have some degree of "bounce," especially spring-loaded fast-make-and-break switches like those in keyboards. Excessive bounce means, effectively, multiple input. You want just one input per stroke of a key. Also, remember, any keyboard is going to have about seventy-five of those switches—that is, seventy-five possible points of malfunction. You can buy cheap keyboards—but can you put up with frequent malfunctions? (A computer hobbyist can; he or she has all kinds of time for dealing with malfunctions.) You want key switches that can take hundreds of thousands of strokes without malfunction. Top quality is what you want. Yes, it costs.

A keyboard is a direct *hand tool*. Try keyboards out. How is the *feel*? How does it feel to your secretary, bookkeeper or whoever else will operate the computer? Is it comfortable to work with, that is, are the keys "live" under the fingertips? Does it take uncomfortable pressure to make positive contact (and see a letter or number displayed or printed out)? Or—the opposite fault—are the keys so hair-trigger sensitive that you "type" errors in because your fingers lightly brush unwanted keys? Are the keys *uniformly* sensitive to the fingers of a touch typist?

Electrically, today's quality keyboards are of the "capacitance" type. Look for them.

Along the way you may meet hobbyists who may tell you that you don't need a keyboard if your computer "has a good front panel." (The front panel is something that you don't need; we'll describe it later anyway.) That's "true"—provided you have unlimited time, like the hobbyist, and can afford to throw the front panel's few switches over and over again in at least ninety-six different combinations of "on" and "off" (ninety-six is the typical number of electric typewriter characters—counting capitals and lower case letters, numerals, punctuation marks, etc.). A front panel is as much a substitute for a keyboard as a bolster is for your spouse. And by the way—a "good" front panel costs more than a good keyboard.

WRITEHANDER™

At least one valid substitute for a keyboard exists. This is Writehander™, a plastic hemisphere about the size of half a grapefruit. Distributed over its surface are twelve pushbutton switches—four for the fingers, eight for the thumb. Thumb and finger pressure on various combinations of these switches send coded impulses to the computer for all the characters a standard keyboard would have, plus machine-control characters. Writehander is made in both right-handed and left-handed versions (and in large-hand and small-hand models either way).

Right-handed (foreground) and left-handed versions of Writehander™. Either version is available in large- and small-hand sizes. The output is standard 7-bit ASCII code (see Appendix A). Finger code charts are available for Cyrillic, Katakana, and most European alphabets.

Courtesy of The NewO Company

Of course the operator has to remember the thumb-and-finger combinations for all the characters—there is no way to mark twelve buttons for one hundred twenty-eight pushing combinations (ninety-six "typewriter" characters plus thirty-two control characters). Yet learning to use Writehander could hardly take as long as learning to type.

Writehander was developed by the NewO Company of Palo Alto, California, originally for handicapped people. Obviously it would be easy for anyone to use. The fingers never leave their four assigned buttons. The thumb alone moves to determine whether a character is a capital or lower-case letter, a numeral, or a control character. For some characters, more than one finger-button must be pressed at a time, but few people if any would have trouble with that. Many right-handed users prefer the left-handed version, which leaves the right hand free for other purposes: pencil wielding, coffee cup holding, page manipulation, etc.

Writehander's electrical output is in **ASCII (American Standard Code for Information Interchange)**, the same as a regular keyboard's or a Teletype's™. The standard keyboard will die hard, if at all, but we think Writehander will, over time, be crowding it closely. One of us authors was an amateur radio operator for many years, and Writehander reminds one of the old Morse key—you could place it any place on the table that left you comfortable, or on the arm of your chair, or strap it to your thigh. You didn't have to *face* the gadget.

TELEPRINTERS, TELETYPE™

A teleprinter is both an input and output device. You can use it to "type" information into the computer. The computer can use it to "type" information back to you. ("Look, Ma, no hands!") The teleprinter has both a keyboard and a printer in its box, and because information can flow either way, the teleprinter serves as a **terminal**. It is, like any computer terminal, a device through which you and the computer communicate with each other. Usually, a teleprinter can also be used *off line*, like a sort of elaborate typewriter, with the computer not involved.

The very "type" of the teleprinter is the Teletype™ machine. This is the old warhorse, the "classic" way of communicating with a big main frame computer. It will work for your small computer as well. Refurbished workhorse models, like the popular Model ASR-33, make relatively inexpensive but rugged and reliable terminals. However, the "classic" Teletype machines are rather slow and have blocky typefaces. For today's computers, the Teletype company itself, like its competitors, offers more svelte models with higher speeds and elegant typefaces, but they cost more.

Two versions of the QUME Sprint 5 "smart" terminal, using daisy wheels for high print quality. The receive-only version at left may be used with a remote keyboard; both versions are microprocessor-based. Using a teleprinter as a terminal does not preclude having a CRT display elsewhere in the system.

Courtesy of QUME Corporation

The classic Teletype™ incorporates a paper tape punch and paper tape reader, thus offering you a second set of input-output devices. You can let the machine punch your keyed data onto paper tape, for reading into the computer later (or for mailing to another computer). You may let the computer punch a tape instead of, or in addition to, producing a printout. There are several things you can do with your Teletype machine, producing or not producing tape, producing or not producing printouts, reading or not reading tape, and so forth. We doubt that you will be interested in paper tape. There are newer devices—magnetic disks and tape cassettes.

The Teletype™ is also known colloquially as "TTY." *TTY* was the old communications-industry abbreviation for Teletype™ when that was about the only brand of teleprinter in use (or at least in common use) for anything. Nowadays, "TTY" *like the name Teletype itself*, is often used to denote any teleprinter. Rightly or wrongly, legally or illegally, the trade-name "Teletype" is going generic—the way "Thermos" went generic.

Does this matter? It could. Teletype™ is an honored old brand name, but you could be sold a pile of junk, and pay Teletype-class money for it, because everybody in the store kept referring to it as a "teletype," and what did you know? Confused use of trade names as generic terms is very common in our society, usually honest but not always, and misleading in any case. A *teleprinter* is what you'll be offered. It may be a good teleprinter (e.g., Teletype™, DECWriter™, QUME, or other good brand) or

A tabletop teleprinter using a dot matrix printer at 30 characters per second: the DECwriter IV.

Courtesy of Digital Equipment Corp.

it may be a bad teleprinter. But a teleprinter is what it is. If the vendor's personnel insist on calling it a "teletype" regardless of its brand label, you may have reason to wonder why.

ELECTRIC TYPEWRITERS

An electric typewriter can be used as an input-output device or terminal, but not in its pristine form. For this purpose, the typewriter needs to have some electronic circuitry—an interface —added. A few specialty companies have converted IBM Selectrics and perhaps other brands to computer input-output use. The better conversions (but not all conversions) leave the typewriter mechanically and electrically unaffected (so the IBM warranty still applies) and the typewriter may be used off-line simply as a typewriter.

A good electric typewriter does produce fine printouts, of course, and a machine of Selectric quality will give you camera-ready originals to take to the offset print shop. (This, we think, is the best way to use an electric typewriter for "mass production" printing.) A Selectric types at a maximum speed of 14.9 characters per second. It will do one double-spaced typewritten page in a minute and a half. That's fine for one page, not fine if you want to turn out one thousand form letters. For doing your own "mass" printout, you'll want one of the fast printer units, described later. We offer some caveats on the use of typewriters later, in the discussion of printers.

CRT DISPLAY

You will find CRT display units among the output devices. They are usually referred to simply as "CRT's." A CRT unit resembles a small television set. And well it should, since it uses a *cathode-ray tube* (CRT) just as a TV set does. The display unit's CRT is a finer, more expensive tube than the TV set's picture tube. This is because the display unit requires higher resolution: greater clarity of detail. The CRT screen will display "typed" characters and fine-line graphics materials with a clarity and sharpness that your line-ridden TV screen cannot offer.

A CRT display accepts entire "pages" of data in a fraction of a second, and holds them in view for you for as long as you need them. You could just as well be reading this book page on a CRT screen. With adequate circuitry and programming, a CRT display can *scroll* the data upward and downward on the screen, so as to locate desired data items quickly, or go back and read something again, or skip ahead, or edit whatever is there.

One attraction of a CRT is that it eliminates the bales of paper that flow from printout-only output. You can continuously monitor your data, the program interaction, and the results, and when you want some particular thing printed out, you can command the computer to print out just that.

Many CRT units incorporate a keyboard, in which case they are called "CRT terminals." Any combined input-output device used primarily for communication with a computer is called a terminal.

OTHER DISPLAYS

Recently some other displays, not based on the TV-like CRT, have shown up on the market. These include *plasma displays*,

The Vector MT Mindless™ terminal: a keyboard-and-CRT combination with a 12-inch (diagonal) screen. With its Vector Flashwriter II control board, it displays 24 lines of 80 characters and has block graphics and many other features.

Courtesy of Vector Graphic Inc.

liquid crystal displays (LCD), and "vacuum fluorescent" devices. One advantage they have is in compactness—they are flat and thin, unlike the funnel-shaped CRT, which generally has to be about as deep as its face is wide.

Plasma displays involve electrically charged particles trapped between special glass plates. Their letters and numbers glow brightly against a black background. Most plasma displays are on the small side, at least in the vertical dimension. The typical plasma screens that came on the market in 1979 were a few inches high and showed only a few lines of "type." The characters, however, were large and bright (and red- to orange-colored). We have heard of one (Magnavox's Orion system) that produces a thirty-two line format of sixty-four characters each—but with a $6,300 price tag.

We are told that the physical design of plasma displays—involving a sandwich of transparent plates—permits rear projection, and that "projection may be from microfiche or transparencies under microprocessor control." (*Computer Decisions* magazine, September 1979.) That certainly could be useful to someone. It may be on the market by the time you are reading this.

You are familiar with the liquid-crystal display from watches and calculators. These are being scaled up to show lines of microcomputer data; early models in late 1979 displayed two lines of 40 characters each. Multicolored displays, featuring one or several colors depending on how electric currents are applied to the character modules, are scheduled to reach the market late in 1980.

These rather new technologies are impossible for us to evaluate without more experience with them. We have a "conservative" preference for the tried-and-true CRT screen with its "nearly square" format ("three-by-four" aspect ratio—three units of height for four units of width) that can display an entire page, or major portion of a page, of data or text *at low cost*. No doubt larger plasma displays and LCDs will become more common, and rapidly, and prices will probably come down. We don't want to put a crimp in progress, but we feel that those who are starting their first affair with a computer should stay with time-tested devices (after all, you are not in the equipment-testing business). Yet, the "low-profile" but bright plasma display format might well suit your purposes; you will have to make your own decisions. The same goes for LCD panels. The true portable microcomputers that were unveiled during 1979 featured plasma displays (except for one with a four-inch CRT).

CASSETTE DRIVE

As you shop for input and output units you may be offered **cassette drives**, which accept ordinary audio cassettes. (Special data tape cassettes are made nowadays, but all cassettes are mechanically identical.) A tape cassette is, of course, a form of magnetic external storage or "memory." The computer cassette drives are usually double: one drive accommodates an input tape and the other an output tape. Wouldn't a single drive be cheaper? Of course—and you could, in principle, feed data into your computer, or accept results out of it, using your little desktop dictating machine.

However, the point of using a computer is the saving of time. Your computer's brain, or CPU, is capable of processing data much faster than your input cassette drive can feed it in. Results are usually ready the moment the final bit of input information has entered the computer. Those results have to be stored some-

A compact word processing system by Artec, using a small plasma display inset into the front panel of the teleprinter terminal.
Courtesy of Artec International

Tape cassettes are adequate where data storage requirements are small, as in this classroom application of a home-and-hobby system. Cassettes are slower than disks for data recovery.
Courtesy of Radio Shack, a Division of Tandy Corp.

where—they may quickly outstrip the CPU's internal storage or "memory." You may as well store them on another cassette that is running at the same time your input cassette is running.

What about reel-to-reel tape for your computer? In principle, your microcomputer could use it. As you know, the big main-frame computers have reel-to-reel units. However, precision tape-reel equipment for any computer is expensive. Neither its expense, nor the mechanical intricacy of its drive mechanism, is appropriate for the microcomputer—the "small business system" this book is concerned with.

Very likely, cassette equipment would be inadequate for your needs, unless you have an extremely small business. You might have various accessory uses for cassettes, but the brunt of your data-storage load will probably be taken by something else: disks.

For business purposes, disk storage is preferred. The computer in this photo is the same machine as in the classroom photo (a Radio Shack TRS-80) but with beefed-up memory, a more elaborate keyboard, and a heavy-duty printer. A microcomputer is versatile. This system (the TRS-80 Model II) has a more elaborate software set than the original home-hobby-classroom version.

Courtesy of Radio Shack, a Division of Tandy Corp.

FLOPPY DISKS, DISKETTES

You will probably opt for **disk files**. Large, rigid glass and plastic disks with magnetized coating have been used with mainframe computers for about two decades. For your microcomputer, the disk file uses **floppy disks** or (floppy) **diskettes**. Both are much smaller than the rigid disks developed for the larger computers. The small ones are termed "floppy" because they are made of a lighter, thinner material than their big-machine ancestors and are flexible.

A floppy disk has a mylar surface treated with magnetic oxide. It records magnetic impulses just as a tape does. But a disk has advantages over tape. A disk has, or at least can have, discrete "domains" of information storage. This means much faster data entry and recovery. There can be definite areas of its surface in which certain blocks of information can be found. A desired byte of information will be in some definite domain, placed there by the computer. Thus the particular information item can have a discrete address on the disk surface. Unlike a grooved music disk (or any kind of tape) there is no need to "play" all prior information through, sequentially, to reach the desired byte.

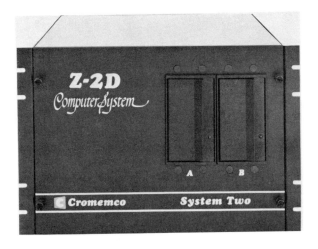

A microcomputer with a pair of diskette drives installed in its processor cabinet. The drive doors open to admit disks, close to keep out dust.

Courtesy of Cromemco

To find a domain, the disk drive rotates the disk a certain number of degrees from an arbitrary zero line. The magnetic reading head moves a certain distance from the edge or center. The domain is, so to speak, at a certain latitude and longitude that are easily reached.

Complicated patterns of setting domains are used to reduce the amount of spinning and head-moving needed to find selected domains and bytes. Different manufacturers use different systems, which in turn require different software **disk operating systems (DOS)** and even different interfacing circuits. A disk recorded on Computer A is not necessarily readable on Computer B because of this. (But any *blank* disk will serve either computer's disk-mapping scheme.)

You are not likely to have problems, however. Your dealer will guide you in making sure that all equipment you buy is compatible with your disk unit and its software.

A disk can be started and stopped at precise intervals, and there is no danger of its breaking — *unlike tape.* And, on a bulk basis, disks have much greater storage capacity than cassettes. Of course disk equipment costs more — but it's probably the way you will go.

A computer with four full-size (8-inch) floppy disk drives. The number of drives a microcomputer can handle depends on the circuitry in its controller card and its software disk operating system (DOS).

Courtesy of Cromemco

Floppy disks superficially resemble 45-RPM phonograph records, even in their size (8-inch diameter). But unlike a record, the disk stays in its paper jacket while being used. The disk rotates inside the jacket. The jacket keeps it suitably rigid, keeps it from wafting off the drive and striking a recording head or other part of the machinery, and—because of a special coating on the paper—it keeps the disk clean. (It is advisable to leave a disk inside its jacket at all times.)

Floppy disk drives come as doubles and even as quadruples, for obvious reasons like those for double cassette drives. It is theoretically possible to work with a single disk drive, but you won't want one.

There is some looseness in floppy disk-diskette terminology, but as a general rule, a floppy disk has a nominal 8-inch diameter, and a *diskette* (still floppy!), 5¼ inches. "Minifloppies" are 5¼-inch diskettes. You will hear of double-density and even quadruple-density disks. "Density" refers to the amount of information that can be stored on a disk's surface. For the most part, the associated equipment (and software disk operating

A double-sided, double-density 8-inch disk drive and a 5½-inch minifloppy drive with its controller. These may be installed in their own cabinets for use as remote peripherals, or incorporated with the central processing unit or CRT display in a larger cabinet.
Courtesy of Shugart Associates

A minifloppy or "diskette" drive can really be compact.
Courtesy of Shugart Associates

system, or DOS), play a greater role in setting the density characteristic of the disk than does the disk itself.

For *word processing* purposes (Chapter 4), currently available disk systems tend to be superior to the IBM mag-card system (on certain of that company's magnetic-memory typewriters) because of the greater information-storage capacity of disks.

Disk drives and their disks are **input-output devices**. You can read information and programs into a computer from a disk, and store output information on a disk. Most programs that you might buy nowadays will be delivered to you on disks. Even if you receive a program in some other form you will probably want to transfer it to a disk for enhanced convenience.

HARD DISKS: WINCHESTERS

Not long ago "hard" (rigid) disks were for the main-frame computer only, and later for expensive minis. Suddenly, the low-cost "Winchester" disks have appeared, and the microcomputer industry has snatched them up and is running with them as if they were minifloppies. Winchesters come in two sizes, 8-inch and 14-inch. *Unlike* floppy disks, they cannot be removed from the disk drives. However, a Winchester can hold up to about twenty million (8-inch) or forty million (14-inch bytes of information. This is the equivalent of quite a handful of floppy disks. Winchester drives cost more than floppy disk drives: on the average, $3,000 to $4,000 more. There is some talk of prices coming down as mass production tools up and competition gets murderous. (As we write, there seem to be more manufacturers of Winchesters than there were of floppies when floppies were first introduced.)

The Winchester cannot be removed from its drive because it is sealed in an airtight (or heavily filtered) unit. Its read-write head, like a floppy disk head, is literally airborne—it rides over the surface of the disk on a cushion of air. But the hard disk's head rides just a few millionths of an inch off the disk. The slightest bit of dust, condensed smoke, or other crud will cause a literal "head crash" onto the rapidly spinning disk with its *thin* magnetized surface. Contamination upsets the aerodynamics of the system.

A Shugart 8-inch hard disk drive with its printed circuit board removed. This unit holds either 5 or 10 million bytes of data. Disk is nonremovable.

Courtesy of Shugart Associates

This 14-inch "Winchester" can hold up to 40 million bytes of information.

Courtesy of Shugart Associates

Backup

That nonremovable feature represents a disadvantage: you cannot store the disk in some other site for safety against fire or other mishap. But of course fire could strike wherever you would keep your floppies, unless you deposited them in a bank vault. The answer is to use an "old technology" backup: floppy disks, data tape cassettes, or streaming tape. Some of the week's data can be copied onto the older storage media at the end of each day: two or three floppies can be loaded in just a few minutes. Manufacturers have been alert to this problem so that several—concurrently with their introduction of their Winchester lines—offer various backup systems involving floppies or tape.

The 8-inch Winchester drives are amazingly compact, and their various manufacturers tout them as "fitting the same hole" as 8-inch floppy disk drives. Manufacturers and OEMs are thus assured that they need not redesign their cabinetry if they want to offer computers with integral Winchester drives.

Will the Winchester make the floppy disk obsolete? How would we know? We don't.

We would guess — probably not. Any more than plug-in bubble memories or anything like them will necessarily make any disk drive obsolete.

Winchester disk technology is so new that our crystal ball is foggy. It seems a natural for heavy word processing applications, or for offices with large data bases (such as large medical and dental clinics, warehouses, parts distributors, etc.).We share their many manufacturers' faith that they are going to catch on. They will push the microcomputer into new markets: into businesses where larger quantities of current data need to be stored than can be conveniently accommodated on floppies. The floppies should retain their place as the medium of choice for smaller, "budget" systems, for businesses that require a smaller data base.

As always, we advise proceeding with caution. Here is something brand-new, and bugs will show up in some units — and will show up commonly in some brands. It happens, however, that the leaders in the introduction of Winchesters (such as Shugart, BASF, IBM, and several others) have been making floppy drives for a long time. Their engineers are familiar with the vagaries of small high-speed motors and aerodynamically floating heads, and their Winchester designs will probably have been lab-tested and lab-evolved over a long time. If you intend to buy from a systems house, OEM, or store putting out its own brand of total system, be sure to ask who manufactured the disk drive. (Ask who manufactured each and every component.) Then find out all you can about that manufacturer while you are considering your choices.

We say that with a little trepidation. We may be slighting some small new house or houses that have top-flight engineers, and rigid quality control, who know what they are doing as well as the "old" houses do. But as a rule, that kind of house is founded by a fine engineer who learned the ropes with an older house, and who may be a brilliant professor of mechanical engineering somewhere who has analyzed everybody else's drive and designed around their bugs. You'll hear about these pluses as you investigate his company.

Question: "I think I can afford a computer with those floppy disks now, but not with the expensive Winchesters. Should I wait—for prices to come down, or until I have saved up more money?" Our categorical answer: don't wait. If the system you can afford can do the job you want a computer to do, acquire it now. You can always upgrade later (especially since your computer will save you money and increase your revenue).

Winchester who?

Winchester is not a brand name, but a generic name denoting economical hard disk units developed explicitly for small-computer use. The origin of the term is obscure. Some people suppose that a "Dr. Winchester" was instrumental in its development. Perhaps it was developed in a loft shop along Winchester Boulevard, which runs through several cities in the Silicon Gulch area near San Jose, California. IBM's labs figure in two legends about the device: that "Winchester" was simply a code name for IBM's pioneering small hard disk, or that (according to Priam Corporation of Cupertino, California, a manufacturer of both 8-inch and 14-inch versions), IBM planned a dual drive with 30 megabytes on each drive; it was nicknamed the "30-30" and that name inevitably became "Winchester."

In the Silicon Gulch area the name "Winchester" has a historic connection with the venerable Connecticut firearms firm: its founder's rich widow settled in San Jose, on an estate along what is now Winchester Boulevard. She built a bizarre mansion there to which she was forever adding rooms, in the belief that if construction stopped, she would die. This went on for years. The house became a sort of labyrinth. But one day she was persuaded to call a holiday in the construction work. The hammers and saws went silent—and on that day she died. "Build thou more stately mansions, O my soul!" The sprawling "unfinished" house is still there, now surrounded by commercial buildings, and is visited by thousands of tourists and local school children every year.

Had you thought that everything about computers was cut-and-dried? The Winchester disk drive is about as old as the latest fuel crisis and the origin of its name—a haunting name in its native haunts—is already the subject of mystery and legend.

"Who's got the disk?" Since Winchester disks are not removeable, Cromemco makes a real black box of its dual hard-disk system. (See "black box" entry in the Glossary.)

Courtesy of Cromemco

PRINTERS

Prominent among the output-only devices are the various **printers**. Modern computers are noted for their high-speed printers; the expensive, horrendously complex printers for the giant main-frames print out thousands of *lines* per minute. Printers appropriate in size and expense for microcomputers are slower — but these are no slouches, at least as compared with the best of typewriters. Some microcomputer printers will do up to 300 characters per second. That is four to five lines of type on standard 8½-inch-width office paper.

The electric typewriter used as a printer is *slow*. The IBM Selectric will deliver 14.9 characters per second. So, it would have taken a computer-driven Selectric nearly four seconds to write that last sentence, which is fifty-eight characters long. "Impressive" when you compare it with the performance of a human typist, but nothing earth-shaking when you compare it with true printers. But more important, no electric typewriter has the endurance of machines designed as printers (assuming comparable quality; cheap printers exist). Fine a machine as the

Selectric is, if you keep it running hour after hour, day after day, you will eventually have a mechanical breakdown. Probably something minor, but when it happens, the machine is down. And so is your computer.

This is not to knock the Selectric or any other quality typewriter. The typewriter is just fine provided you (a) are not in a supersonic sort of hurry, and (b) are not going to give it a heavier daily typing load *via* the computer than you would *via* a human typist. That means, you don't keep it running at 14.9 characters per second hour after hour all day, all week. For heavy-duty printing out of massive data outputs at high speed, in high volume, it would really be more economical to invest in a true printer. (Even if you need the Selectric or other good typewriter for whatever you need it for.)

Daisy wheel

Fine typewriter print quality can be had from some **daisy wheel** printers. The printing component in these machines consists of ninety-six metal strips arranged like wheel spokes or daisy petals. A letter or other character is at the end of each strip. The "wheel" rotates at high speed, and when the desired character is properly positioned, a hammer rod shoots out and drives the strip or "petal" against an inked ribbon. These machines are relatively inexpensive and run for hundreds of hours without even minor malfunctions. Most are slow as printers go, with speeds of thirty to forty-five characters per second. But that is two to three times as fast as the best electric typewriter.

Daisy-wheel printers are available in print-only and teleprinter versions. The "daisy" heads are available with 10-pitch and 12-pitch ("elite") character sizes and a variety of typefaces. The daisy heads are easily removed and interchanged. Leading printer brands, such as QUME, DIABLO, and Nippon Electric, offer an option for alternate-line left-to-right and right-to-left printing. This increases printing speed and reduces wear on the equipment, since the print head mechanism need not fly back to the left margin to begin a new line.

All comments in this book about daisy wheel printers apply equally well to the NEC (Nippon Electric Corp.) *Spinwriter* printers with their "thimble" variation on the daisy wheel principle, unless a specific exception is made.

A compact daisy-wheel printer, the Diablo 1650.

Courtesy of Diablo Systems

The daisy wheel gives high-quality "typewriter" characters without a typewriter.

Courtesy of QUME Corporation

QUME offers a twin-head daisy-wheel printer that can print up to 75 characters per second, print up to 192 different characters on a line, with two different type fonts, type in two different languages in up to four colors. (What more could you ask?)

Courtesy of QUME Corporation

Like any good teleprinter, this Diablo daisy-wheel printer/terminal will work by itself, substituting for a typewriter, or it will control your computer, or accept output from it.

Courtesy of Diablo Systems

Matrix printers

An alternative, offering high speeds but with less attractiveness of print, is the **matrix printer**. This comes in two main types, *impact* and *non-impact*. A matrix printer forms letters by printing patterns of dots. The dots are arranged within a matrix area of, typically, 5 × 7 dots or 7 × 9 dots. The illustration gives enlarged examples of these types of letters, as well as samples of text.

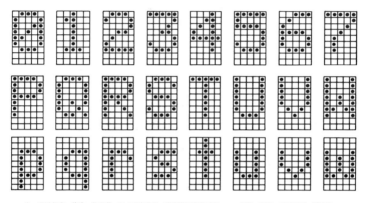

```
1 THIS IS DOT MATRIX PRINTING.  IT IS FINE FOR
2 YOUR IN-HOUSE COMMUNICATIONS, AND YOU CAN
3 GET BY WITH IT FOR THE NUMBERS ON YOUR
4 BILLS AND INVOICES.

12    There was a vogue some years back for sending out
13 everything in dot-matrix print to proclaim LOOK AT
14 US: WE'RE REALLY MODERN BECAUSE WE USE A COMPUTER,
15 but you will probably agree that this practice is
16 no longer even cute.
```

In the impact type of dot matrix printer, very small hammers strike the paper through an inked ribbon. There may be seven or nine or these pin-hammers in a vertical row that sweeps back and forth across the line to be printed — or hundreds of them in a horizontal lineup that will move up or down to generate an entire printed line. Impact printers are typically faster than daisy wheels, running from 30 to 300 characters per second, but are not as fast as non-impact printers. Unlike the latter, however, they can be used for making multiple copies (using carbon paper or whatever).

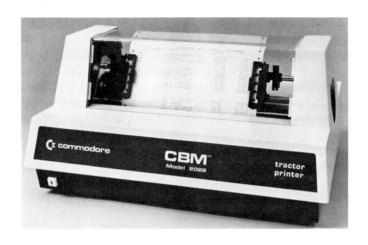

A tractor-feed dot-matrix printer for business use.
Courtesy of Commodore Business Machines, Inc.

Non-impact matrix printers use either heat-sensitive paper or tiny jets of ink. In the former case, a moving print head focuses pulses of heat energy where the dots should be on thermally sensitive paper. In the latter, electrically charged drops of ink are guided by a shifting magnetic field to strike the paper in the right places. Since there are no flying hammers, nothing mechanical to make contact with the paper, speeds can be very high.

Some extremely fast dot-matrix printers have the printing head sweep alternatively left-right, right-left, left-right to make successive lines of print. This means that the machine must print every other line "backwards," but this is no problem for the proper equipment and software.

Options

Printers have various options such as upper and lower case letters or, in the cheaper ones, upper case only; line widths from 20 to 132 characters, with 80 most common; and various speeds. All this involves engineering choices as to the kind, number, and mode of motion of the print heads. Prices may vary widely with the capabilities and quality you are buying. Needless to say, shop for a printer as if you were shopping for a typewriter or a dump truck: look for ruggedness. (Go ahead and ask the dealer challenging questions about mean time between failures,

Very satisfactory quality can be had from a non-impact printer using a
9×12 matrix of dots. This sample was produced by Comprint.
Courtesy of Computer Printers International, Inc.

A Comprint high-speed (225 cps) non-impact dot matrix printer.
Courtesy of Computer Printers International, Inc.

average number of lines printed between failures, and so forth, for any model he is showing you.)

ISOLATORS, NOISE SUPPRESSORS

Power lines are electrically noisy. An ordinary kitchen radio tells you this: you hear all kinds of buzzing and crackling between stations. Computers are subject to interference by electrical noise, too. The noise pulses can amount to spurious bit pulses and clocking pulses. Also, power lines frequently have voltage surges. Computer manufacturers — at least the better ones — do try to incorporate reasonable amounts of filtering equipment in the computer power circuitry to cut out noise pulses, or at least diminish their power. You are probably well advised, however, to invest in an isolation transformer/filter circuit assembly, and preferably one with a *line-voltage regulator*. This will suppress noise pulses, help keep the voltage steady, and remove any incidental shock hazards.

POWER SUPPLIES

Depending on how your computer is assembled, it may or may not have an internal or integral *power supply*. A power supply consists of a transformer, a rectifier, and filtering circuitry that converts the nominal 120-volt AC line current to the 4 to 12 volts of DC needed to run semiconductor ("transistor") equipment. Your TV set, stereo amplifier, etc., come equipped with integral power supplies.

There are good technical reasons for having external supplies on some equipment — especially when *add-on* is contemplated. Even if you buy a small one-box-holds-everything computer having its own internal supply circuitry, the next accessory you buy could demand 4 volts or 12 volts DC — and you have a choice of buying batteries for it, or a power supply.

We cannot guide you here to the purchase of your specific power supply. What you must do is look at the power ratings (in DC volts and milliamperes) of the various gadgets you plan to invest in, and then choose a supply that offers the range of voltages at a total *current* value that exceeds the total current (in milliamperes) that all your equipment items together will require. Now, suppose all your gadgets together demand 1800 milliamperes and the supply your dealer shows you is rated at 2.5 *amperes*? No problem: 1 ampere = 1000 milliamperes. Thus the preferred supply delivers 2500 milliamperes (abbreviated *ma*) and is ample for your needs.

Ask about—and look for on the label or in the technical documentation—the *regulation* of the power supply. A supply that offers you 12 volts DC ± 1% is vastly superior to one offering you 12 volts ± 10%. Better still, is 0.1%, and so on. Don't buy any power supply that does not boast a regulation figure; this applies also to equipment having a built-in supply.

FRONT PANEL

This is the part that doesn't do anything. At least, it does not do anything that would interest the businessman. It may be available as an accessory to your small business computer if the same basic CPU assembly is also offered as a hobby computer.

A front panel holds a number of switches and an array of little lights. Some of the lights will go on as the switches are thrown to enter a "1" bit. Some may also go on as the computer program processes 1 and 0 bits. The lights are arranged in sets of eight, corresponding to the eight bits in a byte.

These collections of eight lights are called display registers. If you are a born voyeur of inanimate objects you may wish to peer obscenely at the workings of your computer's mind. You recognize the front panel now—it's always there in the science fiction movies and TV series. A space ship can't move or the computer can't add two numbers without a thousand lights blinking. Now, the display registers did have a use, long ago, on the old giant main frame computers. When such a computer hit a bone in the meat grinder, so to speak, and stopped computing, the operators could tell from the patterns of lights left on where the program had failed—that is, which line of the program the computer was last executing. This gave them a leg up on the debugging process, which was then frequently needed. Otherwise, when a computer is operating at its normal speed no human eye and brain can follow, much less interpret, the patterns of shifting lights.

A hobbyist may advise you that you can enter program words and data items through the front panel if your keyboard breaks down, or if, on his advice, you haven't acquired a keyboard. Sure you can. It may take all day or all week, but yes, a front panel can be used for that. Ages ago, before somebody dreamed up an interface for a Teletype machine and hooked that up to a computer, the front panel route was about the only way to go. Besides, that is, opening up the computer and actually re-wiring some of its circuitry—the earliest programming was "hard-wired" programming.

Should you get a winking-blinking front panel to impress customers with, if the computer is stationed where they can see it? *Nah!* Microcomputer front panels are too small and simple to impress customers with. Besides, they cost a lot of money. Excellent keyboards cost less.

MODEMS

A **modem** is an electro-acoustic device that couples a computer to an ordinary telephone line. It converts the computer's output data pulses into audio tone signals—and converts incoming tone signals into data pulses. There are modems and modems, but the kind you will be most frequently offered will accept the handset of your telephone in a pair of round openings in the top of the small modem cabinet.

That kind, of course, leaves your phone free for other purposes. You can acquire a modem that will permanently hook your computer up to a **data line**, more or less "replacing" a phone on that line. But data lines are more expensive, and different from, ordinary voice lines. The put-the-handset-in-the-top kind utilizes voice lines for occasional data transfer. Voice lines are "slower" than data lines; they can accept fewer signal impulses per second. However, a small business with its probable low volume of data communications can accept this.

In fact, if you subscribed to a computer service and they gave you a terminal for communicating with their computer, that terminal would usually have a built-in handset modem. The "slow" voice line is adequate for your kind of purpose.

Now, how badly do you need a modem? If you have not yet computerized at all, you don't need one. If you are just getting your feet wet in this field, you won't need one for some time. You may very well *never* need one. With your own in-house computing, you have no direct or immediate need to communicate with somebody else's computer.

If you expand your computerizing, you might find modems very useful. They could be used to network your stockroom computer or branch-store computers with the "main" computer in your office. Some day. This is just to let you know they exist, and what they do.

THE COMPUTER ROOM

A great deal of nonsense has been uttered and written in the past few years about the microcomputer's lack of need for a special computer room. The old main-frames, you will recall, always operated in special rooms in which temperature, humidity, dust, and even vibration were closely controlled. The ancient vacuum tube computers generated so much heat, in fact, that the associated air conditioning was second in expense only to the computer itself. A microcomputer needs no such coddling. It's comfortable where you are comfortable.

But only where you are comfortable. Contrary to what has been said in some books and articles, it is *not* advisable to install it "anywhere, even outdoors." After all, the computing system consists of high-quality, *delicate* electronic equipment. Would you install your Nobody-Touches-This-But-Daddy stereo gear outdoors? Out in the rain, dew, dust, solar heat, night chill? A computer wants to live where your prize quadraphonic stereo lives—which is in a comfortable room where you like to live. It would not do to install your business computer in your plating room next to the acid vats, or tuck it out of the way down in the boiler room, or put it on a bench next to your heaviest punch press. Treat it as another member of the staff—an honored member of the staff, who gets a dust-free, mist-free, quiet environment with decent temperature and humidity conditions to work in.

Yes, there are process-control computers which may conceivably have to be installed in less-than-optimum environments. But such computers are specially ruggedized, with chassis and cabinets designed to keep out dust, moisture, and corrosive fumes. That costs money, of course. However, in the usual process-computer installation, the computer is in a protected spot, remote from the critical operation and connected with the operation by long electric cables—at the business ends of which sit sensors and relays that are the computer's "eyes" and "hands."

"DESK TOPS" AND ACCESSORIES

We have been talking about "desk-top" computer systems, but the top of an ordinary desk is probably not the optimum place for a computer. For one thing, the keyboard should be lowered to standard "typist's" height—which enhances the

A teleprinter terminal desk, with a drawer to catch and form an accordion-folded printout.

Courtesy of Wright Line

operator's efficiency and accuracy as well as safeguarding health and comfort. Most small computers and CRT terminals are "human-engineered" to put the CRT screen at proper height (slightly below eye level) once the keyboard is at proper "typist's height." Having the various components strewn on a real desk-top means the sacrifice of a desk's worth of expensive floor space. Also, you may have use for "stand-up height" computer or terminal stands for some applications.

Your computer system may or may not "come with" a desk. If it doesn't you have your choice among many brands and models of desks and stands designed specifically for the small computer. These put the components at various levels, effectively stacking them to make the installation more compact, and more convenient for the operator. A disk drive or printer, for example, might sit where the conventional drawer-pedestal would be, leaving most of the desk-top free for papers and work. Some offices might prefer to have the computer in a rack-and-panel mount, especially if the computer serves more than one terminal or "work station."

Other accessories

There are fat catalogues listing and illustrating myriad useful accessories for the small computer. You may want a CRT swivel

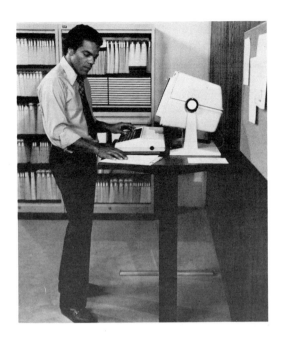

Courtesy of Wright Line

This "Microdesk" comes as a kit.
Courtesy of Computer Systems Design

Courtesy of Basic Time

—no matter where you put the operator's work station in the room, there is likely to be some glare from reflected room lights on the face of the screen. Just angling the unit slightly may fix that. There are many situations in which you might want an auxiliary CRT or an entire terminal out of some employee's direct line of sight but readable if he or she just turns his head slightly. This may require an angled screen.

You will want easy-access storage for floppy disks. There are many "card carousel" schemes, and gadgets resembling the Rolodex™ but swiveling on a vertical axis, with the disk envelopes hanging vertically. You will want similar storage for cassettes, or even reel tapes—that keep the tapes dust- and moisture-free.

Then there are various caddies and trays for disks, cassettes, and folds or rolls of printer paper; self-adhesive address label rolls and folds with tractor-feed (perforated) edges; extra print wheels with different typefaces for your daisy-wheel printer, and so on.

You may need preprinted forms of many sorts to go through your printer. A number of companies specialize in these. If you get your own programming into gear (using a part-time or full-time programmer for custom work) you will need documentation storage. There are some clever binder-and-cabinet combinations for this.

What about a fire safe for keeping irreplaceable disks and other valuables? This, too, is a small-computer accessory.

Courtesy of Eichner Systems, Inc.

Courtesy of Eichner Systems, Inc.

Courtesy of Eichner Systems, Inc.

A documentation drawer.

Courtesy of Wright Line

One of many forms and sizes of the documentation or bound-data file.

Courtesy of Wright Line

Unless you have an absolutely fireproof data backup system, a good fire safe is a must for your disks.

There are electrically conductive floor mats to keep static charges from building up on, or from being carried to, your equipment. Static charges can creep into the computer's electronic innards, sending false signals, churning a memory into chaos, even damaging delicate semiconductor chips. The conductive surface of the mat drains and dissipates charge.

There is hardly a gadget or structure that you could think of for making your computer operation more efficient that somebody hasn't manufactured. Whatever you need, if your dealer hasn't got it he can get it for you, or you can mail-order. If your needs are extensive and frequently repetitive (as for paper, forms, labels, disks, etc.), some of the accessory companies, like paper or stationery companies, have reps who will call on you regularly, survey your needs, take your order, and show you what's new.

Some of the computer accessory companies handle paper; others do not (except for special items). Those that do not will direct you to good suppliers. It is advisable to anticipate your needs, to allow for order-processing and shipment time (always have an extra month's or two months' supply of printer paper and printer forms on hand). As with paper, you should be a bit ahead with small accessories and non-paper supplies. For example, printer ribbons should be ordered five at a time. If you only use up three ribbons a month, you can adjust your repeat orders. Items like extra daisy wheels should be ordered well in advance of expected need.

You will find the accessory companies at the small-computer shows and conventions, displaying along with the computer and peripheral makers. It is worth your while to attend these shows, even after you have acquired a computer. You will probably develop a relationship with your local computer-accessory supplier like the one you have with your local office supplies store.

COST AND QUALITY

Constantly improving semiconductor technology makes the mass production of CPU chips cheaper and cheaper. More and more elaborate CPU and related chips can be expected in the near future, as *large-scale integration* (LSI) technology shifts into higher gear. (It is reliably rumored that the equivalent of an IBM 370 — which is a large main frame computer — exists on a chip in a lab as we write). In the late 1970s the industry was on an economic curve that featured the halving of costs every two years, at least for the basic semiconductor devices.

Do not, however, wait for the costs of entire computer systems, including peripherals and software, to be cut in half. Things like printers or keyboards involve materials and processes that cannot be made cheaper by improvements in semiconductor technology. But system prices will probably trend downward, at least bucking inflation, because of large mass-production runs once the Small Computer Revolution really catches on.

WATCH OUT

The constant lowering of costs of CPU chips and similar semiconductor devices means that anybody can order batches of chips and start building microcomputers in his garage. This "anyone" includes any uninspired soldering iron jockey and any schlock artist. Yes, there is schlock in this field, as there is in any other. Only a few years ago the government and the public discovered schlock even in the aerospace industry — where supreme quality had "always" been the watchword.

There is one thing you have that no computer can have. It's your built-in crap detector, or CD. (In this kind of field, there is no escaping initials and acronyms.) When you are reading the blurbs and listening to the salesmen, you have to keep your antennas extended on that CD. All this computer stuff is heady. But even a shiny new fork-lift is heady stuff. You keep your head when you buy one of those. *Don't* take the position that "I'm not one of those computer guys, I'm a businessman." Don't disdain to understand the jargon or the real principles. Yes, you're a businessman, not a fork-lift man, but you didn't get snowed when you bought the fork-lift, and you made damned sure you weren't stuck with a lemon.

Go for quality. Buy at, or as near, the top of every line as you can. At least, buy the top lines, in a good store. Make sure the store itself is a top store, guaranteeing everything and keeping a good service shop.

"You get what you pay for." As it is you can pay a handsome price for *good* stuff (including IBM's recent version of a "small" computer). If you were unwary you might pay good money for junk. One purpose of this book is to help you recognize the really fine equipment now available at really reasonable prices.

You will buy your computing system the way you buy any other business tool. Also, you will amortize it like any other tool. The amortization of a tool brings you tax relief — and the effects of having this particular tool should bring you enhanced efficiency and profit.

Chapter Nine

THE PROFESSIONS AND THE COMPUTER

The microcomputer has solid uses in professions as disparate as accounting, law, medicine, and writing. We have room here to examine only these four, but the principles illustrated here apply to almost any profession.

THE ACCOUNTANT

The computer will never replace the accountant. There is no substitute for the accountant's professional judgment, and the computer is nothing more than a mechanized bookkeeper. But the computer is an obvious tool of the accountant. It can reduce hours of human research and manual computation to minutes—as with amortization and depreciation problems. The computer can quickly retrieve the requisite information from its magnetic files, and process it with despatch.

Many accountants use computer services or timesharing today, but, if they looked into it, could find acquisition of an in-house small computer more economical. Even more important, the accountant would have absolute control over the data base and over contingencies—such as the computer "going down." (The advantages of owning a computer *versus* renting time or buying services were touched on in Chapter One and discussed in some detail in Chapter Six.) And of course there is the matter of speed—results are obtained immediately with one's own computer. The software can be as you like it, without compromise. Finally, there is absolute security of confidential client data.

The accountant's software needs include programs for charting accounts for all clients, for providing them with periodic updates of their general ledgers, and for sets of journals, income statements, balance sheets, W-2 forms, and so on. Tax-return programs would have to be modified yearly, and for this and other purposes the part-time or full-time services of a programmer might be required. This expense would be offset by the continuous economies in time and increases in efficiency. Just the preparation of a balance sheet or income statement is tremendously faster with computer procedures. Also, since the document can be thoroughly checked out and edited on a display screen before it is committed to print, the very first hard copy will be completely accurate.

While any small business might get along on a set of discrete programs, one for each task (payroll, accounts receivable and so on), the accountant would opt for a more elaborate, somewhat more expensive **data base** system through which a variety of discrete files can be related and updated. The accountant, for example, would want to accumulate data during an entire year, which would be processed quarterly and at year's end for her own and her clients' tax returns. With a data-base system, all files can be searched semiautomatically for relevant tax data.

The accountant's hardware would probably include a quality printer, since most printout is for out-of-house readers. The accountant might prefer a hard-disk system to a floppy disk system (since the hard disks accept a much greater volume of data), or even, a hard disk with floppy backup. The backup disks would be stored off the premises, so that fire or other catastrophe could not destroy all data. Hard-disks hardware adds about $3,000 (and up) to the total cost of the system. Software would include a word-processor or at least a report generator program; the former is more versatile.

As an accountant you will have many uses for a computer, and you are also your client's best advisor on when he should acquire his own in-house computer. You know the particular business and you can judge affordability. Suppose, for example, the business is already buying batch services or timesharing at reasonable cost. The accountant may advise acquisition of the computer even if its initial monthly cost exceeds the service cost by some margin — because the accountant will be able to see what specific additional services the in-house computer can provide. The computer can increase revenue as well as saving business operating costs.

You will find your own computer valuable in forecasting for the client—predicting future business activity on the basis of what the business has done in the past. This would permit adjustment of budgets for enhanced cost-effectiveness and for improved leverage in obtaining new revenue. The greater the variety and volume of data that can be analyzed, the more reliable the forecast, but forecasting can be a crushing burden for the accountant—a burden the computer will help relieve.

The accountant is always concerned with "real" costs or hidden costs. Alert business executives would like to increase inventory turnover and reduce overstocking in order to minimize costs and achieve more effective pricing. However, what an accountant would consider a valid inventory analysis involves information that may pass the manager by. For example, what was the actual cost of certain items in the inventory at their time of acquisition, and what will be the cost of the same items in a reorder? What percentages of the stock of a given item were acquired at different costs? This information permits realistic appraisal of how low a markup can be tolerated for competitive pricing. A similar manual analysis of the inventory would be tedious for the accountant and expensive for the client—but with a computer, you can streamline the procedure, producing the "answers" at reasonable cost and in a short time. Providing *timely* information benefits the client and enhances the accountant's reputation.

THE LAW OFFICE

A law office has business bookkeeping and accounting of its own just like any other business, plus some special needs for information processing—courtroom documentation and support; legal research; checking out costs to be incurred by, or moneys accruing to, clients because of contracts to be signed; and also **word processing**—for correspondence, contracts, wills, deeds, affidavits, briefs, and the many standard forms a lawyer must be concerned with.

It is advantageous if both the partners and the employees keep track of their time. This may be routinely done in most firms as far as the partners are concerned—the senior partners, at least, appreciate frequent analyses of where revenue comes from and *who* is really producing. But the time of clerks, assistants, and paralegal employees tends to be unevenly distributed among cases. It can be of value to know which client to charge for given support time (directly or indirectly) rather than leaving all such time in a vague and amorphous "overhead." Tracking everyone's time manually in a large firm can seem "more trouble than it's worth," but once a computer is on the premises the cost of time-tracking drops to the labor cost of entering everyone's weekly time log into the machine.

Attorneys and law offices were among the pioneers in early word processing, as customers for IBM "memory" or tape-run typewriters. Nowadays, however, the price of a "smart" typewriter will buy a microcomputer system that does word processing *and* data processing, and it does a better, faster job of word processing. (The CRT screen or equivalent display makes a tremendous difference.) Not only that, this single system can have several terminals and therefore several operators; it is the equivalent of as many "smart" typewriters as it has terminals. By means of a quality daisy wheel printer it provides the finest "typewriter" print quality, at *three times the speed* or better.

A stenographer can just as well transcribe dictation through a computer keyboard as a typewriter keyboard. He or she can correct the transcription on the computer's display screen, a much faster process than with any paper copy. What if, once the stenographer delivers the hard copy to the attorney, the latter decides that changes need to be made? The stenographer notes the changes, puts the storage disk back into the machine, brings the document back onto the CRT screen, makes the changes, and commands printing the revised hard copy—letter perfect, and fast.

The computer brings increased efficiency to the law office as it does to any other business. Law offices used to be regarded as staid, rather old-fashioned places where the contemporary mania for efficiency might be tastefully excluded. Only now, the competitive squeeze is on. Rates count; therefore costs count; therefore efficiency counts.

As in the medical office, client invoices and statements must be prepared at frequent intervals. There has to be an audit trail throughout the history of the account. The law office has to watch accounts receivable and accounts ageing. And effective cost accounting involves time management, and analysis of who is doing what: the lawyers' Charges and Receipts Report. The kinds of reports needed are similar or analogous to those needed

A computer system in the professional office. It features full-sized (8-inch) floppy disks and a detached keyboard that can be positioned anywhere the operator is comfortable. The system's software includes a versatile word processing system, plus program modules for data base management, complete accounting, professional billing (for law, medical, or dental office), mailing lists and much more: the system is built around its software.

Courtesy of Alpha Professional Systems, Inc.

in the medical office *(next section)* and the sizes and costs of systems for law offices of various sizes are similar.

Billing becomes much more efficient since the computer can automatically extract billing information from the general data base, where it also extracts information for addressing envelopes (since law offices have traditionally shown disdain for window envelopes). A daisy-wheel printer can write about one hundred typical law office bills per hour.

The advantages of computerized word processing in the law office are obvious, expecially when it comes to contracts and wills; these were discussed in Chapter Four.

There is talk of prepaid legal plans. These are bound to resemble prepaid medical plans in many repsects, including the proliferation of forms. A computer program can tap the data base and fill out a form much faster than any human clerk can—never getting tired, bored, distracted, or making mistakes.

The computer can help the law office step up its scale of operation without proportionate increases in paralegal support staff. It takes over the repetitive, time-consuming chores.

Legal documents and records tend to be so voluminous that the small law office will opt for large (8-inch) floppy disks for data storage, and the larger office for small or large hard disks. The hard disks are not replaceable (each is sealed in its drive mechanism) but each holds one to ten *million* data bytes per disk.

We know of one law office, specializing in aircraft accident cases, that uses a microcomputer to process technical information concerning the accident. They have also worked out a formula and a computer program that more realistically estimates the probable future financial losses to the surviving family of an aircraft accident victim.

Two of the three attorneys in this office are also mechanical enginers. Few law offices may have this level of nonlegal technical expertise in-house, but this firm's use of its computer illustrates the possibilities. In a more conventional vein, they have worked out a storage system that files case information on disks, indexed by a standard ten-character case identifier, adapted from those used in law library citations. (See "The Automated Law Office" in *Interface Age* for October 1978.)

THE DOCTOR'S OFFICE

The medical or dental office (or clinic) has a rich variety of uses for the microcomputer. Any such office has a complex bookkeeping load with a need for constant cross-file updating. But it also needs to maintain patient history files—and to be able to flag patients who need further checkups or further treatment. In addition, the microcomputer has myriad other uses in medicine, from keeping literature abstracts to monitoring the conditions of particular patients, and even to diagnostics.

Business software designed specifically for the medical and dental office has been under development the past few years. Medical people have often been involved in its development, and more than occasionally a program has been developed by a doctor who is also a computerist. The various reports generated by one medical software package include the charges and receipts report, a new accounts report, a new case report, doctor' charges and receipt report, a method of payment report, accounts receivables ageing, patients' monthly statements—and the filling out of insurance forms. An editing program allows for additions, changes, deletions, and program listing for all account data. The package permits a daily report on new accounts, new cases, and new transactions, and gives an analysis of payment type on the accounts. The software also offers a year-to-date listing of all account transactions. Accounts can be listed by number and name, and the account number can be identified for a given name.

The insurance program keeps track of all the requisite information—for patient identity, physician identity and degree, physician code, referring physician, diagnosis, procedure description, etc.

This is only a partial listing of the capabilities. Even mailing labels can be generated by a program in this package. The programs are interactive, prompting the operator (who need not be a "computer person") with questions and instructions for the entering of data or the requesting of a report.

The medical office has to proceed like any other in choosing or designing its business sytem: by analyzing the data-processing needs, and deciding what kind of information must be tracked, what items need to be updated and at what intervals, and what kinds of reports must be generated. This analysis defines the software needs.

The choice of software influences choice of the hardware system. All microcomputer hardware systems are physically equivalent but not identical. They have different memory capacities. Different systems use different versions of BASIC (or other language), and have differing *operating system* software (Chapter Three). A program or software package that would run on one operating system (such as the famous CP/M) might not operate on another. The small-computer consultant, systems house, or dealer can help make sure that software and hardware are compatible.

A moderate-sized microcomputer system could accommodate financial transactions files for several thousand patients. Its limits would be fairly flexible, set by the software and the size and types of the disks or other storage media used. For medical purposes, however, such as patient medical histories, it is not easy to predict what would be needed. The software problem is more difficult, because files have to be much longer, and of varying length.

However, medical histories, like any other documents or data, can be processed by computer and stored in computer media; this is a **word-processing** problem. The office would probably need two files on each patient: an abstract file, and the main, detailed narrative file. Either would be recoverable for changes, study or printout by the same identification number, but through a different command to the computer, and would be stored on different disks.

The physician is constantly reading medical journals and filing information about diseases and treatments. Information keeps pouring in; it is difficult to store and retrieve. Bibliographies and abstracts can be stored on computer disks, and sort programs can be had so that information may be retrieved by invoking any one word in a title. (The computer will then display or print out all titles containing that word—each accompanied by the author's name, publication name, volume and issue number, date, and page number.) From time to time the physician reads some paragraph that has particular weight or significance and he would like to be able to retrieve it quickly. Just as titles and abstracts can be entered in computer files, so can isolated paragraphs. "Just what was it Wilson had to say about melanomas in patients who had excessive exposure to sunlight along with unusual exposure to hydrocarbon vapors?" can be answered by entering the paragraph, labeled or coded as such, in the abstract file or one like it.

A computer program could be devised to pull the paragraph out once it was given any of the key words—*melanoma, sunlight, hydrocarbons,* even *Wilson.* Of course everything else that can be identified by one of these words would also scroll by on the display. (There are ways to make the retrieval more narrowly specific, but too narrow a selection criterion would defeat the purpose of this kind of bibliography.)

That sort of thing has been done on large computers for many years; so has its equivalent in fields other than medicine. The large computer implies an institutional setting. The individual physician, or the local medical clinic, is not the kind of institution that owns a large computer; and the requisite software is usually proprietary. What "suits" the large computer to this application is not the computer itself, but the massive disk and reel-tape storage faclities connected with it. A microcomputer can handle the task—and for the individual physician or the small clinic, the cost of the peripherals need not be prohibitive.

The Size of the System

The size and complexity of a medical business computer system depend directly on the size of the office. An office or clinic with one to three doctors would benefit from a "single user" system, with a single terminal (keyboard and CRT) and a disk memory of one or two megabytes (one megabyte = 1,000,000 bytes). Such an office serves twenty-five to fifty patients a day, and issues between two hundred and one thousand billing statements a month—assuming the use of family billing, in which a single statement covers all members of the family.

This office might get along on a single dot-matrix printer for all uses including billing, although a daisy wheel printer ("nice-looking type") would be useful for many purposes. Good type enhances the legibility of medical record printouts, for example, and the daisy wheel may be used in lieu of an electric typewriter for correspondence and other uses. Such a system might cost $350 to $500 per month for a two-to-three year amortization.

A larger office with three to ten practitioners would require more disk storage space—full-sized (8-inch) floppies with dual density or even quadruple density, or a small hard disk ("Winchester"). Also, the printing demand is heavier. Such an office might have five thousand to ten thousand statements a month. A typical good daisy wheel printer could write fifty to one hundred bills an hour, but this could, in practice, require up to thirty hours. With proper software, a pair of daisy-wheel printers could cut this time. So could a quality dot-matrix printer, which would be much faster than a daisy wheel. A second terminal might also be useful for handling the data-processing load. Such a system would cost $17,000 to $20,000, payable over a term of a few years.

The medium-sized clinic would opt for a larger system, with several terminals (or perhaps several small micro-computer systems networked together, with each serving as an intelligent terminal for the whole system), several hard-disk storage units, and one or more large fast printers. The system might serve forty to fifty doctors, and would cost between $25,000 and $40,000.

A large clinic with up to one hundred practitioners would require a "large" system, based on a minicomputer or advanced microcomputer (the distinction is now very hard to draw) and costing $40,000 to $100,000. This would use hard disks providing up to one hundred million bytes of information, possibly with magentic tape backup (and off-premises storage of the backup tapes). It would require three to twenty terminals, and a 300-line/minute printer using special form stock.

Any investment in a microcomputer for a growing office requires choice of a leading brand with proven software—from a knowledgeable vendor who has previously served the medical and dental professions. The system he offers should be able to handle a variety of insurance forms. Both hardware and software design should allow for expansion of the system—the addition of more and different peripherals (especially mass storage) and the addition of programs to handle additional tasks. The larger the system, the more important the training program offered as part of the package.

For a system of any size, *complete documentation* of the software is indispensible; so are clear, usable hardware manuals. (See Chapter 3). Also, the larger the system, the more crucial the quality of the office's analysis of its data-processing needs and the more critical the choice of a computer systems consultant.

A Profile

Edmund D. Butler, Jr., M.D., is a California urologist who has "graduated" from involvement with large institution computers to employment of his own microcomputer in his practice with a sizeable suburban clinic. Dr. Butler is also a clinical assistant professor of surgery at the Stanford University School of Medicine. He had learned a programming language, FORTRAN, while a medical student. Before acquiring his own computer, he had been storing condensed patient data and literature abstracts on one of Stanford's large computers—an IBM 370/168. He communicated with the computer by means of an office terminal and an ordinary telephone line (through a modem, Chapter Two). The massive 370 system could accept any amount of data he wanted to store, but, as he says, "there was a limit to the amount I could afford to store." In addition, the need to dial up and log on the computer was inconvenient and time-consuming.

Acquisition of a microcomputer in 1977 meant writing software in another language, BASIC. For this, Dr. Butler obtained the help of programmers from the manufacturer of his equipment, Cromemco, Inc., whose plant and headquarters, are, like

Stanford, not far from his office. Butler appreciates that Cromemco's support was beyond what an individual user would normally expect from a manufacturer, but the company and its programmers took an interest in the then-novel applications he wanted. A Cromemco engineer produced a fast **sort** program that displays abstracted patient information; type of ailment, level of severity, date of most recent procedure, result of most recent examination, etc.

A dozen years earlier, while he was a urology resident at Stanford Medical Center, Butler and a colleague had developed a special diagnostic program for urological problems in patients suffering from various degrees of paralysis brought on by spinal injury. The program worked well, and won a prize from the American Urologic Association. The young doctors were happy to demonstrate it. However, a specialist once pointed out that he could accomplish, in ten minutes with ordinary diagnostic procedures, everything the computer had accomplished. Dr. Butler accepted this as a lesson: "Don't ask a computer to do things that people can easily do by conventional means." However, this does not nullify the possible value of computer-aided diagnostics in other circumstances.

Dr. Butler's main interest today is in storing and retrieving summarized clinical information, concerning patients in his own practice. Most physicians with an active practice would be unable, on any given day, to "review" their total experience in regard to a specific operation or their results for a specific mode of therapy. Such reviews can be made with card-file systems, but at costs in time and effort that becomes impractical as the number of patients in a given series increases.

Currently, Dr. Butler's system uses Cromemco's data-base management software, which operates in the menu-driven interactive mode. It can find any one out of four hundred urological patients through a quick menu-sort command procedure. Butler can make his own menu definitions in the data base. He appreciates the security offered by his in-house computer: the data are his and only his.

The developmental system at present has three data bases: Vasectomy, Bladder Tumors, and Prostate Surgery. Each file displays the patient's name, date of surgery, birth date, ZIP code, date of last visit, interval to next appointment, a complication code (e.g., hematoma), review data, comments, and a "flag" for special identification. The system will sort by complication code, giving patient's name, or it will sort by name, listing complications. It allows for rejection criteria for focus on a narrow range of problems.

In its present form, the Cromemco **DBMS** lacks certain desirable statistical features. For example, it does not calculate the total number of patients; nor does it offer a breakdown of the numbers of specific complication cases, or of average ages. Some software options are available but would require special programming and more external memory space. Dr. Butler's original system employs 5¼-inch diskettes, and the solution may involve 8-inch, "full-sized," floppy disks.

The full potential of the system remains to be realized. In 1979, Dr. Butler was treating twenty-six bladder tumor patients. This small number would allow him more than one thousand bytes of data storage for each patient, only this is a non-uniform group, and the highly variable file length would require improvement of the software. "We haven't reached the point where the system is more efficient than hard-copy files — index cards or log books — for small numbers of patients," Butler acknowledges. "The computer really becomes effective when there is large volume of similar data."

Dr. Butler would like to use his computer system also as "an electronic filing cabinet." He is striving to achieve an efficient cabinet that will quickly return specific information he needs, without "losing" any because it may be filed under the "wrong" category. Much of what he wants had been achieved on large computers in institutional settings. Dr. Butler is trying to develop a similar capability for the private physician's office, using microcomputer technology. As more physicians acquire hands-on experience with computers, and put their minds to getting what they need out of them, and begin to publish and swap their ideas, development should speed up.

Not all doctors have the inclination to work directly with the computers, learning programming languages and techniques as did Edmund Butler. But as they deal with software creators and vendors, and define their needs, physicians can create a demand for appropriate software. The general "explosion" of small-business software in the past few years has occurred because businessmen were demanding it. Doctors could trigger a similar explosion in specifically medical software. This would enhance the effectiveness of individual practices, and could ultimately advance the art of medicine.

Direct Medical Uses

The physician and the medical clinic have other uses for the computer, including even diagnostics, which are completely beyond the scope of this book (and the competence of the authors). Another use is in monitoring the conditions of particular patients, in the hospital and out. While this, too, is really beyond this book's scope, a few observations are in order here.

Several seminal articles on direct medical applications of microcomputers appeared in *Interface Age* magazine for July 1978. In one article, Dick Moberg of the Department of Neurosurgery, Jefferson Medical College, wrote of how microcomputers now plot a single vector cardiogram from the separate EKG traces to show a spatial summarization of the electrical activity of the heart. Also, the small computer can separate a raw EKG record into its frequency components by fast Fourier-transform analysis. Moberg envisions a single microcomputer serving as a phalanx of instruments, with the aid of selected sensor modules and programs: cardiac output monitor, arrhythmia analysis monitor, portable EKG computer, vestibular function tester, regional blood flow monitor, pulmonary function tester, and microwave radiometer. This is but a sampling of what is possible, or is being developed in institutions such as the Microcomputer Engineering Laboratory at the Massachusetts Institute of Technology.

In the same issue of *Interface Age*, Robert C.A. Goff, M.D., Fellow in Neonatology at the Children's Hospital Medical Center of Northern California, discusses his use of microcomputers in the intensive care nursery. His system provides "instant processing of, and access to the voluminous laboratory data and event summaries generated by each patient." Goff observes that the sets of clinical problems common to premature and sick infants are relatively stereotyped; as a result, "an estimated 90 to 95 percent of all data and event summary information can be specifically encoded for later search and retrieval." The remaining information would be accessible by manually searching a category encoded as OTHER. The equipment used amounts to a "bedside" computer. Its very small NorthStar disk drives "can be tucked away almost anywhere." Goff uses a pair of disk drives for one or a few patients (changing disks from patient to patient, allowing each patient ninety thousand bytes of information). The equipment, with proper software and sufficient sensors, could service many patients. For more than a few patients the expense of additional floppy diskette storage units would be prohibitive, but the expense of a high-capacity hard disk could be justified. (Some of the new Winchester disks offer about twenty million bytes of storage; see Chapter 8.)

Presumably, not all medical applications would require a complete microcomputer system, right down to a printer. Microprocessor-based sensing and storage devices could be quite compact and inexpensive, and could be connected to full-fledged microcomputer systems for permanent information storage, elaborate processing, and printouts. Many could be operated either on-line (connected to the computer) or off-line, with compact tape cassette or bubble-memory modules for off-line applications. It may be quite some time before we get to Doc McCoy's all-purpose shirt-pocket diagnostic machine, but as Moberg says, the doctor's traditional "black bag" may soon carry quite a few highly sophisticated but *small* monitoring and diagnostic tools. A microprocessor chip (Chapter 9) is the electronic equivalent of a TV-set chassis in a medicine capsule.

Realization of possibilities could be rapid as physicians become familiar with the microcomputer and its potential, and begin to work with local computer and electronics people to develop particular applications.

THE WRITER'S OFFICE

The writer is a human word processor, and he or she is also a small business. Depending on level of success, income, investments, and style of conducting business, the writer might make good use of a computer for business and tax purposes. But **word processing** is the primary application of the small computer for the professional writer.

From the writer's point of view, a small computer system designed expressly for word processing is preferable. The hardware is essentially the same for word processing as for data processing systems—both kinds have a CPU and bus, keyboard, disk or tape drives, screen (CRT) display, and a printer. The difference is mainly in the software (the programs), but the system designed with word processing in mind will have keyboard refinements—replacing software routines with function keys.

(These still evoke a software routine, but you don't have to go through any command procedure, you just press a key: to delete a letter or word, delete a line, add a line, shift a paragraph, or whatever.) The advantages of systems designed expressly for word processing were discussed in Chapter Four. The "dedicated word processor" is still usable as a data processor; it is only necessary to load data processing programs into the internal memory.

Like any other businessman or businesswoman, the writer should shop for a word processing system in a large, well-established computer store, with business systems more prominent than its hobby lines, and with dedicated word processing systems available for demonstration. The small and shakier hobby-oriented store could try to push inadequate systems. We would advise against shopping in a general electronics-goods store that handles stereo, Citizens Band gear, ham radio gear, computer games, and so forth. For such stores, computers are a sideline. Go to a *computer* store, or approach a small-computer systems house. You want to see complete word processing systems demonstrated. You will want to see "either-or-both" systems demonstrated. *Try them out yourself*, at length and at leisure. Take your time, compare, think.

If you buy the wrong system you will quickly go back to using your clunky old typewriter. Then you'll have an entire computer system gathering dust—while you're still making payments. Unless you are a want-ad marketing genius as well as a writer, unloading it will be a nightmare.

What is the "right" system? Somewhere out there is a system that is right for you—or as close to being right as the present state of the art allows. You will decide on what's right for you after you have been through several different system demonstrations. You will not buy the first one offered you (will you?).

Like everyone else being addressed in this book, you, as a writer, need to decide what you want a computer *for*—exactly what you want it to *do*. Then you must shop carefully for a system that can really do it. For most writers, it will be a system that demands the minimum of "computer expertise" on the user's part.

What It Can Do

We defined word processing in Chapter Four as "typing with a computer," but it is much more than that. It is a powerful aid to rewriting, editing, getting a manuscript just right, in minimum time, before a word is committed to paper. While there are word processing systems in which a skilled operator works blind, the typical microcomputer system has a TV-like display screen—the CRT. Everything "typed" on the computer's keyboard appears immediately on that screen. Errors may be corrected either at once, or later, at the writer's choice. Chapter Four mentioned the "Hemingway" system of writing, just getting it all out in a rush, and leaving organizing, correcting, and polishing for later.

Everything that is "typed" is stored on a magnetic disk or tape. The storage medium is "played back" for corrections or for printing out. By use of simple commands—or even of function keys—entire words, lines, sentences, paragraphs, or blocks of print may be shifted to another part of the text ("cut and paste" capability), or deleted. Words may be added or deleted anywhere. Typing errors may be corrected by simple strikeover or by special command. A winking **cursor** on the screen shows where the next character to be typed (or the next line or block of text to be shifted) will appear.

If that location is not satisfactory, function keys will shift the cursor to any spot desired. The screen can be blanked out on command (leaving its contents stored in memory), or the display can be **scrolled**, upward or downward, to bring preceding or succeeding material into view.

The program should allow for left and right justification, and for any kind of indenting, including indenting of entire paragraphs or blocks of text. Many printers are capable of line-and-a-half as well as single- and double-spacing, and the software should be able to take advantage of that. Typically, a writer's word processor will give any column width desired (up to eighty characters for a standard 8½ by 11 page) and good programs allow a column to be situated anywhere across a page. Variable column width may not seem important to the straight narrative writer, but it is important to, say, the script writer. The program should allow for automatic adjustment of top and bottom margins, and for variation of the desired number of lines per page. Some word processor programs give you features like automatic typing of your name and address across the top of every page, along with automatic page numbering.

With length of lines and number of lines automatically set for each page, word counts become much simpler. (Yes, even the word count could be computerized if you got fancy.)

Word processor programs provide ways for breaking words at the ends of lines. There are ways and ways of breaking lines, and some programs will accept a set of rules (or provide one). However, even the best program is essentially stupid. You may instruct it to hyphenate the *-ing* or *-ation* endings of words. Fine, but it will faithfully hypenate *k-ing* and *w-ing* and *n-ation* and *st-ation*. There are ways of getting around that, but perhaps you had better be resigned to making your own decisions.

Good programs allow for proportional spacing, and this gives you an opportunity to decide, before the end of a line, where or whether to split a word. The word will go on the next line if you decide not to, and proportional spacing will dress up the uncompleted line. This is **wraparound** capability.

When the command is finally given to print, the whole or any part of a document will appear on paper — formatted according to instructions entered prior to printout. Since all correction has been done on the display screen before printout, the very first copy can be letter-perfect.

Since the "manuscript" has been stored on a magnetic medium, it is a simple matter to print out a second hard copy for the writer's own archives. Farewell to carbon paper and flimsy onion-skin. The "manuscript" can be permanently stored on the disk, of course. The typical floppy disk or diskette can be plucked from the disk drive and stored away in a drawer.

However, disks cost several dollars apiece, and a paper copy for the file drawer is probably the most economical choice fr most writers, freeing the disks for re-use. Double-density and quadruple-density disks can hold the equivalent of several hundred pages, so that several articles or stories might be filed on one disk. This would require some sort of foolproof indexing system (involving a card file, or another disk and a software routine). We, the authors, confess to a die-hard bias in favor of a hard copy for the files. Perhaps in a few years we shall move with the times and entrust everything to disks or to bubble memories. Then we might even throw away our wastebaskets.

Nuts and bolts

The writer will usually want a single-user system. Of course, if you are prolific and successful you may employ a typist or even a secretary. His or her output can also be enhanced by use of a word processor. A single computer could still serve both of you, by use of separate work stations (terminals). Each of you would have your own keyboard-and-screen setup working with the same CPU. This is called timesharing or multiplexing (Chapters 2 and 3). It is a software function, not a hardware function. All computers inherently have the capability. The leading microcomputer brands now offer it as an option. You could buy a single-user system capable of conversion to dual-user status later.

An essential in the writer's computer system is a keyboard that is as much like a standard typewriter keyboard as possible. (*What*? Aren't they all like that?) Today, most good word-processor keyboards are based on the IBM Selectric typewriter design. The good computer keyboard will have one or more additional rows of keys for computer functions. Do not settle for a keyboard that uses letter keys as function keys with shifting. You want your shifting to take you back and forth between lower case and capitals. Did you know that many small computers, including most "hobby configuration" computers, have no provision for lower case letters at all? Beware!

Suppose "they" offer a four-row keyboard with character keys doubling as function keys, plus "a little software routine" to get you into lower case? Forget it. Anything that doesn't let you type just the way you type on a typewriter will shortly send you back to your typewriter.

There can be apparent exceptions. There are keyboards that seem to have a function printed on the vertical face of just about every key—but in effect have two SHIFT keys, a regular SHIFT and a FUNCTION shift. That would be acceptable.

The Computer's Printer

Another essential for the writer is a quality printer. This means daisy-wheel. Yes, there are quality dot-matrix printers, but the writer's output must look like good typewriter type. The dot matrix printer is adequate for many purposes, but not for the writer's. Its peculiar "typeface" may have a certain chic for enterprises whose printouts must shout "Look a' me, Ma, I'm usin' a COMPUTER!" but your editor would be unimpressed.

Presentation is at least half your battle, as many writers have learned in sorrow. The better your manuscript looks, the more it appeals to the editor even before he or she begins to read it. The perfection afforded by a good printer gives your manuscript the professional look it deserves. Any editor who can pay you any money at all is looking for professionalism. (Okay, you're an established professional, and your editors know it. But send them dot-matrix stuff and you'll get it back with a note: "Arthur, could you have somebody just type this?")

Daisy wheels are rugged, as discussed in Chapters Two and Eight, and they give "expensive typewriter" quality with nary a breakdown. (NEC "thimble" machines are also rugged, reliable.)

What if "something better than a daisy wheel" comes out by the time you are reading this book? Fine, but remember, you are not in the equipment-testing business. When that "something" has been on the market a few years and all the bugs are out of it, you might consider buying one. Provided, that is, that you can bear to part with the faithful daisy wheel that will still be spinning up a storm for you. Daisy wheels have been around for a long time and their bugs are pretty much extinct.

Daisy wheels will allow you practically any kind of type face you like. If you write in Japanese, you can even have Katakana.
Courtesy of QUME Corporation

Again, the NEC Spinwriter printers with a "thimble" are a variation on the daisy wheel idea. Everything that's good about daisy wheels is good about "thimbles" (Chapter 8).

Invest every dime you can in the quality keyboard and the quality printer. Buy as near the top of the line as you can.

Caveats

The writing profession includes a few extroverts and drivers of hard bargains (those guys who get an advance of half a million on the basis of an outline scribbled on a paper napkin over lunch). But it includes a disproportionate share of loners, timid spinners of fantasy, shrinking violets, Milquetoasts. These latter types are to the salesman as the trembling gazelle is to the leopard. *Pounce!* — and the salesman is unloading some Palaeolithic-era keyboard and a system with nothing like lower case in sight. Ask about lower case and you may be informed that lower case is something new in computers and the software for it is hard to get. You may be asked, "How often d'ya need lower case, anyway?" The tone will imply that anybody who is even tempted to use lower case is one of those closet whatchamacallits who ought to be locked up.

Milquetoasts are really tigers at heart, because they will fight like tigers to maintain their Milquetoast status. They can come up with rationalizations like, "I can get the funny keyboard and what you call the primitive system for a lot less money, and besides, the future is here and I've got to get with it — my friend Jack Bytechomper says I'm culturally deprived because I don't know BASIC, and when I learn it I can get around the limitations of the system." Sure. We like to save money ourselves, and we enjoy programming in BASIC. We could argue very forcefully in favor of going thou and doing likewise. But it's not for everybody.

Bring out that inner tiger, then, when you are in the computer store. If they haven't got what you want, there's something wrong with *them,* not you. Shop for a computer the way you shop for a typewriter. If the machine isn't right for you, it's no sale.

At all costs, the writer should — like any other businessman — shun the hobby-oriented system, with its rudimentary software, too-small memory, and narrow choice of peripherals. The hobby system may perhaps be induced to do "real" data processing and "real" word processing, but it will do them in the manner of Samuel Johnson's dog walking on its hind legs: remarkably, but not well.

This may fly in the face of advice the writer may be getting from a computer-oriented friend, whose well-meant and mostly unconscious tendency may be to turn the writer into a computer hobbyist. The friend is confident that with his know-how and the writer's money they can haywire up some kind of *kludge* that the writer can use as a word-processing system, real cheap. Never! It is said that no old-time railroad shop mechanic ever trusted a tool that he had not made and tempered himself. But when you need to use a pair of pliers, you just want a decent pair of pliers made by somebody who knew what he was doing. And you never felt you had to build your own typewriter. (What about that time you decided to write your eighteenth-century historical novel with quill pens? You botched up a few goose feathers and went back to your store-bought typewriter.)

Remember, computer-oriented people, whether hobbyist or professional, tend to be interested in the computer *qua* computer. The writer wants it as a tool. Like most readers of this book, the writer is interested in the computer secondarily. The application, not the system, entices him.

Avoid the kludge; acquire a tried-and-true system. Analyze your needs; scrutinize your budget; shop at leisure. Read all the sales literature carefully. Insist on having the systems demonstrated, with *you* at the keyboard. Are procedures really simple? Are the instructions clearly written? Do your inevitable bungles cause the computer to quit and suck its thumb? You will learn a lot, surprisingly quickly, in just a few hands-on demonstrations. Yes, it takes time to become a really proficient operator of a word processing system (like, a week, or a month — not the years it took you to become a decent typist) but you will quickly become adept at judging and comparing systems.

Remember, first off, the system has to let you "type" the way you type on a typewriter, or all its bells and whistles don't matter.

Most writers pride themselves on being nontechnical, at having studied the liberal arts and the humanities, English Lit rather than Engineering. Some writers reading this section may have flicked right to it, avoiding the "dull and irrelevant technical material" in the rest of the book. (And relying on Jack

Bytechomper to make the "technical" decisions.) But this book is written for non-technical people. Unlike Jack Bytechomper, its authors are writers, as Jack is not. We approach computers from the standpoint of the nontechnical reader, even if we can build our own kludges. We are not implying that other writers cannot learn to build kludges if they should want to, but the kludge is not a tool. We cut our teeth on established computer systems (big systems, pre-microcomputer) and learned on them. No matter what you want to do with a computer, you have to learn, and you have to start somewhere. If you haven't started with Chapter One of this book, we urge you to turn to it. Please study Chapters Two, Three, Four, Five, and Eight before you go out to shop. Don't get your education from a salesman—and as for Jack Bytechomper, use him to distract the salesman with shop talk while you put a demo system through its paces.

THAT BOTTOM LINE (FINANCING)

Computers can be financed, just like cars or typewriters or anything else. (They can also be leased, but let's defer discussion of that.) Dealers and systems houses (or OEMs) offer various financing deals, but often involving a third party who will own the contract, and who demands rather stiff interest and service charges. Your own personal or business bank would obviously be your first choice, though tolerable financing arrangements can be made by many vendors. The problem is, banks have stayed out of the business of financing computers, and your banker will start shaking his head the moment you mention the word. But there are ways of getting around "tradition".

Most professionals have business credit, but some, just getting started, may not. Writers, slaving away Bob Cratchit style in their little corners at home, may not have established any (never having thought to open a charge account at the stationery store). But good personal credit counts, of course. It is easily converted into business credit. The banker can help. He can at least advise. Go to the banker with a concise but well thought out presentation about why you need the computer, how it will increase your revenue, pay for itself. Stress that it's a microcomputer—an office machine, not a God of the Algorithm. Of course you've already been shopping around and can tell him what the computer would cost. You probably won't be sticking your neck out for any more than you would for a new car. The banker will warm to your prudence.

Now, if your credit is good with that banker, you may be able to get an unsecured loan. This has a typically lower rate of interest than a secured loan, because you're considered that good a risk. If they don't think you're quite in the class for *that much* unsecured money, maybe you can offer some collateral (since they won't want the computer) that the bank will like. But perhaps you could swing an unsecured note for, say half the price of the computer, and get the other half from your doting aunt or whomever.

Discount

Once you have a loan or loans, you have cash in hand. Now, if you offer the vendor cash, you can demand a *discount*. The discount will offset, or help offset, interest you must pay on the loan. Furthermore, you can dicker for a "cash basis" that gives you up to ninety days to pay the computer off, without charges or interest. You will have to part with some of it as a deposit, and interval payments at thirty, sixty, and ninety days. You may run into a hard-nosed vendor who will concede only thirty days as a "cash" basis. No sweat, since you have the cash in hand, but you can probably get ninety days down the street.

During those thirty to ninety days, of course, you will have the cash deposited in a savings account, which draws daily or monthly interest, dipping into it whenever you have to make a payment. Now you've got your discount, plus interest. And a motive to push for ninety days.

Of course you will want guarantees that a computer system will be delivered and running within the payoff period. You can't demand perfection as your acceptance criterion—the "turn-key" or "starter" software won't be tailored exactly to your business methods anyway—but you can expect to have a *bona fide* working system. With all the guarantees and warranties that have been discussed earlier. With microcomputer systems, you can usually expect to be in the computing business well within thirty days, even if you have arranged a ninety-day "cash" payoff.

You may find that the vendor doesn't want cash. He'll push his easy-payments plan, for thirty-six months or whatever. Or he may seem to insist that you lease. Either way, it will probably be because he (ahem!) gets a little return from the financial institution that is actually underwriting the deal. But here you are, with that begged or borrowed cash in your hands, so persevere.

If you have cash, most vendors will ultimately give in ("If I don't, somebody else will, and a bird in the hand...").

How big a discount should you ask for? Talk over your strategy with your banker and accountant. Talk with other business people who have bought computers. (It could be worth your while to buy them lunch.) With all your heads together you'll come up with a pretty good estimate of what the traffic will bear: ten percent, twenty percent, or whatever.

Besides, you've been seeing dealers and vendors, getting systems demonstrated. You know what you want and you know the ticket price. So you should already have opened the question of, "What kind of a deal will you give me for cash?" (Now, if you are like most people, a pushover for car salesmen, bring your accountant with you when you open the question of cash. And let's hope you have a real flinty-eyed accountant. Somebody cold and tough who can stand up to the vendor's blandishments for you. Get that cash deal with the discount!) Consider the discount offered as an *offer*. Consult your accountant, banker, etc., and come back with a counter-offer.

What if you have no cash? If your banker and your doting aunt have both demurely turned you away? If your spouse won't let you hock the utilities stock? Then you still have the vendor's something-down-and-easy-payments plan, and leasing. Get all the terms described to you (from several vendors and lessors) and decide what you can live with.

LEASING

Leasing is common with big main-frame computers and with minis, and many vendors offer lease deals for microcomputer systems. There are several forms of lease, and we do not claim to be experts on them. You will just have to look carefully at each kind of lease deal that is offered to you. Your accountant, of course, will be able to give you invaluable guidance.

Possibly the optimum lease plan is *lease-purchase*. As with automobiles, you can usually get into lease-purchase (leasing with a purchase option) with only a first-and-last payment, plus perhaps a moderate service fee. Each month, a portion of the lease payment is applied toward the principal of the system's cost—a lease is just another form of the secured loan. Each month, the purchase-outright price of the system gets a little lower. At the end of the term of the lease, half or less of the original cost will be outstanding. You can then purchase the computer with a balloon-type payment, retiring the remaining principal.

For that payment, you would probably be able to get a loan from your bank with comparative ease. The bank will know that you have been leasing the computer (after all, you'll have to tell them). They will know you have been stable with two or three years' worth of lease payments. They will know that this particular system is a good investment for you—if it were not, you would not be trying to buy it. You will have had a few years of testing it. The loan may well be unsecured (since banks get vexed at the idea of ever possibly having to foreclose on a computer, or to "repossess" a computer). Why not? You've had a history of making payments of similar or larger size and can probably go on making such payments indefinitely. (Obviously this computer has been an asset *and has been paying for itself.*) You are now considered top-drawer, eligible for an unsecured loan.

Usually, you can purchase the computer outright at any time during the term of the lease. They will accept cash (but not tender you a discount) for that. At the end of the lease term, if you still choose not to buy, the lessor must find a way to unload the computer, unless both parties agree to renew the lease. You are still on the hook until the unloading is completed.

If, during the term of the lease, you want to get out, you probably can with little trouble (but check on this beforehand), but the lessor will have to unload the computer, and you are legally involved until he succeeds.

Look carefully into the agreement about the unloading situation. Ethically, it should run something like lease-purchase for cars: if the lessor sells the property for the nominal cash value outstanding (analogous to the automobile "middle Blue Book" value), nobody owes anybody any further money. If he must sell it for less, you make up the difference. If he succeeds in selling it for more, he pays you the difference.

No matter how similar the lease deals are *in form* from dealer to dealer, do examine everybody's offered deal. Leasing is a competitive business, just like selling. A competitive lessor will acquire the system for as low a price as he can get, passing the saving along to you. Somebody taking a flyer in leasing may be high priced compared to someone who has leased out many computers.

There is, of course, the straight lease. You lease the system for a specified term, and when it's over, you and the lessor are quits, unless you both agree to renew. You don't worry about how he is going to unload the system once he gets it back from you. That's his problem. But you'll pay higher monthly payments throughout. And getting out early may not be easy.

TAX BENEFITS

Once you have bought a computer system, whether for cash-and-discount or on an installment plan, you can depreciate the equipment and take a tax break on that. You can take investment tax credit besides. Thus you have a yearly saving, that effectively pulls the cost of the computer down. Or your disposable cash up.

If you lease, whatever you pay for the lease each year is a straight business expense, so it comes off the top. This, too, effectively pulls your computer cost downward.

Dilemmas, dilemmas. What's the best strategy? Buy or lease? We can't help you with that here. But give your accountant all the facts before you decide. What he or she charges for the consultation will be a bargain.

Chapter Ten

THE BUTCHER, THE BAKER, THE CANDLESTICK JOBBER

People unfamiliar with computers may benefit from some examples of what businesses in similar lines have done. Certain things are common to all business computer applications, but every line of business is different, and so all applications are different. The executive contemplating the purchase of a computer may have doubts and questions as to what, specifically, a computer can do for his business. This chapter will present a few sketches of how small computers have been applied in various lines.

The owner or manager of almost any small business could probably benefit from this chapter's section on the small manufacturer. Everyone has problems with inventory control, production scheduling, sales timing and strategy, information gathering and channeling, and adapting the computer and the business to each other. This last involves enlisting the willing cooperation of the staff, and taking care to maintain staff morale.

The computer is a tool that will ultimately make the staff's job easier — not a predator that will eat the staff up. Make sure the staff knows this — especially your key people. You don't want a prized worker's anxiety to cut his efficiency or impair his or her willingness to help you get the most out of your computer. Anxiety comes in two forms: that "the computer will take over my job," and "I'll never learn how to use that thing." The computer cannot substitute for human judgment and skill, and today's microcomputer-based systems are just business machines anyone can learn to use.

Making the computer work for you involves some work on your part before you acquire it. Chapter 5 was devoted to analyzing your business, determining your needs, using a consultant if needed, and coming up with a system that will do the job. It was pointed out that just this pre-installation analysis will tell you many things about your business that you never knew before. Even so, getting the computer settled into the groove of your business is going to take some hands-on experience with it over a period of time.

Marshalling the information is one of your big problems. You have people on your staff who tend to carry entire production flows or inventory turn-around flows in their heads. They have never put these into words or charts. They are going to feel threatened when you insist that they do, when you pester them with questions on just how they get a widget built or how they keep the stock shifting so that the retail customer always sees fresh, stylish merchandise. But much as you appreciate the value of these people, you have had your worried hours about them. What if chain-smoking Harry has a heart attack? What if Florence decides to retire? What's it going to cost the business to train someone to replace them? How can you do it without Harry or Flo around as a teacher? Besides, even if you have a revelation from on high that Harry and Flo will be with you for many years to come, there will be certain analyses you and the computer must keep doing in order to keep costs down and revenues up (that's what the computer is for!). What they know, you and the computer have gotta know.

Various of your employees know certain things that you really don't. Lead times for this or that, optimum order quantities, most reliable sources, useful lore on materials or parts, whatever: all stuff that you and the computer need to know, and that the employees (a) don't realize you don't know; (b) don't realize that they know; (c) forget, neglect, or decide not to tell you. Bessie from Bookkeeping may have grasped intuitively that you are probably losing money by passing up the 10-day, 2-percent discounts but may be timid about "telling you how to run your business." Entice this kind of thing out of Bessie and check it out on the computer. You'll need a cost-projecting program that takes in the relevant information on interest rates, charges for beyond 90 days, etc., but it's no sweat to get one.

There will be countless things that people forget to tell you. Remember when your old college buddy taught you four-on-the-floor shifting? And the different goofs you kept making, with Old Buddy saying at each one, "Oh, yeah—you've gotta do *this* before you do *that*"? And Old Buddy bellowing at you to double-clutch to shift down in his car, without defining "double-clutch" and with you being too embarrassed to ask? Sooner or later you got 90 percent of the information out of Old Buddy and picked the other 10 percent by trial and error. There doesn't seem to be much to shifting a car's gears, but there is more to it than either you or Old Buddy had thought.

It's those unconscious steps, the "instinctive" stuff, that you have got to remember to tell the computer—and have got to cross-examine out of the Old Buddies on your staff. Your "computerizing" won't work until the computer can really follow what goes on in your business.

You may find yourself with a plethora of information that you seemingly can't use, at first. It will take experience with the computer, on the part of you and your staff, before you and your key people realize what the computer can do for you, and acquire some savvy on how to "get it out of the computer." It may take some time before it occurs to some of them—or to you—even to wonder whether the computer might help with a certain problem. You will, in a sense, be breaking in a computer the way you break in a promising new employee. Actually, you will be breaking in yourself and your staff on how to use this versatile new tool.

Share the tool

Try not to envision your computer system as a sort of spider poised at the center of a web, with all information coming to a central point. Your department heads, supervisors, foremen, salespeople, and so on need information, too, and they need to process information, and they need simplified ways to submit reports. *They* need to use the computer. They need access to it—usually right to its keyboard.

They'll be afraid of it. Computers are for experts, aren't they? *Not yours.* Yours has one or more CRT or other display screens that present the user with a menu. The menu asks some question like, "What do you want to do?" and offers a numbered list. Choosing a number causes the machine to present a second menu for the specific task; choosing items off that menu causes instructions and prompts to be displayed. The user pecks a key here and a key there, types in some numbers or words, pecks another key, and the computer keeps guiding him through the process of getting what he wants. See Chapter 3 about how that works.

If your whole operation is one small store, or one small loft job-shop, or one medium-sized warehouse with rather few employees, you can probably get away with one computer work station, and perhaps one employee whose work can be interrupted now and then to operate the computer for somebody else. (But you will find people from the floor rushing in to jiggle the keyboard themselves — why bother Maisie?) But if you have departments, separate rooms and shops, separate floors, and so on, you will want local terminals — keyboard-and-display boxes that put the computer at anyone's fingertips. (Don't worry; you can have this arranged so that that smart kid down in plating won't have access to management secrets; your sensitive-data software can be "blind" to any terminal or terminals you designate; also, sensitive programs and files can be password-equipped.)

You want a terminal station where Harry can step right up and order more steatite from the stockroom. Of course Harry is a great mechanic but can't spell, and the computer doesn't recognize Harry's capricious variations on the spelling of "steatite." No matter. You can go fancy, and have several likely variations programmed in. Or you can stick a card on the computer somewhere that has crucial words pre-spelled for Harry. Or you can have him order it by stock number.

For the retail store, as far as your sales clerks are concerned, the point-of-sale terminals are just "electronic cash registers." There are many versions of these, including UPC scanners (which use the Universal Product Code of black-and-white parallel lines on product labels). The point-of-sale terminal eliminates a normally tremendous paper flow; the information going into the computer goes into the data base for all kinds of running accounting, including continuous inventory update.

Remember, even your *small* computer can have several terminals or work stations, just like the giants back at IBM headquarters.

What if your business is spread out geographically? For example, you are a trucking company, and you consider yourself a small one. But you have terminals (in your industry's meaning of the word) in eight cities in three states. At least you have end-points, turn-around points, and some of them have small local offices. How do you tie them in? Two ways. You can use terminals hooked up to your main office by telephone lines, through modems (see Chapter 8). Or, as some trucking companies have already done, you can let returning trucks carry cassettes or disks of the remote offices' daily reports, requisitions, or raw data back to your main office. The information will get to you overnight, at zero extra cost. How about that? Either way, you will want some form of "smart terminal"—a small, stand-alone, perhaps one-piece computer (everything in one cabinet) at the far-end locations.

"Why not let the trucks carry paper, and have somebody at the home office punch the paperwork into the computer?" Because your clerks at the remote office will have spent time entering that data onto paper. Your headquarters computer will have to spend time re-entering it in the computer. If the boys in River's End or Pocatello have put it directly onto disk or tape, that's that.

THE SMALL MANUFACTURER

The computer is a management tool, especially a production management tool. It has been called "a great hindsight tool," because the computer is no magician. It can't see the future— even though you can use it for forecasting. The computer cannot learn from your mistakes. However, you can, and the computer can come up with the kinds of information you need in order to analyze experience and improve your present and future decisions. The computer cannot tell you ahead of time that you will generate too much scrap on a certain job run. But it can show you immediately how much scrap has been produced, and what this breaks down to in costs for materials and production time. Then it's up to you or your shop manager to find out what went wrong. Perhaps your investigation will turn up information that the computer can use to help you head off a similar mishap.

Again, there is no magic about the computer. It isn't even human, and it certainly isn't wise. How much scrap is too much scrap? There is no way the computer can know that. But you know, or your floor manager knows. The computer can be told that, and can be instructed to flag management any time scrap starts getting out of hand. Sometimes you may not know "how much is too much," because you are doing something new. But the computer has a sharp quantitative memory and filing system; over time it can help you work out what the quantity should be, just by comparing good runs and bad runs. It can summarize in seconds or minutes "experience information" that it would take you days to retrieve from manual records — or that you could never accurately retrieve from the memories of the old hands on the floor who have been running their operations by the seats of their pants.

The computer is not only a record-keeper and calculator, it is a summarizer. You have to specify the summaries you need, and see that the computer can deliver them to you. This is a matter of programming and formatting.

The computer's hindsight can be immediate. It can do its Monday-morning quarterback exercises while the production work is in progress, keeping track of what is going on. You don't have to rely on the after-the-production-run-is-over hindsight, or end-of-the-fiscal year hindsight. You can have fresh information for immediate decisions. So can your floor superintendent, your machine tools foreman, or whoever needs spot information. It's a great searchlight for finding bottlenecks.

Inventory

You want to keep inventory lean so as to reduce both your monetary investment in stock *and* the carrying costs. These typically run 15 to 20 percent per year on the total value of the inventory. Stock that is sitting idle is actually eating up money. The computer can finger the items that are always overstocked. Some items can be sold or scrapped, removing them as liabilities. But you also want out-of-stock and below-minimum information. You want the computer to flag items that need to be reordered on the basis of lead time. Also, if any one part or material will be needed for several projects, one big money-saving order can be made, rather than several small-lot orders. And there will be no need to order an overstock to make sure of having enough. The computer will show the total of what will be needed.

There are established computer procedures for organizing materials procurement and minimizing expense, that are difficult in theory (and impossible in practice) to carry out with manual inventory-control methods. But they work with speed and dispatch as computer procedures, because the computer can relate several different files (provided it has good *data base* software — see Chapters 2 and 4) and summarize information quickly.

You are going to modify products, making design and engineering changes, substituting materials, and so on. The computer can keep updating the bills of materials, so that Purchasing stops ordering teflon for the widget lamination when you've found that mylar will do, and remembers to order the extra 4-40 screws for that corner that gets the most strain.

Production costs

Estimating these is often by "educated guess." An accurate estimate can be expensive and time-consuming by manual methods, especially if there is going to be a serious change in the product or in procedures, in materials or labor, or in lot size. The computer can work out standard costs because it has been collecting and organizing information on current runs. It can "model" how the cost will differ if something is changed. Along with you, the computer needs "experience" about this. Let's say the last run of 1000 widgets cost 2100 hours of directly attributable labor, for an average of 2.1 hours per widget. The new widgets are going to have four more screws, and Harry can reliably guesstimate how much set-up, drilling, tapping, inspection, and screw-in time that will take. So, you and the computer have a basis for working out what the next run should cost. And the computer can give you a reliable labor cost, because it can digest breakdowns of who does what for how long at what hourly rate. Also, after you've done several runs of widgets under various conditions, the computer can show you best case, worst case, and median cost, and offer a figure on what the cost "should be." And you will of course look into your best and worst cases to learn what went right and what went wrong.

Inflation gallops along, and for projected costs, the computer can take into account any inflation rate you give it to work with. If conditions suddenly change, for better or worse, you can get the computer to modify its prognostications instantly.

The computer can't see the future, but you can. You have a sideline of brake-temperature detectors for railway cars, and business is light. But in a period of one month you find that seven major cities have voted in subway systems, and all will be under construction by next spring. With the help of the computer it won't take you long to find out what you'll need in the way of additional equipment, plant, labor, inventory, and financing to cash in. You can model what your revenue will be if you let the subway gadget take over more of your operation, or if you keep other production lines running while you make subway gadgets with an expanded facility, and what this will cost, given the projected trends in interest rates and inflation. You can get accurate bids in, early.

A specific manufacturing industry: Clothing

A clothing manufacturer needs to generate cutting tickets, as well as maintain inventory records. Software already exists for this; one package maintains files on the warehouse location of each piece, the number of pieces in each lot, the original cloth length before shrinking, the width, the shrunken length, the cutting allowance required, the specification of related lining and other materials and buttons or fasteners, and so on. The package offers a model file, with descriptions of the garments, their manufacturing specifications and requirements, special features, etc.

Perhaps with modifications, a software package like this one ought to be useful for manufacturers of tents, awnings, seat covers, sleeping bags, soft luggage, special tarpaulins, or anything that uses cloth or cloth-like materials, and similar processes: stretching, cutting, seaming, etc.

CONSTRUCTION AND LUMBER

A construction company would of course have use for all business functions of a computer — payroll, accounts receivable and payable, general ledger and so on. Like the manufacturer, the contractor needs rapid, accurate job costing, and also equipment management. Some software exists specifically for this industry.

It seems to us that a little demand from the industry would bring forth software on matters like equipment status: a daily report on where every bulldozer or backhoe is, how long it has been there, how long it is expected to be there, which pieces are in the shops for which repairs, which ones are due for routine servicing or overhaul, what operation, maintenance, and repairs are costing on each piece and total, how much revenue each piece is earning, and so on — plus summary reports of original purchase price, amortization, depreciation, salvage value now, salvage value at end of depreciation, insurance costs. Any combination of these items could be diddled into summary reports.

Any construction company would probably appreciate programs for quick analyses of buying *vs.* leasing for special equipment needed only on certain jobs, and for tax-advantage analysis of the optimum time for retiring a piece of equipment and replacing it with a new one.

The job status board can certainly be computerized — going all the way back to preparation of a bid through contract signing and commencement, what stage each job is in, what the holdups and bottlenecks are, cumulative costs to date, flagging of out-of-line cost items, estimated time to completion, and so on.

We cannot say that the software exists for these items we have been speculating about. But it certainly can be generated, as the word gets back to the programming houses that construction firms are asking for it. Of course any firm can have it ginned up in the process of tailoring off-the-shelf business-industrial software packages to specific company use.

Lumber and building materials

Suppose we describe just one program, developed by Jim Schreier, Associate Editor of *Interface Age*, who reported on it in June, 1979. Schreier simply calls the program LUMBER. It calculates board footage, square footage, cost per 100 or cost per each of 35 different items (including hardware); it figures respective costs, adds sales taxes and drayage charges and gives a net total. The format is that of a standard lumber yard or materialman's bid. Thus it is suitable for bidding on total construction and remodeling packages — but could be directly useful to the customer (contractor or homeowner) for working out estimates of what a project will cost. The program allows parameters for figuring costs on sheetrock, insulation, nails and other building hardware. The program is short and sweet as versatile programs go. It seems to us that the general building materials yard could adapt a program like this to ring the same kinds of changes on cement block, brick, tile, glass, construction steel, concrete, prefab doors and windows, and so on, for heavier construction.

WAREHOUSES

A warehouse obviously has inventory problems, and shipping schedule problems, both out and in. A warehouse order involves the customer identity and address, ship-to point, customer purchase order number, invoice number, and item codes. Software exists to cover this, and the item codes may be defined by the user (the warehouse manager). As with a manufacturer, the warehouse has use for programs that track inventory flow, along with other standard business software.

REAL ESTATE

A favorite field for microcomputer programmers the past few years has been real estate (and real estate development). Only a couple of years ago it seemed rather nice to have a simple program for figuring out the mortgage payments on a home loan. Today the real estate office can compute the capitalization rate—the "free and clear" cash flow after debt service on income and speculation properties, divided by the purchase price and expressed as a percentage. Also important is the matter of accounting returns: the sum of all returns less the amount of the initial investment, divided by the term of the investment, *and* the discount factor—how valuable is a payment received one year from now or *n* years from now? The sophisticated real estate office wants a payback period analysis—how many years will be required to recover the investment (the fewer the better, nowadays!). Real estate people are interested in net present value, profitability index, internal rate of return and adjusted internal rate of return. All of these things can be pretty hairy with manual procedures, but routine and quick for a small computer.

What about property management? This involves lease renewal lists, tenant status reports, cash collection reports, income statements and income summaries, disbursements by a general ledger account, and so on. In a manual system the requisite information is probably "all there" in the bales of paper files, but tedious (though imperative!) to extract by manual means. All the same information in a small computer's data base can be marshalled into any kind of handy report as needed, through choice or design of software.

The real estate developer needs to keep track of prices and costs for mechanicals, plumbing, wiring, general contracting, all kinds of job costing, and may even need to process data on surveying and land leveling. The computer can replace tedious and error-prone manual methods and immensely speed up the extraction of information needed *now* in concise reports.

INSURANCE

Program packages are beginning to appear for insurance office use. One fire and casualty package processes dwelling risks for single buildings and apartment houses, and household contents data, including lists for use in apartment houses or even mercantile buildings. It will automatically rate, code, endorse, and renew dwelling policies. This kind of software stands as a model for software for any kind of insurance policy on any kind of building with any kind of contents. The policy maker or underwriter has to specify to the programmer what is needed, what kinds of forms are involved, and the programmer can run with that. The software just described will maintain loss data from historical review and update, produce cancellation notices and status reports of individual risks, produce declarations and endorsement pages, and generate statistical, accounting, and direct billing records.

Remember, a computer can be programmed to produce reports in any format—including the filling out of preprinted forms; and, from boilerplate stored on file disks, generate individualized policies, with lengthy "original" policies printed out in rather few minutes. This is a matter of **word processing** techniques. Word processing software with the "global editing" feature will replace all references to "Jones and Co." with "Smith, Thompson, and Zarevich" automatically, once the operator has specified the change.

A PORTRAIT STUDIO

What about the small retail business? One local portrait studio profiled in *Small Business Computers* magazine for January 1979 has several uses for its microcomputer besides the bare-bones applications of accounts receivable, inventory control, and other standard business concerns. (It also calculates amortization for installment loans, a sort of elementary task for any computer.) Used for cost analysis, the computer showed the owners that they were overspending on photographic printing and finishing that they let out to subcontractors; they profited by doing more of these jobs in-house. In contrast, they were underspending on advertising as compared with the national average for their type and level of business. The computer gave them figures on which they launched a successful campaign. One of their programs keeps track of growth every month, and calculates, months in advance, the gross sales needed to maintain a regular growth rate.

The studio makes heavy use of the computer as a word processor. The computer prints mailing list labels, and produces personalized form letters to customers and prospects. It also produces "Studi-O-Grams" for bulk mailings on specials being offered. A computer file is kept on every baby born in the local area. On birthdays, a promotional is sent to the parents on a special photographic package. The studio gets a 17 percent return on these promotionals, as opposed to a 3 percent national average. A sideline of the studio is pictorial church directories, on which the computer does the typesetting.

Most of the studio's business is on a cash basis, but the computer prints out the 10 to 15 statements needed every month.

PHARMACY

Prescriptions, paperwork, and patient profiles are the worries of the pharmacist. The small computer can streamline operations, enhance accuracy, update files, and lower the cost of recordkeeping.

Imagine a small computer's terminal at the pharmacist's lab station. He enters a prescription through the keyboard. The CRT displays the requisite information. Then, while the pharmacist is filling the prescription, the computer prices it, reduces the inventory on that drug, and updates the patient profile, adding that prescription. Then it prints out a label and an invoice/receipt. The pharmacist snaps the label and receipt from the printer, sticks the label on the bottle, places the bottle on the customer-pickup shelf, and enters the next prescription.

A dream? Pharmacist Ron McClellan of McClellan's Pharmacy has had such a system in operation since early 1979. (He described it in *Small Business Computers* for August/September 1979.) McClellan's system does more. It accurately and *legibly* fills out third-party payment forms (Medicare, Blue Cross, union, etc.) so that none are returned for reworking; this speeds up payment. This is important, since third-party paying agencies take two or three months to honor claims. The system also keeps an updated profile on every patient.

Pharmacists who maintain patient profiles perform a real service, able to blow the whistle if a physician inadvertently prescribes a drug that will react unfavorably with other drugs the patient is taking, or to which the patient has shown past sensitivity. In some states, patient profiles are now legally required. McClellan expects the profile to be required by national law soon.

It is certainly convenient for the pharmacist to have any patient's profile instantly displayed on the CRT before him, or printed out on paper.

McClellan "designed" the system—not the hardware, of course, and not the software. He analyzed his needs and had clear, accurate specifications for what he needed to have the system do. The vendor came up with some initial software, and McClellan retains a programmer to generate additional programs. New applications for the microcomputer keep presenting themselves. "Pre-computer," McClellan thought he was going to have to hire two new employees just to keep up with paperwork, but now keeps his pharmacy running efficiently with its original staff of four, plus the computer.

RESTAURANT

The restaurant computer system can make use of terminals both in the dining room and in the kitchen. The cashier would have a terminal, of course—some form of the electronic cash register. But the waitresses would have one or more terminals also, for entering orders. The orders would be printed out on the terminals in the kitchen.

The order appears in the kitchen with waitress identification, time of order entry, and a complete specification of the meal. The cook would find everything absolutely legible. When the order is filled, the cook so signifies on his terminal. The computer, meanwhile, has priced every item, and ultimately those prices will be printed out on the waitress's itemized check, with total, tax, and grand total.

The "waitress terminal" may come in several forms. Probably the most usable form, for short-order restaurants, is a flat panel (no visible keys) with a translucent overlay divided into rectangles on which up to 90 menu selections are printed. Beneath the rectangles are pressure or temperature sensitive switches (finger temperature) that activate the "key electronics" corresponding to each item. Of course "blank" spaces can be left for daily specials. The waitress doesn't type; she just taps the "Veal Parmeggiana" or "Cheddarburger Supreme" rectangle.

The computer keeps a running tally of what is being sold, giving the manager and chef plenty of warning and lead time for replenishing stock. At desired intervals the computer will give the executives analyses of what sells best when. The computer can also flag menu items that are going out of stock for the day, signaling the waitress.

The equipment exists. We confess to not knowing much about it because, while we have had hands on experience with many keyboards and even the unconventional Writehander™, and all manner of typical big-computer and microcomputer peripherals, we have not worked hands-on with these special restaurant terminals. We have seen a few, and have queried managers about them in what were not good note-taking circumstances. Your vendor will know where to find them all, and can report to you on features and price for a considerable variety.

Would a flat-panel, no-typing terminal enable the waitress to specify things like rare, medium, medium-rare, well done, and so on? Probably. That looks to us like a Mickey Mouse-level problem for both the hardware and software designers.

Restaurants that have used such systems report that the waitress is left with more time for interaction with the customers which enables her to push extras: appetizers, special salads or deluxe dressings, wines, cocktails, desserts. The bar also has a terminal or terminals. Depending on the particular system, the waitress can enter bar orders or just tell the bartender. Either way, her bar bill will be printed out on the customer check. Extras are a rich source of added revenue.

At the cashier's printing terminal, an itemized receipt can be given the customer for his tax or other purposes. Meanwhile, the bookkeeping for the day is being automatically done by the computer, sale by sale and item by item. The entire day's (and night's) transactions are stored on disk, not only for the cashier, but for the kitchen and bar: inventory is under control. Print-outs for executive purposes may be commanded at any time.

FINDING OUT MORE

Much of the information in this chapter was gleaned from computer magazines, notably *Interface Age*, *Small Business*

Computers, and *Computer Decisions.* These three are heavily business-oriented, though many other magazines, including *Byte, OnComputing,* and *Creative Computing,* often carry articles of interest to business. It is worth the executive's time to scan several of these each month, and to subscribe to one or two that seem to meet the needs of one's specific business. By the time you read this book these magazines will have described or announced many new developments in business software, and of course the computer houses that want the business market advertise in them. Most computer stores have a variety of small-computer magazines on display and for sale.

GLOSSARY

absolute value
The numerical value of a real number, regardless of its sign; thus, -5 has the same absolute value as $+5$.

accumulator
A holding register in a computer's **arithmetic logic unit** for arithmetic and instructions for input-output operations. Data words fetched from memory go to the accumulator; final results go from the accumulator to memory.

ALU
See **Arithmetic Logic Unit**.

address
(n.) A number or name that identifies a particular location in **memory**, a **register**, or other data source or depository.

address bus
A unidirectional set of signal lines over which address information passes to identify a memory location or an **I/O device**.

analog-to-digital conversion
The conversion of a continuously variable (analog) value, such as a voltage, into a coded **digital** signal consisting of **bits** of equal length and value.

ALGOL
Algorithmic Language, a **high-level language** for scientific applications.

algorithm
A set of steps or processes for solving an arithmetical problem.

alphameric data

Data presented in both alphabetic and numerical form (such as mailing list entries, or billing data).

AND

A logical operation in which all input conditions must be true for the output to be true, so that the function "*a* AND *b* = *c*" is expressed by the following **Truth Table:**

A	B	C
0	0	0
0	1	0
1	0	0
1	1	1

APL

A **P**rogramming **L**anguage, one of several early **high-level** languages designed to simplify and facilitate the programming of a computer.

applications programs

Programs designed to perform specific problem-solving tasks, such as payroll or mailing list.

Arithmetical Logic Unit

The circuitry within a computer's **central processing unit** that performs arithmetic operations and associated logic functions (abbreviated ALU).

ASCII

American **S**tandard **C**ode for **I**nformation **I**nterchange, an **alphanumeric** code used in most computers and for telegraphic and similar communications using **teleprinter** machines.

assembler

A program that translates mnemonic instruction symbols (from a higher-level program) into binary coding in the particular computer's own **machine language**.

assembly program

See **assembler**.

assembly language

A system of programming notation in which data and machine instructions are represented by mnemonic symbols; an **assembler** will convert the mnemonics into machine language.

audit trail

A series of records that enables a figure to be verified by tracing it back to the original invoice or other record of transaction. The records may be accountants' journals (on paper) or, in a computer system, part of the data base.

base number

The **radix** of a number system: two is the radix of the binary system (base 2); eight is the radix of the octal system (base 8); ten is the radix of the decimal system (base 10). In modern number systems there is never an exclusive symbol for the base number or radix, which is always expressed by combining 1 and 0: 10.

BASIC

Beginner's **A**ll-purpose **S**ymbolic **I**nstruction **C**ode, a **high-level** computer language designed to give nonexperts access to computers; the language most commonly used with microcomputers.

baud

A unit of information transfer; in microcomputers the baud is defined as one **bit** per second.

binary coded decimal

A system of representing decimal numbers numeral by numeral as binary equivalents, so that a number such as 7325 is translated into separate four-digit clusters of binary digits:

7	3	2	5
0111	0011	0010	0101

which are then combined into **bytes** or **words** that maintain the original decimal place value:

01110011	00100101
7 3	2 5

binary coding

The rendering of data into a code that uses only two values or symbols — 1 and 0 — to express all information.

binary numbers

Numbers using only two digits, 1 and 0, to express all numerical values of any size.

binary system

A number system in which the radix, or base number, is **two** and which therefore can have only two digits or symbols, 1 and 0. Like the more familiar **decimal system** the binary system employs **place value** and all values are based on exponents (powers) of the base number.

bistable device

A device that has two stable states and can thus store or express a logical 1 or a logical 0 at any given time.

bit

Binary dig**it**, which can have a value of 0 or 1 (equivalent in electric circuits to "off" or "on"), and is the basic unit of computer memory, coding and data transmission.

black box

Any device whose internal components and design do not matter to the user, because only its function does. A pocket calculator is a black box to most users; they need not care how it works.

Boolean algebra

A system of mathematical logic treating of the relationships (or "operators") AND, OR, NOT, etc., and using only the values 1 and 0 to express truth or falsehood of logical propositions, developed by the British mathematician George Boole in the 19th century.

bootstrap

1. Technique or device that will attain a desired state by means of its own action. 2. *v.* To use a bootstrap device or technique to initiate a process.

bootstrap loader

A simple program containing few instructions which enables a computer to accept a more complex program. The next program to be accepted is usually an "absolute loader" that enables the computer to accept **operating system** and **applications** programs. In older computers the bootstrap loader was implemented by throwing switches in a coded sequence on a front panel. In most microcomputers the bootstrap loader is resident in **read only memory**, where it cannot be erased, and from which it will act whenever the computer is either turned on or reset.

bubble memory

A compact memory device consisting essentially of a thin single-crystal sheet of magnetic material in which tiny, distinct "bubbles" of magnetization may be created. The presence and polarization of the bubbles can represent digital information. Like the magnetization of particles in a magnetic recording tape, the magnetic bubbles are quasi-permanent and a bubble memory is **non-volatile**.

buffer

A memory storage device of limited capacity, used to hold one or a few data words being transferred between the computer's main memory and its **CPU** or between the computer and a **peripheral**. Buffers have various uses including the matching of devices having different speeds or modes of transmitting information.

bus

Essentially a set of connection lines between various components of a computer and between the computer and its peripherals.

byte

A group of eight binary digits (or a memory cell that can store eight bits) usually treated as a unit; the byte is a data **word** in "8-bit" computers or half a word in "16-bit" computers. Some small (usually hobby- or training-type) microcomputers handle data in a four-bit array called a "nibble" (often spelled "nybble" or "nyble" for no defensible reason).

carry

In arithmetic, the operation of adding one or more numerical units to the next higher place (power of the base); in computers, a signal produced when an arithmetical carry has been made.

cassette drive

A tape cassette machine designed for use with a computer and operation by the computer program; typical microcomputer cassette drives use cassettes mechanically identical to audio cassettes.

cathode-ray tube

A vacuum tube with a face, or screen, backed by a lumines-cent coating which can glow when struck by a thin beam of electrons from a "gun" at the far end of the tube. The position and intensity of the beam can be varied so as to produce patterns of light and darkness on the screen, which results in such displays as television pictures, oscilloscope traces, or data characters from a computer. Abbreviated CRT.

Central Processing Unit

The "brain" of the computer, containing the **arithmetic logic unit** and various control and scratchpad registers. Abbreviated CPU.

chip

A formed flake of silicon or other **semiconductor** material containing an **integrated circuit**. A chip is always housed in a protective-connective device (such as **DIP**) that is often miscalled a "chip."

checksum

A problem with a known answer, resident in the computer system, that is used periodically to check for proper operation.

clock

An electronic circuit in a computer that is a source of timing and synchronizing signals. The computer's clock is controlled by a quartz crystal ground to vibrate at the clock's frequency and which keeps its own time — it need not be synchronized with a "real-time" clock.

clock lines, clock bus

The conducting traces, equivalent to wires, of a **bus** structure devoted to connecting the computer's internal electronic clock circuit to the **CPU**.

code

A system of symbols (characters) and rules for representing, transmitting, and storing information; in binary coding, combinations of the symbols 1 and 0 serve for all manner of information.

coding

The particular sequence of code symbols or characters that represents a coded piece of information; the design of a program; the act of rendering information into code.

COBOL

Common Business-Oriented Language, a **high-level** computer language.

compiler

A computer program which translates **high-level** language statements into machine language, usually generating more than one machine instruction for each statement. The compiler translates each instruction once, leaving the translation in the machine for subsequent uses of the instruction during the processing sequence. Compare with **interpreter**.

complement

A number which results from manipulating another number against its **base** according to a set of rules.

complementing

The process of converting a number of any size to one of its possible **complements** according to a chosen set of rules.

control bus, control lines

The signal lines, analogous to wires, in a **bus** structure that carry control signals between the **CPU** and other components of a computer system.

Control Unit

The circuitry in a **CPU** that carries out control functions as distinct from arithmetical functions.

CPU

The **central processing unit** of a computer.

CRT display

A data display on a computer or **terminal** utilizing a **cathode-ray tube**.

CRT terminal

A **terminal** incorporating a keyboard and a CRT display.

cursor

A position indicator in a **CRT display** that shows where the next character will be entered or which locates a character to be deleted or corrected.

cut and paste capability

A feature in a **word processing** program that permits moving a paragraph or other entire block of information to a different location in the text.

DAC
Digital-to-analog Converter.

daisy wheel printer
A printing machine whose moving printing head has a number (usually 96) of radial arms or "petals" with a type character at the end of each; a small piston or hammer drives the character against an inked ribbon, thus printing the character on paper.

data
1. Any and all items of information — numbers, letters, symbols, facts, statements, etc. which can be processed or generated by a computer. 2. Numerical information as distinct from non-numerical information. 3. The processable information content of a computer's memory and storage devices as distinct from the instructional (program) information.

data base
The entire collection of data stored in the computer system, organized so that quick and efficient searching, sorting, analyzing, and relating of data elements can be accomplished by use of key words, subject headings, etc.

data base management system
An elaborate computer program for manipulating all the data stored in a computer system. Abbreviated DBMS.

data bus, data lines
The signal lines, analogous to wires, in a computer bus structure that carry information rather than address or command signals.

data counter
A circuit that can be set to an initial address number and which will sequentially access new addresses for the **CPU** as program instructions are carried out, one at a time.

data line
See **data bus**.

data processor
A device, usually electronic, that can record and handle information. A data processor is not necessarily a computer though all computers are data processors. An abacus and a card-sorting machine are data processors.

DBMS
Data base management system.

debug
1. To search for, correct, and eliminate errors or conflicting statements or procedures in a computer program. 2. To detect and correct wiring or design errors or sources of malfunction in the computer itself.

decimal system
The number system based on the number ten and powers of ten, employing **place value** so that a digit or numeral's position within the number represents a definite power of ten and some definite multiple of it.

dedicated system
A computer system devoted to a single purpose, such as **word processing** or industrial process control.

digital
1. An adjective referring to positive whole numbers (integers) smaller than the radix of a number system — 0 through 9 in the decimal system, 0 and 1 in the binary system. 2. Denoting use of digital values rather than constantly varying or variable values in a computer or other electronic system, for example, the use of 1 and 0 for computer coding to build numbers that can represent any value, integer or non-integer.

digital-to-analog conversion
The process of converting a digital number value into a physical quantity, such as a voltage or a mechanical displacement (turn of a shaft, position of a plotter pen).

digital-to-analog converter
A device that carries out **digital-to-analog conversion**. Abbreviated DAC.

DIP
Dual-in-line-package (often miscalled "chip").

disk
In computer systems, a rotating flat circular sheet of thin plastic or metal with magnetized surfaces, on which data **bits** may be stored in a manner analogous to tape recording.

disk drive
A computer-operated machine for enabling the computer to store data on and retrieve data from a rotating magnetized

disk. The drive contains a motor, read-write heads, and associated electronics.

diskette
A **floppy disk** 5¼ inches in diameter, also known as "minifloppy", "minidisk", etc.

disk files
Organized collections of data formatted and filed on magnetic storage **disks,** either **hard** or **floppy.**

disk operating system
A computer program that permits the computer to work with and operate one or more **disk** storage units and which usually provides other internal computer-operating programming. Abbreviated DOS.

documentation
All information about a particular computer program or set of programs, including user operating instructions, troubleshooting lore, program design philosophy, labeling or explanation of each program step, etc., usually provided as a manual.

DOS
Disk operating system.

dot matrix printer
A printing machine that forms characters as patterns of dots. The dots lie within a grid, or matrix, of definite dimensions: 5×7 dots, or 7×9 dots, etc. Impact printers form characters by use of a vertical array of 7 or 9 rods that strike through an inked ribbon. Non-impact printers either use flying ink droplets (guided by a controllable magnetic or electrostatic field) or beams of heat energy focused on thermally sensitive paper.

dual-in-line package
A small protective housing that provides circuit pin connections for an **IC chip.** Abbreviated DIP, often miscalled "chip."

dynamic RAM
A form of the semiconductor **random access memory** in which stored information must be maintained by **refresh** cycles even while computer power is turned on.

EAROM
Electrically alterable read-only memory.

EBCDIC
Extended Binary Coded Decimal Interchange Code, an 8-bit coding system used in some large computers.

electrically alterable read-only memory
A form of the **read-only memory** that is permanent under regular operating conditions but whose content may be altered deliberately by electrical means. Abbreviated EAROM.

electronic mail
Personal or other messages generated on a computer and stored in the memory of another, usually remote, computer connected to the first by telephone line or similar means.

EPROM
Erasable programmable read-only memory.

erasable programmable read-only memory
A form of the **PROM** in which the contents of a PROM chip may be altered by a technique employing an ultraviolet light source. Abbreviated EPROM.

external memory
See **mass storage**.

even parity
A form of **parity** checking in which a byte containing a seven-bit character code has either a 1 or a 0 (eighth bit) added so that the total number of ones in the byte will be even.

Exclusive OR
A logic function whose outcome is true if any one of its inputs is true, but false if all are true, so that

A	B	C
0	1	1
1	0	1
0	0	0
1	1	0

Abbreviated XOR.

Exclusive OR gate

A logic gate to execute the Exclusive OR function, whose symbol is

$$A - \ \rangle\!\!\!\!\!D\!\!\!\!> - - C$$

A—)⟩D⟩— −C
B—)

field

In computers, a unit of information that serves as a building block for a **record**.

file

In computers, an organized collection of related **records**. A payroll file would have a complete payroll record on each employee.

firmware

Operating **software** permanently committed to a computer by virtue of being stored in **ROM** circuits, or, in ancient computers, by virtue of having been **hard-wired** into the logic circuitry.

flag

A signal consisting of one or more **bits** that conveys and stores status or control information in a computer. A flag has two stable states: it is set or not set (present or absent).

flip-flop

A bistable electronic circuit that has two stable states, and thus may store a 1 or a 0; it will remain in one of these states until it receives a definite signal that will cause it to switch to the other state.

floppy disk

A flexible plastic disk coated with magnetic recording material on which computer data may be stored; the disk is electrically analogous to magnetic recording tape. A standard floppy disk has a diameter of eight inches. See **diskette**.

FORTRAN

A **high-level** computer language for mathematically-oriented applications. The name is an acronym for **For**mula **Tran**slation.

frequency

The repetition rate of a cyclic phenomenon — such as the swinging of a pendulum, the pulsing of a clock, the vibration of a violin string or the arrival of a train of radio waves. Usually expressed in complete repetitions, or cycles, per second. The standard electrical or electromagnetic unit of frequency is the **hertz,** which equals one cycle per second.

friction feed

A technique of feeding paper into a printer or teleprinter that employs the friction between a platen and rollers, as in a typewriter.

front panel

A control board containing a number of switches and indicator lamps, usually arranged in groups of 8 to correspond to **registers;** an archaic way of loading programs or data into a computer.

function key

A keyboard key that involves a computer operating program function, rather than sending a letter or numeral character to the computer. The key is labeled with the function ("escape," "clear," "home," etc.) rather than with a character.

gate

An electronic circuit with two or more inputs and a single output, whose output is true ("on") only when certain input conditions have been met. (For example, in an AND gate, all input signals must be true for the output to be true.)

global editor

A feature of a **word processing** system through which a particular word or phrase may be deleted or replaced by another throughout an entire text through a signal command.

handshaking

The exchange of signals between a computer and a peripheral (such as a printer) indicating that the receiving device has indeed received the transmitted data. Handshaking aids in keeping data exchange synchronized and in preventing data loss.

hard copy

The printed output of a computer, on paper; a permanent physical record.

hard disk

A rotating magnetic **mass storage** device using a rigid disk and having more data storage capacity than a **floppy disk**; until recently used almost exclusively with large computers (but see **Winchester**).

hardware

All electronic, mechanical, and other purely physical components of a computer or data processing system, exclusive of its **programs** and **documentation**.

hertz

A unit of **frequency** equal to one cycle per second, named for Heinrich Hertz (1857-1894), a young German physicist who proved that radio waves could exist, by way of proving that light was an electromagnetic phenomenon (as theorized by a young British physicist, James Clerk Maxwell, 1831-1879). Abbreviated Hz. Compare **kilohertz**, **megahertz**.

hexadecimal system

A number system using sixteen as a radix (base), in which the individual digits are 0, 1, 2, 3, 4, 5, 6, 7, 8, 9, A, B, C, D, E, F, and sixteen is represented as 10. Since sixteen is a power of two (2^4) this system is related to the **binary** and **octal** systems, and translation among them is straightforward.

high level language

A computer language that is closer to human thought and human conventions of expression and notation, and thus easier for human beings to employ for programming than is **binary coding** and the machine's internal **machine language**.

Hollerith card

A machine-readable card on which data are stored in an organized pattern of punched holes. Named for its inventor, Dr. Herman Hollerith of the U.S. Bureau of the Census and first used for the 1890 census. Often miscalled "IBM card."

IBM card

A misnomer: an "IBM card" is a **Hollerith card**; its invention long predates the founding of IBM.

IC
Integrated circuit.

in parallel
Connected to the same set of terminals in the same way (positive to positive, etc.) so that electric current can move over two or more connected paths. Also, simultaneous transmission of data elements (**bits**) over separate signal lines. Contrast with **in series**.

input device
A device for feeding information into another device, such as a computer. Examples include keyboards, front-panel switches.

input-output device
Any device that can both feed data into and accept data from a computer or other system. Examples are **terminals**, including **teleprinters** and **CRT terminals**, **disk drives**, and **cassette drives**. Abbreviated I/O device.

I/O device
Input-output device.

in series
Connected sequentially, so that an electric current passes through two or more circuit elements in turn. (Contrast with **in parallel**.)

instruction register
The **register** in a **central processing unit** that holds the program instruction currently being performed.

integrated circuit
A complete miniaturized electronic circuit consisting of a number of transistors (actually, transistor-equivalents) plus associated circuit components all fabricated together on a single crystal-slice or **chip** of semiconductor material a few millimeters in diameter. Abbreviated IC. (See **LSI**.)

intelligent terminal
A computer **terminal** having considerable stand-alone computational capability, able to operate by itself as a small local computer or to serve as an **input-output** device for a larger computer system.

interactive mode

The performance of data processing or other computer work by a program that carries on a dialogue with the human user, offering alternatives and prompts, asking for specific items of information, etc.

interface

A device used to link two other devices and permit them to operate together. In computers, an interface is usually a circuit that provides electronic liaison between the computer and a **peripheral** device.

interpreter

A program that reads and executes program instructions from another program written in a **high-level** language. (The interpreter is written in **low-level** language.) This translating function is performed with each instruction every time it is used. Compare with **compiler**.

interrupt

A command signal from a peripheral device that causes a suspension of current **CPU** operations. Program control is transferred to an interrupt subroutine that handles the business of the interrupt in some prearranged way (usually according to a priority list) and then restores control to the original program.

inverter

In computers, a device for generating the simple complement of a signal (change 1 to 0 or 0 to 1), also known as a **NOT gate**. In electronics generally, a device that changes direct current into alternating current. The logic inverter symbol is

A— ⎯⎯⎯▷∘⎯⎯ —Ā   with Ā denoting "not A."

kilohertz

One thousand **hertz**, a unit of **frequency**. Abbreviated kHz. Compare with **hertz, megahertz**.

kludge

A computer or other electronic system improvised from ill-matched components (designed for systems having other functions) and having a limited range of performance. Pronounced klüj.

large-scale integration

The construction of extremely complex electronic circuits on a single **chip**, characterized by upwards of 1000 subcircuits (typically, in 1980-era computer chips, about 100,000 circuits on the chip). Abbreviated LSI.

latch

A device, such as a **flip-flop**, that will lock itself into one of two possible stable states until a definite signal arrives to "turn over" the latch and cause it to lock in the opposite state.

least significant digit

In modern number systems, the rightmost digit of a number. This digit represents the lowest power of the base used in the number. In 1044, the least significant digit is 4. In 1044.23, the least significant digit is 3. Abbreviated LSD.

light pen

A hand-held light-sensitive device which permits a human operator to "write" graphics information into a computer by moving the device on the face of the **CRT display**.

line number

A number which begins and identifies a line of programming in **high-level** languages such as **BASIC**.

line voltage regulator

Circuitry in or added to a **power supply** which compensates for fluctuations in the line voltage provided by the local power company; this aids in regulation of the lower but critical computer operating voltages that are the output of the power supply.

liquid crystal display

A computer data display using liquid-crystal technology (as used in wristwatches, pocket calculators, etc.) in place of the usual **CRT display**. Abbreviated LCD.

logic

1. The system of decision and switching functions in a computer. 2. The electronic circuits that carry out the decision and switching functions.

logic circuit

A circuit made up of one or more **gates**, that will perform **Boolean** operations such as **AND, OR, NAND**, etc., and thus manipulate **digital** data for data processing purposes or for device control purposes. Thus, the organized interconnection of switching and decision devices in a computer.

loop

A self-contained series of program instructions in which the final instruction commands the CPU to return to the first instruction, which causes the series of operations to be repeated indefinitely. Inadvertent loops would be programmers' nightmares, but deliberately programmed loops offer great convenience and economy and incorporate loop-breaking instructions, for example, "If N is less than K, go to Y" — Y being an instruction outside the loop.

low level language

A computer language at the machine-language level (a pattern of pure **binary coding**) or somewhat higher, not simple or obvious for a human being to read, understand, or use. Compare with **high-level** language.

LSI

Large-scale integration.

machine language

The particular pattern of **binary coding** required for a particular computer (or model of computer, if many identical machines are manufactured, as is the case with microcomputers). Any machine language is an extremely **low-level** language. Programs written in **high-level** languages are ultimately translated, in the computer, into machine language by **assembler** or **compiler** programs.

magnetic-core memory

An early (1950's) type of **non-volatile** memory using tiny "doughnuts" of magnetic ferrite material strung on wires. Each doughnut or **core** could be magnetized by passing a current through two of the wires. The direction of magnetization (polarity of the field) depends on the direction of the current pulse in the wires. Each core is a quasi-permanent magnet, holding its polarization until a reversing pulse arrives. Since each core magnet can be polarized in either of two ways it may store a 1 or a 0, which can be sensed by a third wire through the core. A great invention, but requiring much hand fabrication (micro-bead-stringing) and expensive.

main frame

Originally, the extensive array of large rack-and-panel cabinets that held the thousands of vacuum tubes of the earliest digital computers. Peripherals, such as **front panels, tape-reel drives,** and so on, occupied other rack-and-panel cabinets and were distinct from the computer, whose structure was the "main frame." Large computers still bear the informal name of "main frame." For the most part, the ancient "main frame" held what we now call a **CPU,** which in a **microcomputer** occupies one or a few **chips.** Compare **minicomputer.**

mass storage

The files of computer data contained in media other than the computer's main memory (RAM) and which are external to the computer, but which are immediately accessible to the computer by means of connective wiring. Obvious examples include **disks** and magnetic tape (reel-to-reel or in cassettes).

matrix printer

See **dot matrix printer.**

megahertz

One million **hertz,** or 1000 **kilohertz.** Abbreviated MHz.

MHz

Megahertz.

microcomputer

A small computer system using semiconductor chip technology, in which the **CPU** occupies one or a few chips and is known as a **microprocessor.** The microcomputer typically is of small size ("desktop") and low price ($500-$2000, stripped down) but has computing power comparable with older **main frames** and lower-priced **minicomputers.** Also, the microcomputer uses semiconductor-technology memory devices in contrast to the **core memories** or other technology used by main frames or typical minicomputers.

microprocessor

1. The **central processing unit** of a **microcomputer,** usually but not invariably consisting of just one **LSI chip.** 2. Any LSI circuit or chip used for control and **logic** functions which involve complex switching. 3. A microcomputer, especially one implemented on a single chip or one small **PC** board.

microprocessor chip

An **LSI chip** carrying a complete **microprocessor**. The chip must be connected with memory and interfacing chips in order to function as the **CPU** of a microcomputer.

minicomputer

A relatively small-sized computer developed from concepts and devices originally generated for main frame computers and compatible with **software** and **peripherals** designed for the large computers, but in recent versions employing **microcomputer** hardware and concepts, so that strict distinctions between mini- and microcomputers become increasingly difficult to make. Today a "mini" is likely to be distinguished from a "micro" by price, brand name, and to an extent speed of execution of instructions.

mnemonic

1. A technique or symbol designed to aid the human memory.
2. In computer work, a **mnemonic code**. Pronounced "nehmónic." Widely mispronounced "pneumonic," originally for the sake of whimsy.

mnemonic code

A system of abbreviations, acronyms, and symbols designed to be easily learned and remembered. Mnemonic codes replace obscure, complex terms in binary coding and thus are easier for a programmer to read, recognize, and use.

modem

Modulator-**dem**odulator device, which enables computers and terminals to communicate by use of data lines (usually telephone-system lines). Some modems are direct-connected: the computer or terminal is wired to the modem and the modem is wired to the data line. Thus the modem is an electrical **interface**. **Acoustic** modems work in conjunction with an ordinary telephone handset: the modem is connected to the computer, and generates and accepts audible tone signals which carry coded data over the telephone line.

most significant digit

In modern number systems, the leftmost digit in a number, representing the highest power of the base present in the number. In 1044, the most significant digit is 1. Abbreviated MSD.

motherboard

A large **printed-circuit board** supporting a wiring pattern and edge-connectors, into which other **PC** boards may be plugged; a microcomputer motherboard accommodates a PC board for the CPU circuit, the **memory** circuit boards, various **interface** boards, etc. In practical terms, a microcomputer's motherboard is synonymous with its **bus**.

NAND

A logic operation, actually NOT AND, the negation or inversion of the **AND** function. The logic proposition A and B = C is true if A and B are both false:

A	B	C
0	0	1
0	1	0
1	0	0
1	1	0

NAND gate

A logic gate to implement the NAND function, actually an AND gate with an **inverter**, whose logic symbol is

negative logic

A computer logic voltage convention in which the lower of two voltages signifies 1 and the higher voltage 0. Thus, in a 0V, +5V system, 0V would signify 1.

non-volatile memory

A memory device whose contents are not lost if power is removed. Examples include **core** and **bubble** memories.

NOR

A logic function, actually NOT OR; the negation and inversion of the OR function, so that the proposition A NOR B = C is true if neither A nor B is true, that is,

A	B	C
0	0	1
0	1	0
1	0	0
1	1	0

NOR gate

A **logic gate** for the NOR function, consisting of an OR gate with an inverter, whose logic symbol is

$$A - \!\!\!\!\!\! \quad \quad$$

$$B - \!\!\!\!\!\! \quad - C$$

NOT gate

A **logic circuit** whose output is the inversion of the input, so that A becomes $\bar{A}$ ("not A"). Synonymous with **inverter**.

numeric data

Data consisting exclusively of numbers or numerals. Compare with **alphanumeric data**.

octal system

A number system whose **base** or **radix** is eight, using the digits 0, 1, 2, 3, 4, 5, 6, 7 and in which eight must be represented as 10. Since eight is a power of two (2^3) the octal system is related to the **binary** and **hexadecimal** systems and interconversion is straightforward. In some computers octal notation is used to condense binary expressions.

odd parity

A form of **parity** checking in which a byte containing a seven-bit character code has either a 1 or 0 added (eighth bit) so that the total number of ones in the byte is odd.

ones complement

The **complement** of a binary number formed, in practice, by replacing all zeros with ones and all ones with zeros.

operating system

A set of computer programs devoted to the operation of the computer itself, which must be present in the computer before **applications programs** can be loaded or expected to work.

OR

A logic function in which the outcome is true if either of two (or any of several) values is true. The logic expression OR is implicitly equivalent to the grammatical **inclusive or**, in which any or all input values may be true, so that

A	B	C	$(A + B = C)$
0	1	1	
1	0	1	
1	1	1	
0	0	0	

output device
Any computer **peripheral** that receives data signals from the computer, such as a **printer, teleprinter, CRT display, disk** or **cassette drive** system, etc.

parallel connection
See **in parallel.**

parallel in, parallel out
A way of loading and unloading data in a **register**, in which each data cell **(flip-flop)** in the register is fed a **bit** through a distinct signal line, simultaneously with all the other cells; all bits exit from the register simultaneously on a set of parallel output lines.

parallel in, series out
A way of loading and unloading data in a **register** so that all data bits arrive simultaneously on separate input data lines, and depart sequentially on a single (series-connection) data line.

parity
A system of checking for accurate transmission of data characters by means of adding a spare bit, as that the number of ones in the **byte** is either odd or even; see **even parity, odd parity.**

parity bit
The extra **bit** added to a data character **byte** as a means of checking accuracy of transmission.

PASCAL
A powerful **high-level** computer language for business and general purposes, often used on microcomputers; named for Blaise Pascal (1623-1662), French mathematician and philosopher, who at age 19 invented a mechanical calculator.

PCB or **pcb**
Printed circuit board.

peripheral devices, peripherals

Input, output, and **input-output** devices designed to work with a computer but not essential parts of the computer, such as keyboards, printers, CRT displays, etc. The computer is indifferent to the kinds of devices connected to its input and output ports, so all these devices, while necessary for human convenience, are **peripheral** to the computer itself and are interchangeable with others.

pixel

An element of a display on a CRT screen: the smallest picture element, using a tiny square or rectangle of some shade of gray; a matrix of pixels makes up a picture resembling a coarse halftone.

PL/1

Programming Language 1. An early high-level computer language.

plasma display

A data display using a rarified electrically charged gas trapped between conductive glass plates, instead of the glowing solid phosphor of a **CRT** screen.

point-of-sale terminal

A computer **terminal,** often resembling a cash register and functioning as one, used for recording transactions, calculating totals, printing an itemized receipt, and transmitting all transaction data to a central computer, which keeps track of inventory, sales volume, etc.

positive logic

Computer logic circuitry in which the higher of two reference voltages is interpreted as 1 and the lower as 0. Thus, in a 0V, +5V system, +5V constitutes the digit 1.

power bus

The conducting lines, analogous to wires, in a **bus** structure that carry operating voltage and current to the system components, as distinct from data or command lines.

power supply

A device consisting of a transformer, rectifiers, ripple filters and regulating circuitry, for converting the usual 115-volt (or 230-volt) AC supply voltage to lower DC voltages needed by computer components (typically, +5 volts, −5 volts, and

+ 12 volts DC). The power supply may or may not be housed in the same cabinet as the computer.

printer

A device for producing paper copies (**hard copy**) of the data output of a computer. The printer is operated entirely by signals from the computer or other source of coded character signals.

printed circuit board

A thin insulating board or "card," postcard-sized or larger, on which conductive paths (analogous to wires) can be deposited by photolithographic processes analogous to printing. Electronic parts (such as resistors, capacitors, and **DIPs**) are mounted on the boards and interconnected as a circuit by the pattern of conductive lines. Abbreviated PC, **PCB**.

program

A coded set of instructions in a computer language, to be loaded into a computer's memory and used to operate the computer system itself or to carry out data-processing tasks.

program counter

A register in the **CPU** that holds the next instruction to be executed, which constantly updates itself as each instruction is fulfilled.

programmable read-only memory

A form of the **read-only memory (ROM)** which a computer manufacturer may program for his computer's purposes by electro-optical means. Abbreviated PROM.

programmer

A person skilled in a computer language or languages who writes programs.

programming

1. The act of writing programs for a specific computer or application. 2. The existing or projected sets of programs for a computer.

programming consultant

A professional skilled in interpreting the programming needs for an application and in designing the specific programming procedure.

PROM
Programmable read-only memory.

radix

The **base** of a number system, literally (in Latin) the root. A modern number system is based on exponents or **powers** of the radix: 10^0, 10^1, 10^2, 10^3, 10^4, etc., which in the **decimal** system correspond respectively to 1, 10, 100, 1000, 10,000, etc. In a modern number system, the number of digits exclusive of 0 is always one less than the radix, so that the decimal system has the digits 1, 2, 3, 4, 5, 6, 7, 8, and 9, and the binary system only 1. The zero in all systems is really a place marker, since zero signifies "nothing," and nothing is not a power of the radix. The place marker is essential, as every digit position has place value representing a power.

RAM
Random-access memory.

random-access memory

A **read-write memory** in a computer. The term refers specifically to a memory on a semiconductor **LSI chip**, although non-semiconductor memories such as **core** memories are also both read-write and random-access. Through "random access," the computer can retrieve or deposit information instantly at any memory **address**, without combing through other memory items written at earlier addresses. Abbreviated RAM; compare with **sequential access**.

read-only memory

A form of random-access memory in which information is permanently stored and cannot be erased or replaced. Abbreviated ROM. ROM chips store certain indispensable operating instructions for the computer or allied device, providing **firmware** (compare with **software**). In microcomputers the term refers to a semiconductor device (LSI chip) though broadly speaking even a phonograph record is a read-only memory.

read-write memory

Any computer memory system in which information may be retrieved or entered at any time under program or operator control. Semiconductor **RAM** and magnetic **core** memories are read-write memories; so are recording tapes and **disks**.

record

An organized collection of data **fields** and an ultimate component of a **file**.

refresh

The process of repeatedly reinforcing or restoring the contents of certain memory devices, such as **dynamic RAM**, in which the electric charge or other means of recording a data **bit** tends to determiorate rapidly with time.

register

A small temporary data storage device capable of holding one or a few **bytes** or **words** of data for purposes of computation, or data interchange between a computer and its **peripherals**. A **CPU** contains a number of registers that variously hold data to be manipulated and individual program instructions.

Reset-Set flip-flop

A simple **flip-flop** with two inputs and two outputs, wired so that a true reset signal sets the prime output (which may be the only accessible output) to zero, while a true set signal will set the prime output to 1. The set and reset signals are equivalent to A and $\overline{A}$ (not A). Each time the R-S flip-flop changes state it latches in that state until a new input signal turns it over. Also known as **set-reset** flip-flop; abbreviated R-S.

ROM

Read-only memory.

R-S flip-flop

Reset-set flip-flop.

scratch pad

A small area of high-speed memory used in conjunction with computation and whose contents are ever changing.

scrolling

The movement of a displayed pattern or text upward or downward on the display screen for rapid reading or rechecking. As lines of text or data disappear at one edge of the screen, new lines are generated at the other edge by rapid retrieval of data from memory.

semiconductor

A material, usually a metal (silicon or germanium) with properties between those of conductors and insulators, whose electrical restivity can be changed by action of an electrical charge, light, or other stress.

sequential-access memory

A storage device in which all data items up to n must be read before n is reached and read, and random retrieval is not feasible. Examples include phonograph records and recording tapes.

series-in, parallel out

A way of loading a **register** so that data bits move into the register sequentially, with the first bit passing through all cells before reaching its designated cell, but, on reading out, each cell feeds its bit onto a separate data line so that all bits leave the register simultaneously.

series in, series out

A way of loading and unloading a data register in which all bits enter and leave the register sequentially on a single input and a single output line.

series connection

An electrical circuit in which a current flows through each circuit element sequentially and in which there is a single current path from the source, around the circuit, and back to the source.

shift register

A **register** in which all data bits may be moved to the left or to the right one register cell at a time, in the manner of people playing musical chairs.

silicon

A metallic chemical element with **semiconductor** properties, related to the element carbon.

software

Programs and their **documentation**, though the word is often used as a quasi-synonym for "program" or "programs."

sort program

A program in which items in a data **file** may be arranged or rearranged according to some desired scheme (alphabetically, by age, by amount, by zip code, Social Security number, part number, etc.), and retrieved according to some such criterion or according to a key word, etc.

sprocket feed
A means of feeding paper through a printer that uses sprocket pins that engage precisely spaced holes in tear-away strips on the side edges of the paper sheet.

static RAM
A type of **RAM** using flip-flops or their equivalent so that recorded data bits are stable until deliberately changed, and which thus requires no **refresh** cycle.

string
A sequential set of data items or characters stored in contiguous units of memory.

system
1. An organized collection of devices or parts, such as a computer and its **peripherals**. 2. A set of service routines or programs for operating a computer and its peripherals. 3. The computer hardware and software taken together, since some parts of the "computer system" may be virtual parts—items of software that perform what could have been hardware functions (for example, device selection).

systems consultant

A professional capable of analyzing the data processing needs of an enterprise (business, engineering, scientific, medical, etc.) and prescribing the hardware and software components of a system configured to meet the particular data processing needs.

teleprinter

A Teletype™ or other electrically operated printing machine having a keyboard as well as a printing mechanism, suitable for use as a computer **terminal** or as a station in a communications network.

tens complement
The **complement** of a number achieved by subtracting the number from ten.

terminal

An **input-output device** used for two-way communication with a computer, having a keyboard or its equivalent and a printer, CRT, or other display mechanism.

text editor

A computer program that permits ready correction or modification of the contents of memory, including program material as well as textual material.

truth table

A tabular listing of the outcomes of Boolean algebra operations for all combinations of true and false input conditions; similarly, a table showing the 1 or 0, "on" or "off" states of a logic **gate**.

TTY

Abbreviation for Teletype™ terminal; sometimes used to signify a teleprinter regardless of brand.

turnkey system

A data processing system ready to use for applications upon delivery and installation, with all **hardware** and **software** fully developed, tested, and debugged.

twos complement

A **complement** of a number achieved by first forming the **ones complement,** adding one to the least significant digit, and executing all carry operations that ensue from the addition.

UART

Universal asynchronous receiver-transmitter.

universal asynchronous receiver-transmitter

A general **interface** device which converts parallel-transmitted data to serial output form, and serial input data to parallel output form and performs other tasks to enable non-parallel-transmission devices to work as computer **peripherals** and to eliminate the need for having them synchronized with the computer's clock. Abbreviated UART.

vacuum fluorescent

Denoting special display devices not using an electron beam or charged plasma.

volatile memory
A memory device that stores data only while power is applied and whose contents are lost once power is removed.

Winchester drive
A generic term for small (8-inch to 14-inch) **hard disk** drives of relatively low cost but appreciable capacity (5 to 40 million **bytes**) developed for use with small computers. The origin of the name is obscure.

word
A minimum-storage element in a computer memory and the smallest data element worked on by the CPU. Word sizes vary with the design of the computer, varying from eight **bits** (one **byte**) to 12, 16, and up to 64 **bits**.

word processing
The manipulation of human-language textual material rather than numerical data by a computer or other electro-mechanical writing-editing machine.

word processor
1. An electromechanical aid to writing, modifying, and editing human-language texts, often but not always consisting of a computer and peripherals with a word processing program. 2. A computer system dedicated to word processing. 3. A program written for word processing.

X-OR
The **exclusive OR** function.

Appendix

HOW IT ALL WORKS

This has been a non-technical book. This "technical" section will not be much more technical. It is intended to help you enhance your layman's understanding of what goes on inside a microcomputer. If you want to learn more, study the books listed in the menu at the end of this appendix.

You already know that a computer is, loosely speaking, an organized collection of switches. Each switch may be *on* or *off*, and a voltage will be *present* or *absent* at the switch's output. The switch position may be used to represent opposites: yes and no, true and false, one and zero. You already know that computers employ a number system that has only two numerals, 1 and 0. The computers' number system is called the binary system.

What really counts in a computer is not the numbers, but the *logic*. In all logic, in the final analysis, every statement is either true or false. Questions must be answered yes or no. A thing or an attribute either exists or it does not. Anything that exists is a unity, and what does not exist is nothing. Obviously, a true statement can be represented by 1, and a false statement by 0. A number system that recognizes only two digits, 1 and 0, has a close relation to stripped-down logic.

Now, the everyday meaning of "logic" refers to the science of organized reasoning. That is the meaning we have just employed. However, in computer lingo, "logic" usually refers to the systematic connection patterns of switching circuits. To keep the computer and its hardware logic simple—or even workable—designers are restricted to switches with only two states, on or off. Simple on-off switches may be combined in any pattern that will perform a desired task. As we shall see later, those combinations can be elegant.

Since everything depends on on-off logic and a one-and-zero number system, it might seem reasonable (logical?) to start off with consideration of that number system. But it might be better to consider number systems in general.

You are about to discover that you understand the binary system perfectly.

TEN ISN'T SACRED

Suppose we start by killing off The Big Lie. Well, not a lie, just a myth. An Old Schoolteachers' Tale. And that is, "we reckon by tens because we have ten fingers." Or "ten fingers and (ten) toes." So, a decimal system is a natural system, right? Everybody just naturally counts by tens, right?

Wrong. Various peoples at various times have used number systems based on a variety of numbers, such as 6, 8, 12, 16, and 20. Ancient priestly brotherhoods used number-system bases as unwieldy as 7 or 60. But common people were as comfortable with a number base like twelve as you are with your base of ten.

The real reason you have a base-ten system is that you indirectly inherited one from the Romans by way of the Arabs. Our modern civilization inherited many things from the Romans, including a preference *among educated people* for base-ten systems. Unschooled or "common" people long preferred to reckon by ones, twos, fours, and threes and sixes; or halves, quarters, eights; they went by multiples of two. (Computers go by powers of two.) Their favorite systematic number was *twelve*—giving them the *dozen* and the *gross* (12×12). Twelve is a very convenient number. You can divide it by 2, 3, 4, and 6, and get a whole-number answer, and you don't need schooling to do it in your head. Splitting up a dozen of anything is easy, and the dozen dominated petty commerce for centuries.

What makes our modern "tens" system so slick and easy is not that it is based on ten, but because it has certain other features, notably:

1. A quantity of distinct number symbols, and that quantity is equal to the base number: 0, 1, 2, 3, 4, 5, 6, 7, 8, and 9. (*No* symbol for ten!)
2. A *zero* symbol, which permits
3. Place Value, which requires

4. Reckoning by successive powers of the base number, that is, B^0, B^1, B^2, B^3, and so on.

In the decimal system, B^0, B^1, B^2, B^3 work out respectively to 1, 10, 100, 1000, and there is no limit.

In the binary system, these B-powers work out respectively to only one, two, four, and eight, but there's still no limit. By the time you get to the end of a 32-bit big-computer word, the value for the last place is 2^{31}, which works out in Base 10 as 4,278,190,080, a respectable number. Make every bit in that word a 1 and the whole word is worth $8,556,380,159_{10}$. (The subscript obviously means "in base-ten notation," since in binary notation this number comes out as thirty-two 1s in a row.)

Number systems compared

Computers use two auxiliary number systems, the octal and the hexadecimal, to help the computer to condense cumbersome numbers. The octal is based on eight and the hexadecimal on sixteen. Both of these bases are powers of 2, so they are closely related to the binary system, and conversion back and forth is easy.

Now, these "exotic" number systems likewise have (1) a number of digits or symbols equal to the base number; (2) a zero; (3) place value; and (4) consistent use of powers of the base. They use the same powers of their bases as are used in the decimal or binary systems. Suppose we compare:

POWER BASE	B^6	B^5	B^4	B^3	B^2	B^1	B^0
2	64	32	16	8	4	2	1
8	262,144	32,768	4,096	512	64	8	1
10	1,000,000	100,000	10,000	1000	100	10	1
12	2,985,984	248,232	20,736	1728	144	12	1
16	16,777,216	1,048,576	65,536	4096	256	16	1
20	64,000,000	3,200,000	160,000	8000	400	20	1

The bases 12 and 20 were included only because they help illustrate the principles and because they have been used by other cultures. (We are confident, however, that only one, the Mayans' base-20 system, used place value "our way.") In computer work, only bases 2, 8, 10, and 16 matter.

A human objection to the binary system is that working with large numbers (the national debt? the price of a new house?) is clumsy. The octal base helps only a bit: $8^6 = 4096$. The good old decimal base has us at $1,000,000$ by 10^6. Base 12 has us almost into 3 million by that power. Base 16 would seem to be undesirable, because it has us at 16.7 million by the sixth power — values increase "too fast." And base 20 is out of sight.

We have a "comfort factor" in regard to these bases. Only in base 10 do powers seem to "round off neatly," with the numbers coming out as strings of zeros, the way we are accustomed to. But we have been expressing all those other-base powers in Base$_{10}$ numbers. They would all neatly round off with zeros if we expressed each power with numbers generated by its own base. That is,

BASE	\multicolumn{7}{c}{POWER OF BASE NUMBER}						
	B^6	B^5	B^4	B^3	B^2	B^1	B^0
2_{10}	1000000_2	100000_2	10000_2	1000_2	100_2	10_2	1
8_{10}	1000000_8	100000_8	10000_8	1000_8	100_8	10_8	1
10_{10}	1000000_{10}	100000_{10}	10000_{10}	1000_{10}	100_{10}	10_{10}	1
12_{10}	1000000_{12}	100000_{12}	10000_{12}	1000_{12}	100_{12}	10_{12}	1
16_{10}	1000000_{16}	100000_{16}	10000_{16}	1000_{16}	100_{16}	10_{16}	1

Please notice three things about the last two tables:
1. The base number to its zeroeth power is always 1, regardless of the base. (*Any* number to the zeroeth power is 1: $n^0 = 1$. We haven't room to prove the theorem here and you haven't time. Regard it as a mathematical law.)
2. In its own notation, the base number is always expressed as "10." This involves another mathematical law, plus a practical reason: *it's the only way place value can work.*
3. The base number to the first power (B^1) is always the base number itself: $2^1 = 2$, $8^1 = 8$, $10^1 = 10$, and so on. (*Any* number taken to its first power is itself: $n^1 = n$. Otherwise all workable number systems fall apart.)

This means, obviously, that there is no numeral 8 in an octal system, no symbol for twelve in a duodecimal system, and no symbol for sixteen in a hexadecimal system. But that's nothing new: there is no numeral for ten in the decimal system, or for two in the binary system. Binary-two has to be expressed as a one and a zero, a decimal-ten is a one and a zero, and so on.

Numeral symbols

The decimal system uses all ten available digits, 0 1 2 3 4 5 6 7 8 9. To make a duodecimal system (base 12) we would need to invent or borrow additional symbols, to represent ten and eleven — since "10" must represent twelve. Suppose we borrowed A and B. The duodecimal system's digits would be 0 1 2 3 4 5 6 7 8 9 A B — twelve symbols.

The hexadecimal system does borrow letters of the alphabet to represent the numbers ten through fifteen. The hexadecimal numerals are 0 1 2 3 4 5 6 7 8 9 A B C D E F.

One comparison table is probably worth 2^8 words:

Notation in Different Systems

Familiar Decimal Quantity	BASE				
	2	**8**	**10**	**12**	**16**
1	1	1	1	1	1
2	**10**	2	2	2	2
3	11	3	3	3	3
4	100	4	4	4	4
5	101	5	5	5	5
6	110	6	6	6	6
7	111	7	7	7	7
8	**1000**	**10**	8	8	8
9	1001	11	9	9	9
10	1010	12	**10**	A	A
11	1011	13	11	B	B
12	1100	14	12	**10**	C
13	1101	15	13	11	D
14	1110	16	14	12	E
15	1111	17	15	13	F
16	**10000**	**20**	16	14	**10**
17	10001	21	17	15	11
	. . .	. . .	. . .	. . .	. . .
30	11110	36	**30**	26	1E
31	11111	37	31	27	1F
32	**100000**	**40**	**32**	28	**20**
36	100100	44	36	**30**	24
54	110110	66	54	46	36
80	1010000	**120**	**80**	68	**50**
1000	1111101000	1750	**1000**	6B4	3E8

Just looking at the boldface numbers in the last table and reflecting for a moment on *why each is where it is* will give you the benefit of the entire table.

Did you notice one thing? An even number in any system is an even number in all the others. Any odd number is an odd number in all systems. When you go from system to system, you are not "changing numbers." You are merely expressing the same number differently.

You are familiar with doing that. You have no trouble with:

1	2	3	4	5	6	7	8	9	10
I	II	III	IV	V	VI	VII	VIII	IX	X

although you boggle at expressions like MCMLXCIII. (No place value! No zero! And there *is* a symbol for "ten" in this ten-based Roman system! Again, it isn't the use of "tens" that makes a system easy to use, or "natural." It's the modern system of notation.)

Carrying

The octal system has the digits 0 1 2 3 4 5 6 7. You may add up to seven in the "ones place" of a number — but try to add more, and you have to carry over. You must add the extra 1, or 2, or more to the "eights place" and replace the 7 with 0. This goes, of course, for any place in a number. (You can add up as high as 9 in any place in a decimal number, but then what can you do?) We carry and use replacement zeros in the binary system, the same way.

That is,

$$\begin{array}{ccc} 1 & 1 & 1 \\ +9_{10} & +7_8 & +1_2 \\ \hline 10_{10} & 10_8 & 10_2 \end{array}$$

Worries, worries

Some bothersome questions could present themselves at this point.

1. To use a computer, would I have to make conversions from my comfortable decimal numbers to those crazy binary or hexadecimal numbers?

No. You would always deal with your familiar decimal quantities. For you, it's decimal in, decimal out. However, if you were a programmer, and working one level higher than all-binary machine language, you would use hexadecimal as a shorthand. It would become second nature to you.

  2. How does the computer know when a letter is a letter, and
     when it is a hexadecimal value between nine and sixteen?

Easy. The operating program reserves part of the computer's memory for numerical data and other parts for alphabetical-character information. The computer knows what's what just because of where things are addressed.

Remember, when the computer gets down to computing, it will translate *everything* into binary code. Hexadecimal numbers "recode" into binary very readily.

What do we really do?

When we read, write, or think of any decimal number, we are unconsciously taking place value into account. For example, 4032. We know that means four thousands, no hundreds, three tens ("thirty"), and two ones ("two"):

10^3	10^2	10^1	10^0
(thousands)	(hundreds)	(tens)	(ones)
4	0	3	2

By convention, we "read" or say the largest number (greatest power of ten present) first, and go from left to right. But we build the number from the right, actually. At the rightmost place will be some quantity of ones — zero (or "no" ones)), or some number up to 9. The decimal system allows us ten choices for any "power column," or "power place."

We do exactly the same thing with the binary system. Or rather the computer does, since we would find the binary system so awkward to work with. The binary system uses the same kind of ploy: take 1010 — one eight, no fours, one two, no ones:

	2^3	2^2	2^1	2^0	
	(eights)	(fours)	(twos)	(ones)	
	1	0	1	0	(ten$_{10}$)
or	0	0	1	1	(three$_{10}$)

which is no eights, no fours, one two and one one. That adds up to three. But the biggest number we can use in any place is 1.

We read any number from left to right, and unconsciously add as we go. We know how "big" a number is by looking at the leftmost digit (the "most significant digit"). The rightmost digit in any place-value system is the "least significant digit."

All right, the largest a "most significant digit" can be in the binary system is 1, but *where it is* tells us how large the number is. The largest MSD in the decimal system is 9, but we still depend on the place value to show us the magnitude of the number.

A zero, by the way, isn't really a number, it's a placeholder. Exactly the same principles are at work in the octal system (not used very much in microcomputers) and the hexadecimal system. These same principles would work if we went ahead and invented a base-12, or duodecimal system.

That means *all modern number systems work in the same ways*.

And that means, *you understood the binary system perfectly all along*. You may have thought you didn't.

From the back of the class

An objection might be raised: the decimal system gives us the convenience of decimal fractions: 0.1, 0.01, 0.001, etc. We may use that handy decimal point, or we may express them, physicist-style, as negative powers of ten: 10^{-1}, 10^{-2}, 10^{-3}, and so on. What about that?

Objection overruled. The binary system can work with binary fractions and a binary point, or with negative powers of 2. Our hypothetical duodecimal system would have a duodecimal point, duodecimal fractions, and negative powers of 12. The hexadecimal system has...but there's no use flogging a dead horse. They all can work with ordinary fractions, too — ½ or ⅙ or $\frac{1}{n}$.

Converting

You probably already have figured out a simple rule for converting decimal numbers into binary. What is the biggest binary place value that will fit into, say, a base-ten 19? That would be 16_{10}, or 2^4. That leaves you a remainder of 3_{10}. All you can get into 3_{10} is a 2, with a remainder of 1. So you would have a fourth-power 1, a zero (no 2^3 value), another zero (no 2^2), a first-power 1, and a zero-power 1, for 10011. That's "a sixteen, no eight, no four, a two, and a one." In proper "byte form," of course, you would write that 00010011.

Or you can have successive divisions by 2, with quotients and remainders. You would keep dividing the successive quotients by 2. The remainders — all of them either 0 or 1 — become your binary digits, starting in the rightmost, or 2^0 column. You work the opposite way from your off-the-cuff method.

For example, 31_{10}:

$\dfrac{31}{2} = 15$, with a remainder of 1. This will be your *least significant digit*, placed all the way over on the right. You already know you're aimed straight since that place is the "ones" place and 31 is an odd number.

$\dfrac{15}{2} = 7$, again with a remainder of 1. Put that in the "twos" place.

$\dfrac{7}{2} = 3$, again with a remainder of 1. It goes in the "fours" place.

$\dfrac{3}{2} = 1$, with a final remainder of 1. It goes in the "eights" place.

$\dfrac{1}{2} = X$. That is, it's forbidden! There is no way you can divide 1 by 2 and come out with anything that makes sense in binary notation. You are stuck with that final remainder as a 1, which you put in the "sixteens" place.

You may add up in either direction, but you have 1 sixteen, 1 eight, 1 four, 1 two, and one 1: 11111. ($16 + 8 + 4 + 2 + 1 = 31_{10}$).

That was too neat. Suppose we try 36.

$\dfrac{36}{2} = 18$, with 0 remainder. Your least significant digit is 0.

$\dfrac{18}{2} = 9$, with a remainder of 0. Your "twos" place is 0.

$\dfrac{9}{2} = 4$, with a remainder of 1. Your "fours" place digit is 1.

$\dfrac{4}{2} = 2$, with no remainder — your "eights" place gets 0.

$\dfrac{2}{2} = 1$, with no remainder. Your "sixteens" place gets 0.

$\dfrac{1}{2} = X$; you can't do this; the remainder remains undivided; your "thirty-twos" place gets 1.

You have written 100100.

Now you have 1 thirty-two (2^5), no sixteen (2^4), no eight (2^3), 1 four (2^2), no two (2^1), and no one (2^0).

Obviously, $32 + 0 + 0 + 4 + 0 + 0 = 36_{10}$.

A nagging question might be, "what if we wanted to handle an expression like one half? How can that be expressed? Can't there be halves and quarters in the binary system? Of course. Try $\frac{1}{10}$, $\frac{1}{100}$, even $\frac{1}{11}$, or $\frac{1}{1001}$. Or even, $\frac{1}{1010}$!

Binary to octal

Although octal numbers are rarely used in microcomputer systems — despite their honorable history with older computers — it is worthwhile to know the trick of binary-to-octal conversion.

The highest number that can be generated by any three binary digits (or **bits**) is seven. Try it: $111 = $ one four, one two, one one, or $4 + 2 + 1 = 7$. The biggest octal digit is 7.

Suppose you take a larger binary number and split it into groups of three:

$$101100101001 = 101 \ 100 \ 101 \ 001 \quad (= 2857_{10})$$
$$\downarrow \quad \downarrow \quad \downarrow \quad \downarrow$$
$$= \ 5 \quad 4 \quad 5 \quad 1 \ = 5451_8 \ (= 2560_{10} + 256_{10} + 40_{10}$$
$$+ \ 1_{10} = 2857_{10})$$

We used a 12-bit number, because a dozen, remember, is so easily split. But it works on an 8-bit number:

$$11010011 = 11 \ 010 \ 011 \quad (= 211_{10})$$
$$\downarrow \quad \downarrow \quad \downarrow$$
$$= 3 \quad 2 \quad 3 \ = 323_8 \ (= 192_{10} + 16_{10} + 3_{10} = 211_{10})$$

A zero is implicit at the leftmost place of the "first" or leftmost group. Also implicit here is that the groupings of three digits always start from the right.

A computer that uses octal numbers has little hardware tricks for storing them. (No room in this appendix to describe them.)

Octal-to-binary reconversion is straightforward. No octal digit can be greater than 7. Each octal digit represents three binary digits:

$$742_8 = 111_2 + 100_2 + 010_2 = 111100010_2 \ (= 482_{10})$$

Binary to hexadecimal

The trick is the same as for binary to octal, except the binary numbers are split into groups of four digits:

$$000111110101_2 = 0001\ 1111\ 0101 \quad (=501_{10})$$
$$\downarrow \quad \ \downarrow \quad \ \ \downarrow$$
$$1 \quad \ \ F \quad \ \ 5 \quad = 1F5_{16}\ (=256_{10} + 240_{10} + 5_{10}$$
$$= 501_{10})$$

Going "back" is just as easy:

$$2B6_{16} = \ 2 \quad \ \ B \quad \ \ 6 \qquad\qquad\qquad (=694_{10})$$
$$\downarrow \quad \ \downarrow \quad \ \ \downarrow$$
$$0010\ 1011\ 0110 = 001010110110_2 \quad (=694_{10})$$

Of course you could go directly back and forth between decimal and hexadecimal for programmers' low-level purposes (base purposes?) but this book does not purport to teach you programming. We gave you a taste of high-level programming in Chapter 3.

And now, a ringer

The ringer is **binary-coded decimal** or **BCD**. It is convenient to have the computer able to code or store decimal numbers in a *digit-by-digit* binary equivalent. Thus, if the decimal number was 27, the computer would store the 2 and the 7 separately in binary form. A pair of decimal digits can be stored this way in a standard 8-bit byte. Three- and four-digit numbers require two bytes, and so on. No problem here; when it comes time to remember the decimal 27 the computer will consider the place value of the binary coded digits, that is,

$$0010\ 0111$$
$$2 \qquad 7$$

and the single byte can store anything up to 99: 1001 1001. Each four bits can store any number up to 15_{10} so storing numbers from 0 to 9 is no problem.

In straight binary coding, the computer would render 27_{10} as 00011011. *But no law says it must do so.* Sooner or later the computer will have to give you back your 27_{10} as plain 27, so somewhere it may render a byte as 00100111 rather than 00011011.

An analogous process is used when the computer must work with hexadecimal notation. There is always a way to skin another cat.

STILL MORE CATS

The computer skins quite a few variegated cats, as when it must use eight-bit bytes to read or store characters from your keyboard, or tell your CRT or printer to display those characters. Let's consider just one of them, the letter M. Now, if you have anything more than a Mickey-Mouse hobby computer, you have a capital M and a lower-case m. And your computer may use letter keys as control-function keys: you press a CONTROL key and a letter key to make the computer do some particular thing (instead of displaying a letter). So, you need three codes for M. In the standard microcomputer code, those codings come out

$$M = 1001101$$
$$m = 1101101$$
$$Control\ M = 0001101$$

Those codings as binary numbers would translate respectively as 77_{10}, 109_{10}, and 13_{10}. (Notice that the rightmost four bits always $= 13_{10}$, which is consistent: M is the alphabet's thirteenth letter.) But the computer isn't using these codings as numbers.

In fact, when it comes to numbers, the code for the numeral 1 is 0110001, and for the numeral 9 is 0111001. These would work out as decimal 49 and 57, if used as binary numbers. Let's compare these with the coding for A and I, splitting bytes for clarity:

1	011 0001	A	100 0001
9	011 1001	I	100 1001

It's the first three bits that tell the computer what to use the byte for. The final four digits do translate as decimal 1 or 9 (I being the ninth letter). That's consistency, designed into the code.

Three bits? Doesn't a byte have *eight* bits, four-and-four? There's a reason for not using the leftmost bit as part of the code that we'll get into later. (Ultimately the computer will not be cheated: it will receive the leftmost or "final" bit, at least as an implicit zero.)

Confused? Don't be. You don't have to "remember" any particular detail. Our purpose here is only to show you that the computer can use strings of ones and zeros for many purposes — not just for crunching binary numbers. Computer design is economical: it does much with little.

You can do more with even less because of hexadecimal expressions. Suppose you are a programmer, writing away at your desk or keyboard, and you want to specify a colon or the letter J somewhere. The code for *colon* is 0111010, and for *J*, 1001010. Tedious to write out (or key in) all those ones and zeros, certainly. But if the computer will let you input hexadecimal, you can write "3A" for *colon* and "4A" for *J*. (If you want to memorize the symbol table, it's easier to remember things like "4A" rather than "1001010.")

Computer coding is "an entire subject." We shall glance at it again later. And we shall examine computer architecture, for its own sake and because coding and architecture impinge on each other. (The computer's central processor, or CPU, has different "doors" through which variously coded items enter and exit.) But first we ought to consider computer logic.

This section has not covered binary arithmetic. But addition, multiplication, and so on proceed as they do in the decimal system. For some purposes, binary arithmetic uses a few tricks not normally used in decimal arithmetic, though they could be. All that will come later. Now it's time for logic.

COMPUTER LOGIC

You recall that those on-off switches, and the symbols 1 and 0, not only serve to represent binary numbers, but also symbolize the truth or falsehood of statements. "In all logic," it was asserted earlier, "every statement is either true or false." There is no room here to argue the truth or falsehood of that assertion. We have to offer it as a "given."

However, back in the nineteenth century, a British mathematician and philosopher named George Boole published a book on the laws of human thought in which he supported that proposition. Since he could symbolize "truth" or "falsehood" by 1 or 0, he was able to work out a form of "algebra" that used only these two numerals. Boole found he needed only the logical operations AND, OR, NOT-AND, and NOT-OR. And Boole worked out a system of **truth tables** to summarize the connections clearly. (Boole sharply distinguished between "inclusive-Or" and "exclusive-Or," and we shall follow him, later.) Boole's purposes had nothing to do with computers, but it turns out that Boolean Algebra is an immensely powerful tool for the design of computers. In fact, it is *the* tool.

Yet it's simple. (How complicated can it be, having only 0 and 1 to figure with?) And it's practical: if you want to design a computer decision gate — a small part — you diddle up some Boolean algebra and generate a Boolean truth table. You design the computer by choosing decision gates to wire together.

Simple and practical. Yet Boole was just playing an intellectual game, as Einstein was when he came out with relativity and $E = MC^2$. (And look what *that* led to.) Look not askance at the "idle" philosopher, the "impractical" pure scientist. If the particle physicists find that quark that they are hunting, don't ask "What good is it?" You may never know. But your grandchildren will.

Just what Boolean Algebra is all about, and how it clarifies the laws of human thought, need not concern us here. We can go straight to applications.

First, those switches

You are aware that an electric current must have a complete path, usually made of metal, out of the source, through the bulb, and back to the source (Figure A-1). If this is the case, and the battery and bulb are "good," the bulb lights up. Break the path anywhere, and the bulb goes out.

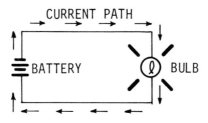

Figure A-1. The basic electrical circuit.

A switch is a device for breaking the path, or making it. The simple knife switch is just a swinging bar of copper. (As a friend of ours puts it, "If you know how a door opens and closes you understand switches.") See Figure A-2.

We can illustrate Boole's AND and OR operations just by considering simple electric circuits having a pair of switches.

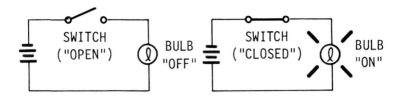

Figure A-2. Circuit with switches, "on" and "off."

The AND operation

The diagrams show a truth table as well as the lamp-and-switch setup. Each "on" or "true" switch position is represented by a 1; each "off" or "false" position is represented by 0. If the lamp is on, the output is 1; if it is off, the output is 0. See Figure A-3.

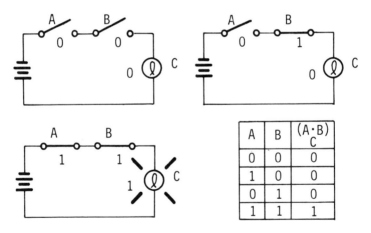

Figure A-3. Logic AND circuit and truth table. (A·B)

For the AND circuit to work, both switch A *and* switch B must be closed, or "on." If either switch remains open, the circuit is open, incomplete. The lamp remains "off."

If we call a lighted lamp "true," the entire lamp circuit is true if *and only if* Switch A AND Switch B are true.

We could have more than two switches in the circuit. In a three-switch circuit, the circuit is true, and the lamp lights up, only if switches A AND B AND C are true. See Figure A-4.

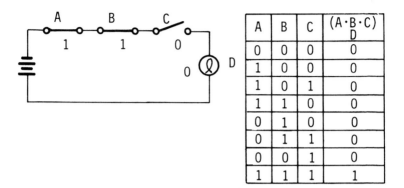

Figure A-4. Logic AND circuit and truth table for three switches. (A•B•C)

Remember, all this follows from Boolean Algebra. The truth table leads us to a theorem, and the logic designer finds the theorem useful:

$$A \cdot B = L$$

That's a mathematical multiplication dot in ordinary math, but it means AND rather than "multiplied by" in Boolean Algebra. Boole borrowed a convenient symbol but not its meaning. We may also write the theorem AB = L. Again there is a resemblance to multiplication, but it's best to stick with the dot — because we *must* use function symbols for other logical "equations." So A•B = L it will remain.

The OR operation

We can wire a lamp circuit another way. Here are two switches connected *in parallel* — one wired across the other (Figure A-5). The current path will be complete if either switch is closed. The lamp will light. Thus, the entire circuit is true if switch A OR switch B is true.

This is one of two possible OR logic circuits, the inclusive OR. The lamp will light if *both* switches are closed, and of course stays off if both are open. The inclusive OR operation covers either or both of the alternatives.

Any number of paralleled switches may be used in this OR circuit.

The truth table, you will notice, uses a plus sign, + , to denote "or." Here, this does not mean addition — just as the AND

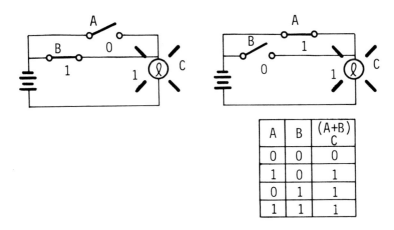

A	B	(A+B) C
0	0	0
1	0	1
0	1	1
1	1	1

Figure A-5. Logic OR circuit and truth table. (A + B)

operation's multiplication dot does not mean multiplication. George Boole borrowed these symbols and endowed them with their special meanings. Why these? Why didn't Boole use some more obscure symbols, so as not to generate confusion? Because, in the working out of Boolean Algebra problems, the manipulations are very simple, very straightforward, if these particular symbols are used. The logical flow is *analogous to* multiplication for AND and addition for OR.

The exclusive OR

We have just looked at an inclusive OR circuit, which implies that there must be an exclusive OR somewhere. In English, in logic, and in computer logic we indeed find the exclusive "or."

What, first, is meant by "inclusive or"? Suppose you say to a friend, "You need to eat some protein. Have some meat or cheese." You are gratified if he orders a cheeseburger. He understands that you mean "meat or cheese or both." You have spoken inclusively. He can get protein from meat OR cheese OR fish OR eggs and so on — and there can be many input switches in any OR circuit.

But suppose you say to your friend, "Have a cheeseburger." And the friend replies, "I am an orthodox Jew. I may eat meat or cheese, but not both at the same meal." His dietary law prescribes an exclusive or.

An exclusive OR circuit is not simple to illustrate or explain using simple knife switches. It is made up of other, complete logic circuits. Suppose we defer discussion of the circuit itself till later. However, the exclusive-OR truth table can be useful here and now (Figure A-6):

A	B	$(A \oplus B)$ C
0	0	0
1	0	1
0	1	1
1	1	0

Figure A-6. Exclusive-OR truth table. $(A \oplus B)$

Notice that in this truth table, the plus sign used to signify OR is circled, to specify exclusive-OR.

What about an AND/OR circuit? No such circuit. The expression "and/or" is an abomination in English, a chimera in logic, and a nonentity in computer logic. It serves no function. In English, the inclusive or is all a writer means when he gets fancy-shmancy with "and/or." Anyone who tries to design an "and/or" circuit learns that there is no way to do it, because "and/or" isn't even a *concept* — the term is illegitimate, meaningless, empty, null. *Ex nihilo nihil* — "out of nothing comes nothing, nohow." We have spoken.

The NOT operation

Computer circuitry frequently employs little devices called inverters. An inverter is a NOT circuit, delivering at its output what it did NOT receive at its input. Give it a 1, and it will deliver a 0. Give it a 0, and it will deliver a 1. The inverter generates the complement of the input signal. Its input, A, becomes NOT A at the output. (NOT A is symbolized $\overline{A}$.) Conversely, $\overline{A}$ in will cause A at the output.

We mention the converse, "obvious" as it may seem, because we are dealing with an electronic device, not just a logical concept. All kinds of electronic devices will give you nothing out when you put something in — if they have malfunctioned, or somebody forgot to turn them on. But it's a rare device that gives you something out when you put nothing in — and in most devices, "something for nothing" *also* indicates a malfunction. The inverter is a device deliberately invented to give the output patterns it does. Here's its symbol and truth table, in Figure A-7:

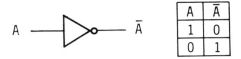

A	$\overline{A}$
1	0
0	1

Figure A-7. Inverter symbol and truth table.

Haven't we just made a solemn pronouncement about "out of nothing, nothing"? If there is a 0 at the input of the inverter, that presumably means no voltage there. So how can the inverter have a voltage (that 1) at its output? Remember that the inverter is an active electronic device, and it has more connections than its stripped-down logic symbol reveals. It has connections for its operating voltage, and also for the system logic voltage (typically 5 volts). So, that logic voltage is in there, ready to be switched. The "switch" in the inverter is "normally set" so that the logic voltage is switched to the output. That's just one way of doing an inversion. (All the ways are irrelevant — *function* is what counts.)

Combining inverters with AND and OR gates gives negative functions: NOT AND and NOT OR. The gate names are usually abbreviated to NAND and NOR.

We shall not bother with a switching diagram, but comparing the truth tables for AND and NAND is useful. See Figure A-8.

AND$= A \cdot B$

A	B	C
0	0	0
1	0	0
0	1	0
1	1	1

NAND$= \overline{A \cdot B}$

A	B	C
0	0	1
1	0	1
0	1	1
1	1	0

Figure A-8. AND and NAND truth tables.

In the NAND circuit, when all the inputs are 1, the output will be 0, which is NOT-1, $\overline{1}$. If any or all inputs are 0, the output will be 1.

In a NOR circuit, the normal operation of an OR circuit is inverted. When any input is 1, the output will be zero. "One OR one gives NOT-one," or, $1 + 1 = \bar{1} = 0$.

When all inputs are 1, the output is still 0. Only if no input is 1 — all are zero — will the output be 1. $(0 + 0 = \bar{0} = 1.)$

Here, for comparison, are OR and NOR truth tables, in Figure A-9:

OR=A+B

A	B	C
0	0	0
1	0	1
0	1	1
1	1	1

NOR=$\overline{A+B}$

A	B	C
0	0	1
1	0	0
0	1	0
1	1	0

(NOR=A⊕B)

Figure A-9. OR and NOR truth tables.

It is possible to learn a great deal quickly by comparing the AND, NAND, OR, NOR, and Exclusive OR (X-OR) truth tables together. See Figure A-10.

AND=A·B

A	B	C
0	0	0
1	0	0
0	1	0
1	1	1

NAND=$\overline{A·B}$

A	B	C
0	0	1
1	0	1
0	1	1
1	1	0

OR=A+B

A	B	C
0	0	0
1	0	1
0	1	1
1	1	1

NOR=$\overline{A+B}$

A	B	C
0	0	1
1	0	0
0	1	0
1	1	0

X-OR=A+B

A	B	C
0	0	0
1	0	1
0	1	1
1	1	0

(NOR=$\overline{A⊕B}$)

Figure A-10. All logic operation truth tables compared.

We have long abandoned those little switching diagrams. But each of these circuits has a distinctive symbol. The symbol stands for the operation rather than for the actual device. (The device symbols would have to show all the connections for supply voltage, ground, etc., not just logic input and output.) The logic symbols, being just that, are distinguished by their shape. The shapes are arbitrary. See Figure A-11.

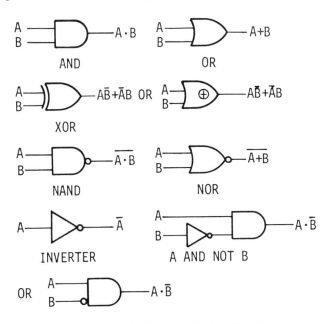

Figure A-11. Logic operation/device symbols for all primary operations and a modification, A AND not B.

Figure A-11 had an "A and NOT B" symbol in it. This was just to show that any logic gate (or logic operation) can be modified for special purposes. In a computer there will be occasions when some particular thing should NOT be happening in order for something else to happen. A direct example would be complicated at this point. But everyday life offers an illustration.

A modern car's radio will not work unless the ignition key switch has been turned at least as far as the "Accessory" position. But we want the battery even further protected — its load lightened — if the starter is operating. Then we want the radio briefly off. We can have an enabling signal, A, from the accessory switch-point, and a signal, B, from the starter switch-point.

We want it arranged so that the radio will *not* have power if B is true. The control device could be a modified AND gate, for "A and *not* B." An inverter is added to the AND gate as in Figure A-11. If B comes along, the inverter will convert it to B̄, "false." The output of the gate will go false. While B is absent, that "perverse" inverter provides a true signal. The gate stays true, and the radio works.

In present-day practice, an AND gate and its inverter would be parts of an integrated circuit — for all the key-switch functions — on a single chip.

Other gates and devices

The logic gates are combined in many different ways to make other, more complex devices. For example, memory modules — either RAM or ROM — for the computer. Clocks, and multiplying and dividing timers. Counters. Shift registers — which are small temporary memories each holding a word of data that is being worked on at the moment. Or a whole microprocessor.

We said, "more complex devices," not necessarily larger devices. Anything from a single AND gate to an entire microprocessor may appear on one tiny silicon chip, and be packaged in about the same sized little dual in-line package or DIP.

It would be tedious for you (and for us) to show you how a number of logic gates would make up a microprocessor or even a partial RAM module. But the principle of combining the simple gates to make complex devices can be illustrated with very simple real combinations. For example, the **flip-flop** and the **X-OR** (exclusive OR) gate.

The flip-flop

Suppose you are a computer designer and you need a small logic circuit that will go true when a certain input goes true (1 out for 1 in) and will stay that way — even if the input voltage changes or disappears. And you want to be able to kill the output voltage on command. And you want it to stay killed until you command otherwise. You want a stable device.

A wall switch is like that. It is spring-loaded, so it is "hard" to make it change state. But push it with a certain minimum force and it will flip to "on" and stay there. It is not likely to turn off accidentally. It requires a push of equal force in the opposite direction to make it flip to "off." By itself, it then stays off. The switch has two stable states: it is a **bistable device**.

You want a bistable device that will automatically change state when it receives a definite voltage pulse on an input, and change state again when it receives a pulse on another input. A flip-flop is such a device.

Flip-flops come in many forms, with various degrees of complexity. Let's consider a simple one, the *reset-set* or R-S flip-flop. This is also called a *latch* for reasons that will be obvious. It is diagrammed in Figure A-12.

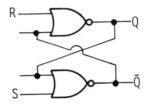

Figure A-12. A simple (RESET-SET) flip-flop circuit.

The R-S flip-flop has two inputs and two outputs. The "second" output is available just because of the symmetrical nature of the circuit, and it can be put to good use. (Or it may be ignored if the computer designer should choose not to hook it up.) The inputs are labeled R and S, and the outputs, Q and $\bar{Q}$. The outputs are complements of each other; a 1 at either means a 0 at the other.

This flip-flop consists of a pair of NOR gates cross-connected as shown. Now, we have to suppose that the circuit is turned on and working. Let's say a 1 had appeared at some time at input R. If either or both of the inputs to R's own NOR gate is 1, the output is 0. So, Q = 0. Because of cross-connection, that zero will appear as an input at the other NOR gate. Also, as yet S has had no input — an implicit 0. A pair of zeros at a NOR gate's input make for an output of 1. Therefore $\bar{Q} = 1$.

$\bar{Q}$ becomes, because of the cross-connection, an input at R's NOR gate. But R itself is already 1. A pair of 1s going into a NOR gate means 0 coming out. The entire situation is confirmed. The circuit is stable, *latched*, with a 0 at Q. (The circuit has been *reset*, is waiting to be *set*.)

Then somebody or something sends a voltage pulse — a 1 — to S. *Whammo!* S becomes 1, so $\bar{Q}$ is forced to go to zero. The value of $\bar{Q}$ is cross-connected over to R's NOR gate, giving a 0 at one of its inputs. Now, the original RESET signal at R is probably long gone; it was just some triggering pulse. R is sitting there at 0 level. Two zeros at the NOR-gate input demand a 1 output. *Flippety-flop!* Output Q is now at 1. The latch has turned over into the "set" state.

All over the computer, various devices may have been waiting for "Q to go to 1" in order to start doing their thing. Other devices are now waiting to learn when Q is *off*; the $\bar{Q}$ output provides this signal when Q is reset to zero. But flip-flops have many uses — such as storing one bit in a shift register, or in a RAM cell.

At last, Exclusive OR

Remember our reluctance to diagram an exclusive-OR gate for you? It takes a combination of logic gates to make one; representing it with simple switches would have been hairy. But now we have the wherewithal to keep it simple (see Figure A-12).

There are several possible combinations that could make an X-OR gate, but the least sophisticated involves two AND gates, two simple inverters, and an OR gate. As the diagram shows, one input of each AND gate is cross-connected to the other AND gate, through an inverter. The incoming A signal will put not-A ($\bar{A}$) on one of the B gate's inputs, and the B signal will put $\bar{B}$ on one of the A-gate's inputs.

Imagine a 1 at A and a 0 at B. Because of the inverter, B's AND gate gets a second 0 input. The output of this gate is therefore 0.

In like manner, A's AND gate receives a second 1 input. With both inputs at 1, its output is 1. The OR gate now has a 1 input, and gives an output of 1.

Exactly the same kind of thing happens if we start with a 0 at A and a 1 at B. The final output will be 1, or "true."

Try it with 0 at A and 0 at B. What happens to each AND gate? What does the OR gate receive? Plainly, a pair of zeros in causes a zero out. So far, the gadget is acting like an inclusive-OR circuit.

But now try it with a 1 at A and a 1 at B. The AND gates are each going to receive *unlike* inputs. Their outputs will be 0. The

OR gate, receiving a pair of zeros, will give zero out. This circuit will give a 1 output if *either* A or B is 1, but *not both*.

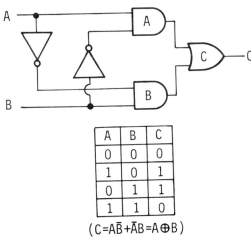

$$(C=A\bar{B}+\bar{A}B=A\oplus B)$$

Figure A-13. The X-OR (exclusive OR) logic gate and truth table.

MORE STATELY DEVICES

It turns out that all kinds of computer circuits can be designed almost entirely through the combination of either NAND or NOR gates, with an occasional extra inverter here and there. This was not learned through random experimentation at a workbench. Most of it was learned because people used Boolean Algebra to simplify all that truth-table stuff, boil it down. It is by algebraic analysis that the way was shown to use *fewer* gates for any given level of complexity, and to use fewer kinds. Don't scorn those "theoretical" guys with the far-away look in their eyes. They keep coming up with better mousetraps.

We have shown the shapes for the various elementary logic gates. What are the shapes for flip-flops, shift registers, RAM modules, clocks, counters, timers, microprocessors and the like?

Almost all look like this (Figure A-14):

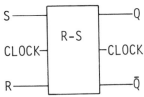

Figure A-14. A clocked flip-flop symbol, the type for most other complex logic-device symbols.

except that the number of input and output connections varies. They look very much like the connection diagrams for the pins on the DIPs they are housed in. They don't need shapes: labels will do. Each of the complex devices is a **black box**, that is, a device with "unknown" contents; only its *functions* matter to the user. Do you really know what's inside the automatic transmission in your car? Do you care? What matters to you is what the transmission *does* for you. The automatic transmission is a black box.

LOGIC VOLTAGES

Throughout, we have worked on the assumption—explicit or implicit—that when one of those logic switches was thrown, a voltage appeared somewhere to give us a 1. Conversely, when a switch was opened, the voltage disappeared. Zero volts gave us our zero. Logic circuits and computers are indeed built this way. In a typical microcomputer, a logical $1 = +5$ volts, and a logical $0 = 0$ volts. This is called positive logic.

Actually, computers would be mighty temperamental if voltages had to be exact. Engineers and designers strive to achieve a 1 with any voltage higher than 3.0 or 3.5 volts, and a 0 with anything lower than 2.5 or 2.0 volts. That allows a little slop in the system. All electric circuits have the property of *resistance*, which eats up electric power and gnaws voltage downward. And for many reasons, a sharp series of computer data or clock pulses that looks like this

can wind up, after fighting its way through too many transistors, looking more like this:

But of course ways are found to refresh that waveform here and there in the computer.

A little slop is okay, but a serious overvoltage can burn out transistors, gates, entire LSI chips. A serious undervoltage can give the computer difficulty in recognizing 1s. That is why, in Chapter 8, we stressed the desirability of *regulated* operating voltage power supplies for the computer.

Now, we can have *positive* logic using *negative* voltage. That is, the voltage can swing between 0 and − 5 volts instead of 0 and + 5 volts. By a technical convention, a zero voltage is considered *higher* than a negative (or "minus") voltage. If you are counting the zero level of a data pulse as 1 and the − 5V level as 0, you still have positive logic. The 1 state is the *higher* voltage level.

This means, however, that you have chosen to call it 1 when you have no voltage present, and to call it 0 when you do have voltage present. That's okay, because the negative voltage, when it gets there, is mathematically "less than" zero voltage.

That's not hard to understand. Consider your banking account. You have + 5000 dollars in it. Fine. You have 0 dollars in it. Not fine. You are overdrawn, and have − 5000 dollars in the account. Goshawful — and you are aware that with an overdraft, you have *less money* than when you had "zero" dollars. The *absolute value* of that overdraft is just 5000 dollars, the same as " + 5000" dollars, which is what you'll put back to get back *up* to zero dollars. Okay, "minus 5000 dollars" is less money than zero dollars, and "minus 5 volts" is a lower voltage than zero volts.

Does this matter? It probably won't, to you, if you buy any kind of integrated system. (Not necessarily with everything in one cabinet — we mean if all components of your system are designed to be compatible.) Whether a computer engineer decides to use + 5 volts or − 5 volts is exactly like an automotive engineer's deciding to use negative-grounded or positive-grounded battery protocol in a car.

But suppose you decide that you have got to have a PDQ printer and it was designed for minus-to-zero logic while your existing computer uses zero-to-plus logic. (Or maybe somebody sold you a PDQ second-hand and skipped town.) You would have an interesting interfacing problem.

You would have an even more crucial interfacing problem if PDQ used *negative* logic and your computer used positive logic.

NEGATIVE LOGIC

In negative logic, the *higher* voltage is a logical 0 and the *lower* level is a logical 1.

If you have a zero, plus-five system, when you have 5 volts at an input you have a zero. When you have zero volts, you have a one.

This can be justifiable. It's one way of knowing that the computer is definitely *on* even if everything is "all zeros." Let's say you've just taken the computer out of the crate and the memory is empty, and so on. (That's the way it used to be, on the big computers, and before ROM firmware came along.) You find the +5V at every test point and you know it's ready to go. The first "one" bit you punch in just punches a 1-sized hole into that +5 volts.

There's little to stop an engineer from deciding that 0 volts is 0 and −5 volts is 1, if he wants to. As long as you decide that the *lower* voltage is 1, you have negative logic. (Remember, −5 is lower than 0.)

It all works just as well as positive logic. The computer works with ones and zeros and it doesn't care how you define them — so long as you are consistent.

This upside-down-logic convention mattered to one of us authors many years back, working with a negative-logic system. Not only that, it was a zero, minus-five negative logic system. For a particular manual-writing purpose, it was necessary to know not only the logic level but the voltage at given circuit points. So there you were, tracing a signal labeled K. Fine. When K was true it was 1 and that was −5 volts. Sure. But very soon K went through an inverting gate and became $\bar{K}$. Then it hit another inverting gate and became $\bar{\bar{K}}$, or not-not K. And yes, it got to $\bar{\bar{\bar{K}}}$, not-not-not K, and the voltage was again zero (was it?); and meanwhile K itself was running loose elsewhere; and along with K, it was necessary to track L, which unfortunately had been begat by $\bar{K}$ but went through a different set of gates and ran a few clock-pulses behind $\bar{K}$ anyway — but everything was fine until the phone rang or I sneezed.

The worst part of sneezing was that I lost all possible track of M, which had been begat by $\bar{L}$ and was equal to $\bar{L}/8$, since it came out of a time-divider circuit. (When I left that job I ran off and wrote *biology* books for a few years.)

It's interesting that gate functions go upside-down and backwards in a switch from positive to negative logic. That is, an OR gate becomes an AND gate when you switch from "high = 1" to "low = 1" logic. In spite of the way they "wired" those "transistor switches" inside to build one gate or the other!

How important are the permutations of positive and negative logic to you? Not important at all—except, perhaps, when some snowy computer salesman tries to blizzard you with things like, "We use negative logic, you know"—implicitly the finest kind. Negative, shmegative.

MICROCOMPUTER ARCHITECTURE

Chapter 1 described a computer system as consisting of "an input device, an output device, and a central processing unit (CPU)." The **CPU**, of course, stands between the input and output devices.

All three of these components were treated as black boxes—their innards didn't matter; only their functions did. The input device accepts data and instructions and feeds the CPU. The CPU processes the data according to instructions and feeds the output device. The output device might be a printer; the input device might be a keyboard. Some **I/O devices**, or **peripherals**, can fill either function: a magnetic disk, for example, can accept data coming out of the CPU or read data into it.

The CPU, then, is the computer proper. The peripherals can be "anything." They either give or receive from the CPU strings of coded data. So, the peripherals can be ignored while we study the action of the computer.

The microcomputer CPU resides (as a rule) on one semiconductor chip, the microprocessor. But the CPU cannot work alone; it must have some random-access memory (RAM), and it needs a clock and a few other accessories. These reside on other chips—or on collections of chips mounted on circuit boards. A decent microcomputer for business purposes also has ROM chips, so that the computer's own operating system programs are permanently in residence. All of these electronic devices must be connected together by a set of signal lines known as a **bus.**

If you searched, you could find a "microcomputer on a chip." Large-scale integration (LSI) has proceeded that far. However, for various good technical reasons, microcomputers for business purposes do not rely on a single chip. They spread their eggs through a number of secure baskets.

At the first level of complexity, then, a microcomputer sans peripherals could be diagrammed as in Figure A-15.

Of course, there are more than six bus lines in a real microcomputer. We are showing *schematic* connections here, not a

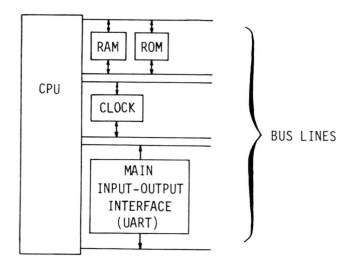

Figure A-15. The microcomputer's bare bones.

wiring diagram. The **RAM** and **ROM** boxes represent memory: RAM for read-write memory, ROM for resident operating-system programs. (The big main-frame computers have nothing but RAM, which holds everything; they simply use a very large RAM, and it is *not* an inexpensive semiconductor RAM.) ROM, you remember, is a "read-only" memory, and is **non-volatile**: its contents are always present, whether the power is off or on (Chapter 2). The clock consists not only of a clock circuit (on a chip) but a quartz crystal: a thin slab of quartz specially ground to vibrate at a certain rate, the clock frequency. The "main input-output interface" is actually a device called a UARTS, for "Universal Asynchronous Receiver-Transmitter." Not shown here are bus lines for low-voltage electric power, nor the ground return line for that power, nor the low-voltage power supply.

The clock keeps everything in the computer marching in step. Its output is a series of voltage pulses, all of equal length. The thousands of transistor switches in the over-all computer circuit will each go "high" or "low" at the leading or trailing edge of a clock pulse. A typical clock rate for a good microcomputer is 4 MHz (megahertz), which means 4,000,000 pulses per second.

The UART, being "asynchronous," enables peripherals which are not precisely in time with the computer's clock to work with the computer anyway. Let's say you are a hunt-and-peck artist on the computer's keyboard. The UART will accept your peckings as they come. Whenever the computer asks it to (many more times during a second than you could possibly "peck") it will send a burst of data bits that represent the coding of the last character you pecked in. It will also translate the computer's bursts of bits into signals that a relatively slow device, such as a printer, can use. The interface circuits connect the UART with the particular peripheral.

The UART is also a "series-parallel, parallel-series" interface, but that will be examined later.

The clock and the UART can be dismissed now as black boxes; what's inside them doesn't matter. (Nothing there but transistor "switches" and logic gates anyway.)

However, the CPU shouldn't be regarded as a black box. It should be looked into.

Inside the CPU are an **Arithmetical Logic Unit (ALU)**, a **Control Unit**, and several **registers**. This is indicated in Figure A-16:

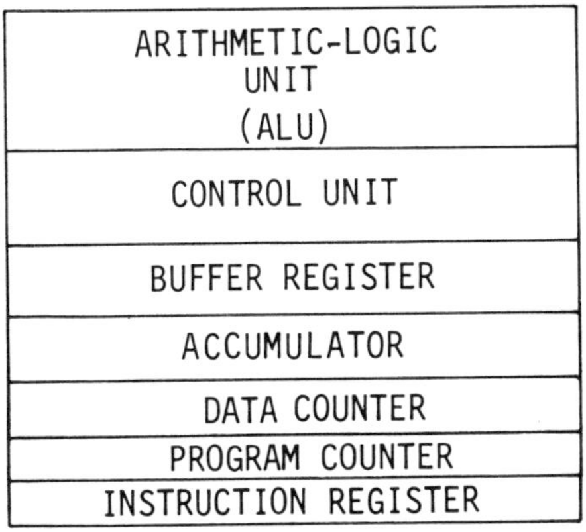

ARITHMETIC-LOGIC UNIT (ALU)
CONTROL UNIT
BUFFER REGISTER
ACCUMULATOR
DATA COUNTER
PROGRAM COUNTER
INSTRUCTION REGISTER

Figure A-16. The CPU or "processor."

First, the registers. A register is a small "temporary" memory unit. Usually, it holds one or two bytes of data (8 or 16 bits), that is, a word or two, possibly more depending on specific computer design. Physically, a register is a series of flip-flops connected together. They are grouped eight at a time, for obvious reasons.

Information *passes through* a register, but is held long enough for a given operation (for example, addition). The *Buffer* Register (or simply "**buffer**") holds data being transferred between the computer and its peripherals. The Accumulator accepts data to be worked on, so that the CPU does not have to work disruptively inside the memory. (The word to be worked on is fetched out and stored in the Accumulator.) The Data Counter holds the memory address of the next word to be worked on. The Instruction Register holds the program instruction to be performed. (Remember, all program instructions are very brief coded statements.) The Program Counter addresses program-memory locations; program information is stored in a different part of the memory from the data words. Every time an instruction is executed, the Program Counter advances one program step, by advancing one program-address step. That opens the door to the next instruction.

There are other registers inside a computer, even inside a CPU (there will be more than one Accumulator, for example). The more registers a computer has, the faster and more versatile it is. Therefore the higher its quality and cost. Registers can be regarded as **scratch pads**. They hold the moment-to-moment instructions and data.

The Control Unit reads whatever is in the Instruction Register and translates it into a pattern of switching bits that put the ALU through its paces. The Control Unit has its finger in all the pies — registers, ALU components, internal and external data buses — and is generating an organized hailstorm of switching bits.

The Arithmetic-Logic Unit, with the help of all these friends, does the work. It performs Boolean logic operations — AND, OR, etc. (No matter what kind of arithmetical operation you can think of, there is a Boolean algebra pattern for it.) It does binary addition. It also does binary subtraction — but not directly. It cheats with an operation called **complementing**, that we shall look at later. Multiplication and division are just sophisticated forms of addition and subtraction (just as they are for you, working with your pencil and paper). Taking a number to a power, or anything else, is just more sophistication. Another thing the ALU does is shift a data word to the right or left, as for multiplication or whatever. It shifts the word one bit's worth at a time, as needed. See Figure A-17.

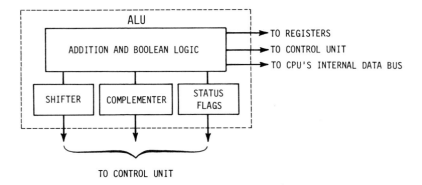

Figure A-17. Inside the ALU.

Finally, the ALU contains flip-flops for **status flags**. If some special operation has to be carried out, such as carrying, there is a status flag for that. Suppose there was a two-word number being worked on. The results of the operation on the first word may have necessitated a *carry* into the second word. (The first word's Most Significant Digit went greater than 1 — which must be added to the second word's Least Significant Digit.) The carry flag is set, and when the ALU operates on the next word, it will be reminded to carry. Once the carry has been completed, the carry flag will be reset.

So now we are able to take a different kind of look into the CPU, as in Figure A-18.

The arrows in Figure A-18, of course, indicate flow of data and instructions.

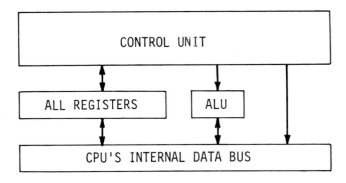

Figure A-18. A new view of the CPU's insides.

But so much goes into and out of a CPU. Information flows back and forth along various sets of bus lines (all of them parts of the over-all computer bus). In a typical microcomputer using an 8080 chip, for example, there will be eight lines — known collectively as "the data bus." (These are distinct from the CPU's internal data bus.) There will be sixteen address lines, to allow for all the different ways to address what's in the memory. (Remember all those address codes just for keyboard characters — 000 for control, 100 for a capital letter, 110 for a lower-case letter, and so on?) The address lines have to handle the RAM memory (with its differently allocated areas for data and program), the various ROM memory chips, and all the peripherals. With that many address lines, the microcomputer could theoretically handle a couple of hundred different peripherals. They would all work rather slowly, however, if they all attempted to work at once. (Just getting the CPU's attention takes a slice of time.)

The sixteen address lines collectively are called "the address bus." Then there are ten control lines, for various signals out to the peripherals and for a few signals in. (The computer and each peripheral in use have to keep exchanging handshake signals — "Yes, I'm here and I heard you" — and the peripherals need to keep sending **interrupt** signals to tell the computer they need attention at this moment.) So, there is a "control bus." Finally, a two-line "clock bus" and a "power bus," four lines. All this is shown in Figure A-19, a connection diagram for the 8080 chip.

The pin numbers are not in order in Figure A-19; we chose to group the pins' *functions* for simplicity in labeling. As you realize, the pins are on the 8080's package, or DIP, and the chip inside has etched on it quite a maze of microscopic "wires." If address line 10 happens to come off the chip surface at one place, and address line 11 someplace else, the DIP designer is going to use the nearest pins. Thus, line 10 has pin 1 and line 11 has pin 40. It all does work out well as a physical layout on the computer's bus-board or "motherboard."

Most 8080 microprocessors are plugged into an S-100 computer bus (Chapter 2) which has 100 lines. But the 8080 has only 40 pins. This leaves an ample number of extra bus lines for other purposes: expanding the memory by fan-out add-ons, for example; or powering and controlling special features of peripheral

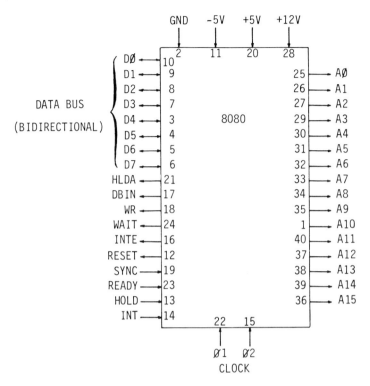

Figure A-19. Pin connections and signal lines for an 8080 micro-processor chip.

interfaces. It also allows for a 16-bit microprocessor setup instead of an 8-bit setup, using some more elaborate descendant of the 8080. (That descendant exists as we write, and is distributed in limited quantities for developmental work.)

The address lines are unidirectional: address signals go out to the memories or peripherals, but nothing comes back through these lines. All return signals will come along the data bus or the control bus. When the CPU addresses a device, all bits of the address go out *in parallel* — marching abreast, as it were, rather than single file: each bit to its own line. This not only saves time; it simplifies the interconnection in many ways.

Notice that the bits (and lines) are not numbered 1 through 16, but 0 through 15. The bits in a byte, or in a two-byte word, are numbered the same way. The bit numbers, of course, reflect powers of 2.

The data lines are bidirectional, allowing an entire byte of information to run in either direction. The CPU itself decides which way the information will go: at any given moment, the CPU is either "talking" or "listening." If it has addressed some place in the memory, it can extract a memory word or send back a new word. If it has addressed a peripheral, it can accept information or give out information, over the same set of lines.

A sampling of signals

It is customary in a computer "handbook" like this to take the reader through each and every signal going into and out of the CPU. But those books are written for the reader whose intentions are more technical than yours. Here, a sampling ought to be enough. The computer may command RESET to "set everything to zero" in the system, in preparation for a new cycle of data processing. It sends out $\overline{WR}$ ("Not Write-Read") when it is ready to read rather than write information on the data bus. It signals WAIT (actually, "waiting") when it has stopped processing and has given some peripheral untrammeled access to the memory. (It will signal WAIT if it has interrupted processing for any reason.) A peripheral will signal INT (for "interrupt") when it needs the computer's attention – it either needs data or has some to give. The peripheral signals READY when the CPU addresses it and it is ready to interact. These are handshake signals, mentioned several times in this book.

Now, every major component in the computer system is hung across the same address lines and data lines: the memories, RAM and ROM, and all peripherals (through the UART). All are always *physically* connected, and they all share all the wires. Yet only one of them is really connected at a time (or perhaps two if they can be connected without mutual interference). It is as if the CPU were plugging them into itself and unplugging them repeatedly. This is accomplished through the addressing.

When a particular device's address goes out over the address bus, various logic gates in that device go "true" and the device is awake and "on." Corresponding gates in the CPU are "true" only for the pattern of address bits that mean *that* device. The corresponding gates in other devices have gone "false" – the devices have been switched off the address and data lines. As far as the CPU is concerned, *only the selected device exists*. The rejected devices may still be operating in some meaningful way.

For example, the keyboard interface may be preparing a pattern of bits for sending down the data bus to the CPU. But the CPU has forgotten it has a keyboard. (We told you computers were stupid.)

Interrupts

That leaves all the non-selected devices hanging out there in the blue sky, with a CPU that has not only forsaken but forgotten them. But they prod it gently with "interrupt" (INT) signals. When it receives an interrupt, the CPU stops its processing operation as soon as it safely can, and peeks at the address lines, in effect asking "Whozzat?" (Actually it's asking, "Whatzat?" because it doesn't know there's a neglected device out there to prod it.) The computer then recognizes a "new" device. It decides whether it can afford to service that device — there's a built-in priority protocol that it follows. If it can't, it will put the prodding device "on hold" and go back to what it was doing.

When it can, it will, in effect, put a bookmark (interrupt flag) in its current processing operation and turn its attention to the interrupting device. When it is finished with that device, it will consult its bookmark and pick up where it left off. (That is, the operating program will feed it the next instruction address for the program segment it *had* been running.)

Now, there are several different ways of arranging interrupt priorities for the CPU, and it would be tedious here to go into them. Just rest assured that elegant logic circuits and the operating program guarantee that "everybody" will get to interrupt the computer in some rational order.

The CPU can select devices any time it "wants" to without an interrupt; all it needs is READY signals from the devices. These are stored in flip-flops until the CPU gets around to seeing who's ready for work. It can send each one INTE, "interrupt enable," which tells them "I'm ready any time you are."

Fast Figaro

All this is happening at lightning speed, of course; each device is remembered and forgotten many times each second. The CPU receives hundreds of interrupts each second: it is a little electronic Figaro, getting demands from all sides. Unlike Figaro, it is too stupid to get tired, bored, or vexed. It has no accumulated weariness because it has no past. It can't even conceive of a future. It knows only "now."

Its pace might seem frantic to us humans, but remember, the CPU lives on a different time scale. It hears four million ticks of its clock during any one of our seconds. It requires just a few ticks to perform any task and may spend most of its time waiting for interrupts. On the computer's time scale, its job is leisurely. Fortunately, it is too stupid to get bored or to have a taste for excitement.

Remember when we said that multiple use of a computer — timesharing or multiplexing — was a software problem, not a hardware problem? (Chapter 2.) This is why your computer system could have several terminals, accepting inputs from several keyboards and displaying results on several CRTs all at once. And each terminal operator is the "only" operator of the computer. All those terminals are connected across the same set of address lines and the same set of two-way data lines. The CPU works with each terminal for a split second, exchanges data with it, accesses program segments for it, processes a snippet of data, and accepts an interrupt from the next terminal. No terminal is actually connected to the CPU unless it has been addressed.

It's as if the computer had a motor-driven rotary selector switch, going constantly from terminal to terminal. Only the "switch" is in the *software*, not the hardware. The "switch" is a set of peripheral addresses, selectable by the program.

To accomplish this, your computer needs sophisticated operating system software (which is distinct from the applications-program software) and plenty of fast-acting RAM. But in principle, even a little four-bit hobby computer with a gnat's memory could do it, if you were prepared to have it done *slowly*.

Of course your human operators go typing away at their keyboards, completely out of synchronization with the computer. No matter; each character they type will wait in a buffer register in the keyboard interface. When the computer is ready to accept that keyboard's latest interrupt, it will grab the buffer register's contents through the data bus.

Buffers

Buffer registers are just devices that isolate the computer from devices working with a different time scale. Like any registers, they are arrangements of flip-flops, with one flip-flop for each bit in the word being stored. When the computer needs the information, it will command all the flip-flops to turn over, spilling the data they were storing onto the data lines. When the computer wants to give out information, it will set all the flip-flops in the buffer accordingly. Then it will go on to the next buffer (for another device).

Buffer registers (or any registers) can be designed to accept data *serial-in, parallel-out*, or *parallel-in, serial-out*, or *serial in-out*, and so on as desired. A Teletype™, for example, works with serial data. The eight bits in a character byte are generated one at a time and go down the output line one after the other, "in single file." The individual bits will be clocked through a serial-input buffer, the first bit going through all eight flip-flops, the second bit through seven flip-flops, and so on. When the buffer is full, the clocking stops. But this buffer can have a parallel output: when it is time to read the buffer's contents, each bit is spilled out "sideways" on to one of eight parallel output lines. Any register, remember, is physically a string of flip-flops, each one of which stores one bit of data – a 1 or a 0 depending on which way it is set. The register may have other flip-flops for auxiliary purposes, like going from series to parallel. Figure A-20 rings a few changes on the serial and parallel register possibilities.

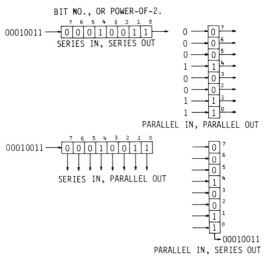

Figure A-20. Register configurations.

Codes

As has been seen, not everything that goes into a computer (or comes out) is straight binary-number data. There are program instructions; there are memory and peripheral addresses; and there is the plain decimal data that you type in and want out, and you have alphabetical data, too: words here and there, or an entire 100-page proposal being word-processed.

Your input and output devices are on your side, accepting and giving back homely decimal numbers and plain words. No matter that everything is converted to a real or virtual "binary number" deep down in the computer. As far as you are concerned, you and the computer "converse in decimal" and you even "converse in English."

Two major codes exist for computers. One, used on certain, usually older, main-frame computers, is an acronym-writer's triumph: **E**xtended **B**inary **C**oded **D**ecimal **I**nterchange **C**ode, or **EBCDIC**. The other, more commonly used today and always used in microcomputers, is **A**merican **S**tandard **C**ode for Information Interchange, or **ASCII**. (Yes, everybody vocalizes ASCII as "Asky," but you're on your own with EBCDIC.) ASCII was originally worked out for telegraph and news-service purposes, using Teletype™ and similar machines. It was adapted and refined for computers as Teletypes became more and more commonly used as input-output devices (replacing all those lights and switches on the front panel).

Under the old telegraph and ASCII conventions, the capital letter O was just an oval; to avoid misreading, a zero was an oval with a virgule or "slash" through it: Ø. Then along came good old IBM, which said, more or less, "Our computers print out countless numbers and rarely a letter; it is tiresome to read whole columns of figures made up of numbers like '$1ØØØ2Ø5.7Ø,' and therefore, computers should print out '$1000205.70' and if the number is word-labeled, e.g., PAYOLA, that will be printed PAYØLA to insure clarity."

Reversing the convention *a la* IBM still has a wild vogue among computer people. They use the slash-oh to mean the letter O even when working with a pencil and paper. "Out to lunch back soon" becomes ØUT TØ LUNCH BACK SØØN. You know. And of course, if a program segment or subroutine needs an acronym like BOTTOM, it comes out BØTTØM. Or how about, ØBØE?

Why names like that? Well, subroutine names are preferably mnemonics, and the favorite American mnemonic form is the acronym. Nothing is more cutesy-cute than the typical programmers' acronym. Programmers work as hard on acronyms as the military guys do, but whereas the lieutenant likes to be obscure, the programmer likes to be cute. It's okay, of course, until you run into a list of subroutines all called OBOE (oops! ØBØE) but distinguished by number, and you find ØBØE Ø1, ØBØE Ø2, ØBØE Ø3, ØBØE Ø4, and so on. We're using slashed Os to be IBM-*chic*, and we're using ASCII zeroes to make it plain we've written a zero. Cute-squared, right? And very one-uppish. After all, if you can't figure *that* out. . . . (Be warned that one-uppishism is rampant in the computer industry, including the microcomputer coterie; that's why most microcomputer manuals and documentation are still pretty bad. When it comes to *any* point where the user requires clarity, the habitual attitude is, "Oh, well, if he can't figure *that* out. . . ." But at least, printed microcomputer documentation will stick to the ASCII convention. It's only whatever isn't obvious that the documenter is reluctant to tell you.)

ASCII has undergone a change; the New International ASCII, promulgated in 1978, will soon be standard here. For international purposes, Ø has to be reserved for one of the Scandinavian-alphabet Os. (The Scandinavians also have Ô, Ö, and things like that.) That means the zero has to be the plain oval: IBM has won! Then what about good old red-blooded American O? That has to be an inverted Q: not a rotated Q, but a flipped-over Q, Ó. Already, especially on dot-matrix print-outs, you can see O rendered as Ó. Of course there is no reason under Heaven why an O for American-English text can't be just O.* (When we have to buy typewriter elements and daisy wheels with a flipped Q for O, we're going to move to Japan.)

Be that as it may, ASCII does everything, with an economy of means. As was seen earlier, jiggling a few address bits and a few "number" bits enables ASCII to do everything with numerals, punctuation marks, capital letters, lower-case letters, control characters, whatever is needed, all in one byte per character. It

---

* Well, there is, really. That reason is optical text readers or scanners, which read pages of ordinary print and render them into computer coding. The automatic scanner needs a sharp distinction between the letter O and the zero. Now you have seen this book's first and only footnote.

even leaves a spare bit in the byte, for accuracy-checking purposes (coming later).

It is customary (mandatory?) in a microcomputer "handbook" to present a table for the entire damn' ASCII code — control characters, capitals, lower case, everything. Do you care about the whole damn' ASCII code? Good.

Checking

At any given time your computer has countless bits zipping through it: character bits, control bits, status flag bits, and so on. Now, computer circuits can hiccup. Even a cosmic-ray particle from outer space zapping through a microtransistor on a chip may flip a 0 over into a 1 or vice-versa. Here and there — and especially in the interfaces between the computer and its peripherals — the computer needs to make sure all bytes are accurate. There are several ways, the two best known being **checksums** and **parity**. Checksums can be loosely described as a way of feeding known dummy numbers through a circuit to make sure it is behaving properly. Parity is simpler and more interesting.

Parity makes use of what are sensibly called **parity bits**. Take that unused bit at the start of an ASCII code-byte. A parity system will eyeball the ASCII byte, count up the number of 1s, and decide whether it is odd or even. Then it will put something in that spare bit as a label.

Now, a parity system may be even-parity or odd-parity. Either way, it is consistent throughout the computer. An even-parity system *decrees* that the number of 1s in a byte shall always be even. If the passing byte already has an even number of 1s, the parity system puts a zero in the spare bit. If the byte has an odd number of 1s, the system puts a 1 in the spare bit.

Thereafter, some gizmo in the computer circuit checks every moving byte to make sure it has an even number of ones. If it hasn't, the checker wakes up and blows a whistle. Processing stops. A PARITY ERROR message may be displayed. Or there may be a software routine that automatically identifies the faulty byte and calls on the source to run it through again. If all is well, processing restarts.

An odd-parity system, of course, decrees that all bytes shall have an odd number of 1s, and behaves accordingly.

For various technical reasons, most microcomputers do not use parity. They have still another system of checking accuracy.

Do you care about its details? Good. But at least you have an idea of how checking systems work.

You're home

Now you have been through the computer, and you have a layman's idea of how it works. It is an accurate idea, just not detailed. You are not ready to sit down and design a computer, but you probably don't care to. There are other books for that if you do; courses you can take. Or you can buy a computer kit and a soldering iron and start putting burn-scars in the kitchen table.

If you plan to do programming, this layman's picture of the computer is a good start, but not really enough. You can do simple programming in a high-level language, like BASIC, but to do fancy programming you want a *little more* detail. Mainly you will look into exactly what is addressed where, and precisely how, in the *particular* computer you are programming for. You still won't care about the nuts-and-bolts aspects; you won't have to learn electronics. Nor will you have to understand semiconductors. (Notice that we have "failed" to tell you how semiconductors work? Almost a first in a book of this kind.) You will just need a more specific knowledge of data paths and destinations.

Probably all you want to do is your payroll on the computer.

And you want to shop for a computer. You now know enough that it will be hard to snow you. And to that end, dear neighbor, we have labored.

COMPUTER ARITHMETIC

Suppose we take a parting lick at computer arithmetic. That's what a computer is all about at bottom (BØTTØM), isn't it?

Binary arithmetic works like any other arithmetic except that you have to start carrying almost from the word go. Suppose we try just adding 1 and 1, or rather, 0001 and 0001:

$$
\begin{array}{r}
0001 \\
+\,0001 \\
\hline
0010
\end{array}
$$

That was an immediate carry. "One" is the largest digit we have in binary arithmetic. So we had to drop our largest digit in the least-significant-digit place, replace it with a zero, and carry the

1 over into the next place. Suppose we try "one and two," or 0001 and 0010:

$$\begin{array}{r} 0001 \\ +\,0010 \\ \hline 0011 \end{array}$$

No carry involved there; we can fit a 1 into the "place." We get 0011 which means 3_{10}. So now we try "two and three," or 0010 and 0011:

$$\begin{array}{r} 0010 \\ +\,0011 \\ \hline 0101 \end{array}$$

First no carry, then a carry, to give us the binary equivalent of 5_{10}, or "a four and a one."

Trivial, right? Worse than elementary, right? Insulting, no? No. Because the computer does it in exactly this same form. Suppose you have a couple of registers. Each has a number in it, and the computer's instruction is going to be to add. Now, regardless of where these registers are, physically, on the CPU chip, they are "wired" together just as if one of them were vertically stacked above the other. Trying to move a 1 from a cell in Register A "down" into the same cell in Register B, which already has a 1, causes B's flip-flop to turn over to 0 — and to signal the neighboring flip-flop that it has. By virtue of this, that next flip-flop receives a 1 at the SET input. If it does not already contain a 1, it will set itself to 1. If it already has a 1, it, too, will turn over and send a 1 (a carry!) to the next flip-flop over.

Subtraction

Binary subtraction is not quite so straightforward. It can be done, but with the use of flip-flops and so on it is best to do it indirectly. Subtraction is accomplished by taking the complement of the subtrahend, and then adding it to the minuend.

The **complement** of any number is just its opposite — A and $\overline{A}$ are complements. So are 1 and 0. We subtract by taking a complement of the subtrahend and adding it to the minuend.

Simply inverting a quantity, however, turns it into its **ones complement** in binary notation. We need something more. We need a "base complement," that is, a **twos complement**. It's easy to get. But to keep this clear, suppose we do some complementing in decimal arithmetic.

You don't have to complement in decimal arithmetic, because you have that flock of digits, 0 through 9, to work with. Your teachers probably never bothered you with it. But a decimal example will show you what complementing will do. To get the tens complement of a subtrahend, you just subtract it from ten. Thus, $\overline{3} = 10 - 3 = 7$. "The tens complement of 3 is 7."

Suppose we want to subtract 3 from 9. We add 7 and 9 and ignore the carry. Because we have gone through this complementing mumbo-jumbo, the answer will put us in teens country, which is absurd. So we'll bracket the carry, and see what it leaves:

$$\begin{array}{r} 9 \\ +7 \\ \hline (1)6 \end{array} \quad \text{which we may compare with} \quad \begin{array}{r} 9 \\ -3 \\ \hline 6 \end{array}$$

That will work with any pair of numbers between 0 and 9. Just subtract the subtrahend from 10, add, and forget the carry.

Roundabout? Of course. But with binary subtraction in a computer, complementing is the only non-hairy way to go.

To get a twos complement, we first form the ones complement of any binary number:

$$1101 \rightarrow 0010$$

and then add 1 to it. That's all!

$$\begin{array}{r} 0010 \quad \text{(ones complement)} \\ +0001 \\ \hline 0011 \quad \text{(twos complement)} \end{array}$$

Suppose we try it with another number: 0101.

$$0101 \rightarrow 1010 \text{ (ones)} + 0001 = 1011 \text{ (twos complement)}$$

Very well, we're ready to try a subtraction. Suppose we want to subtract 0101 from 1110 (it translates as decimal $14 - 5$):

$$\begin{array}{r} 1110 \\ +1011 \quad \text{(twos complement of 0101)} \\ \hline (1)1001 \end{array}$$

We discard that bracketed carryover, and our answer is 1001. $1001 = 9_{10}$. $(14 - 5 = 9.)$
It works!

Multiplication

The microcomputer multiplies just as you do, starting off with the least significant digit in the multiplier, multiplying the multiplicand with each more significant digit in turn, and *shifting* each successive result one place-value. Then all the subresults are added.

$$
\begin{array}{cccc}
\text{You:} & \begin{array}{r} 45 \\ \times 27 \\ \hline 315 \\ +90 \\ \hline 1215 \end{array} & \text{Computer:} & \begin{array}{r} 1101 \quad (=13_{10}) \\ \times 1010 \quad (= 5_{10}) \\ \hline 0010 \\ 1101 \\ 0000 \\ +1101 \\ \hline 1000001 \quad (=65_{10}) \end{array}
\end{array}
$$

Remember, the ALU in the CPU has a *shifter*. And it has registers to hold intermediate and final results in.

What if the computer is multiplying 111110101110 by 101010011? How many intermediate registers would it need? Mighty few. We'll get to that in a moment.

And how can the shifter make things shift? We'll get to that, if you haven't guessed.

Division

The microcomputer divides the way you do, too, shifting and subtracting as needed. No need even for an example.

But how does it shift?

Easy. By use of shift registers. Remember that in a series register, the various bits can be clocked through the register. Just by pushing a bit in at one end, every digit can be made to shift one space over. As each flip-flop in a register cell resets, its output sets the next flip-flop. The flip-flops used in the registers are, by the way, somewhat more complex than the simple R-S flip-flop we showed you, having more inputs and outputs (including clock-pulse inputs, divided-time pulse outputs, and so on), so they can be quite versatile. We could diagram the shift-register logic, showing the daisy chain of interconnected flip-flops. We could then start with a 0 or 1 on the first bit's input, and take you through the logic. But wouldn't that tell you more about shift registers than you wanted to know?

Economy of registers

A simple addition would seem to require three registers:

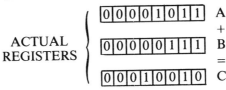

but it doesn't. The results of adding registers A and B can simply be stored in A. This destroys the original value in A, of course — but that original value is still on file back in the RAM until the computer chooses to change it there. So, for simple addition, the computer can get along with just registers A and B. (Most pocket calculators do, too.)

What about those successive additions of subresults in multi-digit multiplication? The microcomputer can successively multiply the multiplicand by two digits of the multiplier, add, store the result; multiply the multiplicand by the next digit in the multiplier, add the result to the former result, and so on. Thus only two registers, *for the addition currently being performed*, are needed. What's the limit? The limit is the *size* of the registers: the total number of bits each can hold. "How many bits wide are they?" The final result is only as "wide" as the storage register.

Any bigger result causes an overflow. In a pocket calculator, an overflow gives you an error indication. The computer *may* have means of storing the overflow, shifting the number one place to the right (dropping the least significant digit) and restoring the overflow bit at the left of the register.

You will notice, however, that your computer has limits to the size of the number it can display: you can't keep on multiplying any value by 1000 (or even by 10, or 2) indefinitely. You will keep losing low-order digits.

But when you try that, you're playing. The microcomputer will deal with any *real* number that has significance in your business. And that's all you want.

BIBLIOGRAPHY
a small menu of books

Chirlian, Paul M. *Understanding computers.* Portland, Oregon: dilithium Press. 1978. Paper.

Lewis, T. G. *How to profit from your personal computer.* Rochelle Park, N.J.: Hayden Book Company, Inc. 1978. Paper.

Miller, Merl K., and Charles J. Sippl. *Home computers: a beginners glossary and guide.* Portland, Oregon: dilithium Press. 1978. Paper.

Moody, Robert. *The first book of microcomputers.* Rochelle Park, N.J.: Hayden Book Company, Inc. 1978. Paper.

Osborne, Adam. *An introduction to microcomputers: volume 1: basic concepts.* Berkeley, California: Adam Osborne and Associates, Inc. 1978. Paper.

Solomon, Leslie, and Stanley Veit. *Getting involved with your own computer: a guide for beginners.* Short Hills, N.J.: Ridley Enslow Publishers. 1977. Paper.

Townsend, Carl, and Merl Miller. *How to make money with your microcomputer.* Portland, Oregon: Robotics Press. 1979. Paper.

Warren, Carl, and Merl Miller. *From the counter to the bottom line.* Portland, Oregon: dilithium Press. 1979. Paper.

Zaks, Rodnay. *An introduction to personal and business computing.* Berkeley, California: Sybex, Inc. 1978. Paper.

INDEX